NIGHT FIGHTER

NIGHT FIGHTER

CF Rawnsley and Robert Wright

A Goodall paperback
from
Crécy Publishing Limited

First published in paperback by Collins in 1957

This edition published in 1998

ISBN 0 907579 67 1

Photographs courtesy of Imperial War Museum
and The Hulton Getty Picture Collection

A Goodall paperback

published by

Crécy Publishing Limited
1a Ringway Trading Estate, Shadowmoss Road, Manchester M22 5LH

Printed in Great Britain by The Guernsey Press Co. Ltd,
Guernsey, Channel Islands

Contents

Acknowledgements 7

Foreword..9

1   "If you want peace..."....................................11

2   Unskilled Labour..22

3   The Tools..31

4   The Trade...37

5   That Elusive Echo 47

6   The Prentice Hand.......................................54

7   The Shop that Brown Built 60

8   Customers!..69

9   The Open Market 78

10   Command Performance..............................85

11   Our Big Friends 93

12   Stock-taking...100

13   Stalemate 109

14   Three Cornered Contest 115

15   Under the Counter.....................................121

16   The Dreaded Rest......................................128

17   Second Innings 134

18   Swing High – Swing Low 143

19   Fast But Not Furious 151

20   Midsummer Fires 160

21   The Enemy Within 169

22   Tough Customers.......................................180

23   The Odds Against Us 191

24   New Tools – New Tricks 200

25   Tour Expired..209

26   The Great Day 219

27   Weapons of Revenge 227

28   The Foreign Shore.....................................235

29   Master Craftsmen......................................242

30   No Joy...253

*To all those whose work on the
ground helped so much to bring
about success in the air*

Acknowledgements

THE AUTHORS wish to express their thanks and their gratitude to Mr. J. C. Nerney, ISO, Head of the Air Historical Branch of the Air Ministry, and to the members of his staff for their assistance so readily given in the research that went into the preparation of this book.

Acknowledgements are also made to Messrs Macmillan and Company, who published *The Changelings* by Rudyard Kipling and to William Heinemann Ltd, who published *Selected Poems*, by Maurice Baring.

Foreword

TWENTY YEARS ago, shortly after I had learnt to fly in the Auxiliary Air Force, Jimmy Rawnsley became my air-gunner in the two-seater Demon fighters with which we were then equipped. That was the beginning of what was to develop into a close association as a team that lasted throughout the years of the Second World War.

I would say that during the long time we spent together as an operational night fighter crew Jimmy Rawnsley knew me better than anybody else. And it was perhaps natural that I, in turn, should have come to know and understand him very well. Jimmy – "The Little Man" as we used to call him – has in his make-up a rare quality of sincerity and modesty combined with a great sense of humour and outstanding ability, and that is what has endeared him to all of us. So far as I was concerned, I could not have asked for a more able and enthusiastic partner in the work we did together in night fighters. From being my air-gunner he became my navigator, and his quiet but unbounded enthusiasm for, and belief in, the possibilities of the radar-equipped night fighter did a very great deal to bring to a real state of efficiency the somewhat primitive forms of radar with which we had to work in the early days of the war. In flying with him I found over the years that his keenness never diminished, and that to the end he set himself a standard from which he would never allow himself to lapse. If there was one man upon whom I knew that I could always rely it was, fortunately for me, my navigator, Jimmy Rawnsley. And I am happy that out of that experience of the war years which we shared there was established a firm friendship.

I read this book that Jimmy and Bob Wright have written about our wartime experiences in its manuscript form, and it is possibly a measure of my appreciation of it that I can say that it recalled for me in the most vivid way many things that I thought I had forgotten but which, I suppose, will always be a part of our common experience. The descriptions of the air combats and the way in which the story is told are all factually correct and true – as well as being very revealing – and capture, to my mind, most effectively the mood and the tempo of our lives at that time.

JOHN CUNNINGHAM

Hatfield,
Hertfordshire

CHAPTER ONE

"If you want peace..."

ALTHOUGH at the time I did not know what it was going to lead to, it all started, as I suppose it ended, with a bonfire. It was not until many years later, after I had had a chance to get things sorted out into what I hoped was some sort of perspective, that I came to realize that. And the bonfire that led me, a peace-loving engineer who had at one time verged on being a conscientious objector, into the back seat of a night fighter in the Royal Air Force was what the Germans called a Sonnwendfeuer: one of the traditional fires which their children light on the hilltops on midsummer night.

My family name of Rawnsley came from my father's Yorkshire origin; my mother was from the West Country. I was born in London in March 1904, so that I was of that generation which had, from the time of our childhood, become accustomed to the sounds of war. And because of that we were, by the early 1930s, adult and experienced enough to start feeling uneasy and apprehensive about the ominous threat of yet another war which seemed to be taking shape. There were many of us who could not bring ourselves to pin our faith in absolute pacifism: most of us, I think, still had high hopes about the League of Nations. Along with many others, I had actively campaigned for the cause of collective security, but that had turned out to be an uphill and discouraging struggle.

It had seemed to me at the time that the greatest hope for peace might come from the same source as that which held the greatest threat to it, and that was in the German people themselves. It was true, I knew, that they were imbued with a certain craving for revenge after their defeat in the war of 1914–1918, and that the misery of millions of unemployed and the bogey of Communism were driving more and more Germans to seek comfort in the empty slogans of their new and fiendish political creed. But there was also in Germany the bright promise of a vigorous and exciting youth movement – the Wandervögel – and I felt that there must be some hope in those sun-tanned, healthy youngsters whose songs rang through the woodlands and mountains as they hiked from hostel to hostel, carrying with them as they went a spirit of brotherhood that spread far beyond their own frontiers.

In an effort to find out for myself what was happening, I took to spending my all too short annual holidays in Germany. Walking or motor-cycling with my wife, Micki, we travelled through the northern beech woods, along the Rhine, and over the mountain tracks of Bavaria. Our first impressions of the people and the country were very favourable. We found everything wonderfully clean and bright and efficient, and we made many friends.

But after a while we had to face up to the discouraging fact that a change was steadily creeping over the country we had learnt to love, a change that was becoming more and more apparent and unpleasant with each succeeding year. A bewildering number of flags began to appear on all the buildings, and more and more uniforms were sprinkled through the crowds. Storm Troopers and SS men bashed about in their stamping boots. And the men of the newly reformed German Air Force – the Luftwaffe – could be seen preening themselves in the cafés and saluting one another at every street corner. The Germans were beginning to strut again.

We were on what was to be our last trip to Germany. Sad and heavy in heart, we arrived one glorious midsummer evening at the little village of Jaub, on the banks of the Rhine. Dusk was falling, and there was a sense of expectancy in the air. We could see, further along the village street, the children forming up for their traditional torchlight procession up the steep, wooded hillside to their bonfire – the Sonnwendfeuer. We ordered our supper in a café, and then we went outside to join the other people waiting to see the procession.

Up in the woods the nightingales sang sweetly, and behind us the river gurgled past in a quiet yellow flood. Our flagging spirits revived a little. Here, at any rate, was peace, with children who still kept the old happy ways of life. Soon we heard the sound of their voices as the procession started, with the ring of little iron-shod boots on the cobbles. But there was a chilling, unnatural harshness in those childish voices, and an ominously martial rhythm about the stamping feet. The torches lit the scene, and as the children filed closely past us our hearts sank. These were not the happy, laughing children we had hoped to see: here was the Hitler Youth, children in form only. There was no laughter on their lips; rather there was on their faces a look that was frightening. The light from the torches flickered on heads uplifted in some mystical trance, into eyes glazed with fanaticism. They marched past in stern military ranks, their boots stamping together in time, their young voices harsh and shrill as they spat out the gritty words of the Horst Wessel song. They marched away up the hill, their torches twinkling as they wound between the trees, and from the darkness the words of the Nazi hymn came stabbing back at us in staccato, venomous gusts.

My wife and I glanced at each other, horrified, and then we looked around at the parents of these little monsters. They stood there with us, their faces aglow with a smug and arrogant pride.

We turned back to the café, and a drunk sitting at a table beside us looked up and leered.

"England...finish!" he announced thickly. "Frankreich...finish! Amerika...bah!"

He peered about, furtively looking for support; those around us smirked, embarrassed, but not altogether displeased.

"Nur Deutschland," the drunk went on. "Deutschland über Alles!"

I had already begun to realize that it was much later than I had thought. Now I suddenly knew for certain that the hour was indeed late, and that I should have to make my own personal decision as to what I was going to do about it.

The heroes of my boyhood had been the fighter pilots of the Great War of 1914-1918. I was fourteen years of age when it finished, old enough to have read avidly everything I could get hold of about those pioneers of air fighting. And although I had long since lost any boyish illusions that I might have had about the glamour of war, I nevertheless felt that the air would still hold some measure of compensation for all the beastliness of warfare. And surely it was going to be in the air that the decisive battles would be fought?

I took stock of my chances. I was thirty-two years of age, and married. I weighed 7st 12lb, and in height I stood 5ft 3½in. These, I knew, were not impressive figures to place before a selection board. In addition to that, I was an electrical engineer, my job being to help maintain the supply of electricity for the Hendon, Golders Green, and Mill Hill districts of London. If war should come, I knew that it was quite possible that I would be ordered to stay at my job.

Hendon aerodrome was very close to where I lived, and three squadrons of the Auxiliary Air Force were stationed there. The flying at Hendon had always had a great fascination for me, so eventually I went along to the town headquarters of one of the squadrons. These were in a sedate old mansion overlooking Hampstead Heath. On the wrought iron gates outside hung the badge of No. 604, County of Middlesex, Squadron. The motto below the badge read:

Si vis pacem para bellum

It seemed to me that that was a singularly fitting start to things. "If you want peace, prepare for war." Registering 5ft 4in, I rang the bell.

Before the war the Auxiliary Air Force was run on rather an exclusive basis. I had to wait five months before I was summoned, along with a dozen other men, for an interview. A hawk-eyed Flight Lieutenant, a regular officer of the Royal Air Force, shrewdly looked us over as he explained the sort of job we were proposing to take on. He left us with no illusions. We were to join as aircraft-hands, general duties, and our work would be to sweep out the hangars, clean the oil-trays, and push the aircraft around. We would be required to attend at the aerodrome every weekend, and two evenings a week for lectures at Town Headquarters.

Out of the corner of my eye I saw that one or two of the youngsters were beginning to falter. I realised that the Flight Lieutenant was merely trying us out, eliminating at the outset the faint-hearted and those who had delusions of glamour. I struggled hard to maintain an expression of intense enthusiasm, even at the find blow.

"You realize, of course," he said, "that you won't have any chance of flying?"

To myself I made the reservation that we would see about that, and within a month of the interview I was accepted as an aircraftman for ground duties. I had the foresight to realize that the Christian names Cecil Frederick which my parents had bestowed upon me were not the sort that would go down with a swing among my comrades in the ranks, so I introduced myself to them by my nickname of "Jimmy", a name which remained with me throughout my Service career.

It took another nine months, until September 1937, before I could get myself accepted for aircrew training, and during that time I religiously did my drills and my share of the chores. I even started to learn a trade as an engine fitter. It was a case of doing anything that would get me nearer the aircraft. When finally I managed to make the change from engine fitter, a highly technical trade, to the lowly and despised one of aircraft-hand, air-gunner, the instructors, who were all regulars, thought I was crazy, and did not hesitate to tell me so.

But I had already cajoled my way into the back seat of our Hawker Demon biplane fighters for a few short and blissfully happy flights. As a new boy, I had to fly with any pilot who happened to be short of a gunner, and it was a decided shock to me to find out how much the different pilots varied in skill and natural aptitude.

The privilege of flying with the Commanding Officer and with the Flight Commanders, and the kudos which went with that, naturally fell to the senior gunners. When it came to my turn to be crewed up it was, therefore, no surprise to me to learn that I had been allocated to the youngest pilot in the squadron. But I was more than satisfied for I had already made up my mind that, in spite of his youth, John Cunningham was the keenest and the ablest of them all. I felt quite sure that I need have no misgivings about flying with him.

John was born in 1917 in South Croydon, where he lived with his widowed mother. He was only eighteen when he joined the squadron in November 1935. With his blue eyes and his crinkly fair hair, his downy pink cheeks and slim, boyish figure, it was not altogether surprising that this young Pilot Officer should be nicknamed "Boy" by his fellow-officers. But the name did not stick. Young as he was, there was a certain quiet determination in his manner and a steadfastness in the gaze of those blue eyes that soon made them think of him as more than just a boy.

Learning to fly with the squadron at Hendon, John's training was done on Avro 504's, and he went solo in March 1936, just before I first made application to join the Auxiliary Air Force. He quickly won the respect of the men who serviced the aircraft. Here was a pilot, they found, who asked shrewd questions, and whose criticisms were always constructive. This young Pilot Officer was no flying club weekender to be turned aside with smooth answers or a bit of technical double-talk. After leaving Whitgift School, John went to the Technical School of the de Havilland Aircraft Company, and he was just as competent as any of the mechanics to discuss technicalities in detail.

And so, in 1937, I was crewed up with John Cunningham as his gunner. I was in luck because I knew that if, by any chance, anything did go wrong, it would not be through any fault in my pilot. What lay ahead for me was the formidable task of making myself worthy of being the other half of that team.

By the time of the Munich crisis in August 1938, I could not honestly feel that I had got very far with the job I had taken on. I had become a leading aircraftman, and I had managed to scrape past an air-gunner's board at Eastchurch. But I was woefully lacking in experience. I was waiting to go to an Armament Training Camp for air to air firing, and although I had done a lot of gunnery on the ground, my actual gunnery in the air had consisted of firing only a few rounds. Most of my air to air shooting had been done with a camera-gun. And they say the camera cannot lie!

The suddenness of the call-up over the Munich panic shook us quite a bit. Within a few hours of receiving our telegrams we were all sitting around our aircraft, at readiness, waiting for whatever was going to blow up, and cheerfully wondering who would be the first to die. At the back of all our minds there nagged the thought of the untidy tangle of loose ends we had so hastily left behind.

In my own case, my wife, feeling as I did after our experiences in Germany, was not only in complete sympathy with what I was doing but also had yearnings of her own towards the air. Shortly after it was formed, she joined the Civil Air Guard and started her training as a pilot.

As I progressed with my training in the squadron the closest friendship I formed was with a keen, thoughtful youngster thirteen years my junior named Gordon Thomas. We had joined within a month of each other, although Tommy had already been in the Territorial Army for a short time.

Tommy flew with Alistair Hunter, a big, sleepy-eyed, soft-spoken man, a fine shot and a great sportsman, who was a close friend of John Cunningham's. Tommy was just as fiercely possessive about his pilot as I was about John, and whenever another gunner flew with Hunter in his place Tommy would go around muttering darkly:

"It'll get him you'll see. If he goes without me it'll get him. I'm the only one who can keep that jinx in order."

Our time at readiness came to an end – to our relief mingled with our shame – when Neville Chamberlain returned from Munich and waved that piece of paper at the cheering crowds. We all felt the day of reckoning had merely been postponed, and that no political claptrap about "peace in our time" could stall off much longer the clash that was bound to occur so long as the Nazis were allowed to continue having their own way.

But the year of the respite we had between the false hopes of Munich and the bitter facing of its reality was, in fact, put to good use so far as the squadron was concerned. By the time we were called up again – on the 24th of August 1939 – we had been re-equipped with Bristol Blenheims. These twin-engined, all-metal monoplanes, designed as medium bombers, had been turned into long-range fighters by bolting four forward-firing machine-guns to the underside of the fuselage.

In this new aircraft the gunner was housed in a power-operated turret just aft of the wing, leaving a vulnerable blind spot behind and beneath the tail where an attacking fighter could neither be seen nor fired at. We pretended to overlook this defencelessness at first, happy in the excitement of being surrounded by so much expensive machinery. And there was the novelty of being able to swing the gun with the touch of a finger instead of having to battle mightily with the effects of wind and the force of gravity. But we could not overlook the fact that we still had only one small machine-gun to match against the much larger and more powerful cannon of the modern fighters.

There was nevertheless for the gunners one great consolation: we still had two-seaters. Had the squadron been given more modern single-seater fighters, as most of the pilots had hoped for, we should have been out of a job. So it was with thankfulness that we stoned and oiled our new guns, and hoped that the rumoured new two-seater fighters would appear before things got too hot.

That week before war was declared was our last at Hendon. Along with the rest of the country, we sat around and waited, and from the aerodrome we could see all day long the trains steaming north, crowded with children being evacuated from London. Time was heavy on our hands. But after a few days the squadron was moved from Hendon to the aerodrome at North Weald, in Essex, our pre-arranged war station, and it was there, on the 3rd September 1939, as we stood on the grass by our aircraft, that we heard the tired voice of the Prime Minister as it came from a portable radio set. Now there could be no more pieces of paper, and the time for words had passed. We knew that at last we were in for what we had been expecting, and as we listened in silence Tommy and I turned and looked to the empty sky away to the east.

Eight months passed before any of us even saw an enemy aircraft. I was on leave when we heard, early in May, the news that the Germans had invaded Holland. When I got back to the squadron I found that they had had their first and rather colourless encounter with the Luftwaffe when they shot up some abandoned Ju 52s on the beach at The Hague. It was a very low level affair, and one of our crews somehow managed to crash on the beach; but the pilot and the gunner walked away from the wreckage of their aircraft, and they got back quite safely to England.

It had been eight months of alarms and discomforts, of losses, and of frustration. Up to this time only a few of the pilots had done any appreciable amount of night flying, and even that had been mainly in peace time in slow and stable aircraft in clear weather, flying from one brightly lighted town to another. Now that we were at war it was all very different. All the familiar landmarks were swallowed up in the blackout, and winter had come to east its shroud over the comforting horizon, bringing with it an increasing blindness.

We were rated, officially, as day and night fighters. We had our full share of the day work: long, dreary, bitterly cold shipping patrols – our aircraft and our flying-suits were not heated at that time in any way at all – up and down the North Sea. We shared these patrols with the day fighters; but the night watches we had to ourselves. Fighter Command wisely decided that the few Hurricanes and Spitfires in service were far too precious to risk chasing about in the winter nights. Our Blenheims had two engines to their one, and a longer endurance. The Blenheims also had less general usefulness which made them – and us – more expendable.

Night after night our crews launched themselves hopefully into the unfriendly darkness. Night after night we chased around after rumours and found nothing, and then had to grope our way back through the weather, which, that winter, was horrible. It was with sighs of relief that we bumped down on those small grass airfields dimly lit with paraffin flares and primitive flood lights.

But although the Germans failed to show up, we did not lack an adversary. We had no homing beacons and there was no system of blind approach, no way in which we could be talked down to a safe landing. Our radio was feeble and short-range, and the blind flying instruments were astonishingly temperamental. Our pilots fought a war that was far from phoney against an enemy that was much deadlier than the Luftwaffe. Human frailty and inexperience, and inadequate and unreliable equipment joined forces with the relentless and ever-present law of gravity, and a foe so implacable just had to be given a name. We called him Sir Isaac Newton. As the bitter months wore on and the score slowly mounted against us, always on the debit side, I had good cause to be thankful that I was flying with a pilot who appeared to be as near Isaac-proof as any man was ever likely to be.

But we were learning about night flying, even if it was the hard way.

We found, for instance, that it was quite impracticable to operate at night in formation. We found that it was no good sending up more fighters than the control system could comfortably handle: a swarm of aircraft, milling around on their own, only confused the plotting. And we were dismayed to find that the searchlights, directed by obsolete sound locators, were quite incapable of picking up and holding a fast aircraft taking evasive action even when the weather was quite clear. And we soon realized, with some bitterness, how utterly hopeless it was to try and find our quarry at night with nothing more to rely on than our own eyesight.

It was all very different to what we had expected. Now it seemed that it was going to be a war of individuals, each crew blind and deaf, working in its own little world of noise and darkness, chasing after meandering beams that flickered across the empty sky, fighting always the numbing cold and the little devils of lethargy and exhausting frustration.

In the middle of January 1940, the squadron was moved from North Weald to Northolt. The aerodrome was under snow when we arrived there. In addition to the flying he was doing with the squadron, John was put on to the job of doing the flying trials for a new photo-electric bomb. Although I continued to fly most of the time with him as his gunner, I was not on board when he had one narrow escape: a new bomb they were testing exploded prematurely just after being released.

Early in February I was suddenly grounded when a routine medical examination showed that my blood-pressure was far too high. I was told not to worry about it, but I was forbidden to fly until I had been before a Central Medical Board at Halton. I was turned down as still unfit for flying and told to report back in a month. At the end of the month I spent a week at Halton under observation, and after all kinds of elaborate tests they finally passed me fit again for aircrew and I went back to flying.

I was just in time to get back into the swing of things before the war started warming up, with the Germans invading Holland, Belgium and Luxemburg. On the 15th of May the squadron went from Northolt to Manston, a forward aerodrome on the North Foreland, and a few days later all the air-gunners were promoted to the rank of Sergeant.

The move to Manston brought us into the thick of things, and for the next few weeks it was all a whirling nightmare of disaster, a kaleidoscope of incongruous contrasts. It was the time of Dunkirk. We saw sinking ships and upturned lifeboats and between patrols we had ice cream on the beach at Margate. There was the smell and the taste of burning oil and battle-stained soldiers danced in Margate's Dreamland. By day we played a grim game of hide-and-seek in the clouds with the elusive enemy bombers and at night we ranged over Thanet and the Pas de Calais while the fires raged all along the French coast. They were the real fires of a real war.

The squadron had several inconclusive skirmishes with the Luftwaffe, most of them over the Strait of Dover, but Alistair Hunter and Tommy had the first successful combat.

It took place on the night of the 18th of June. Nothing much happened until midnight, then suddenly they were ordered off. We were at that time doing elementary intruder patrols over northern France. The weather was clear and there was a bright moon, and from 16,000ft over the Channel they could see for miles. They had patrolled as far as Cambrai, and were flying along the French coast from Griz Nez towards Calais when Tommy saw a small light move out from the coast and over the sea. Hunter could not see it, but finally Tommy managed to convince him that it was an aircraft and they went down to 2,000ft to investigate. They found it but could not recognize it, although it was obviously a German, since we had nothing that resembled that large, twin-engined seaplane flying along with its navigation lights on. They followed it for about five minutes, only 30 yards behind and just below it. Then Hunter pulled up and opened fire with a good long burst.

The enemy aircraft wobbled about, as Tommy put it, and spewed out oil, which came back on to the windows of the Blenheim. Hunter pulled up on a parallel course and very close to the other aircraft, and Tommy got in a good burst amidships. The enemy replied by firing a multiple white signal cartridge, which rather put Tommy off his second burst.

The Germans still left their lights on, and Hunter came around to make a second attack. But by that time they were too low for him to be able to use his front guns, and Tommy got in two more short bursts as they went past. Then the German seaplane crashed into the sea and the lights went out. Tommy went on firing as the Blenheim passed low over the crashed aircraft, for which he was later reproached on the grounds of cruelty. That was, of course, utter nonsense. As he pointed out himself, it was clearly laid down how the gunners were to deal with enemy aircrew over their own territory and what procedure was to be followed. He was doing no more than obeying instructions.

As soon as they were able to check the recognition chart Tommy and Hunter realized that they had destroyed a Heinkel 115, a float plane. The popular press got hold of the story, and it was said that this was the first enemy aircraft to be destroyed by night fighters operating from a home base. But the thing that became a standing joke with us was a quotation from the write-up in the newspapers. 'Diving 9,000ft to the attack!' was a shout with us enough to start a war dance, or a free fight or drinks all around, depending on the mood we were in.

And then suddenly it was all over, before most of us had even had a crack at anything. With the fall of France we were withdrawn to Gravesend, and we went back to the old night watches, chasing shadows, straining our eyes in the darkness as the flak puffs drifted past in the moonlight.

The lull in the battle gave us time to take stock. There were new faces in the squadron – replacements for those we had lost through casualties, postings and promotion – and we had to get to know them.

The new gunners were from the Volunteer Reserve, and some of them looked rather askance at what was known as Auxiliary exclusiveness. And there were new pilots: stocky, tough Peter Jackson, a Sergeant, full of self-confidence; and two very new Pilot Officers who had just finished their training,

Edward Crew and Keith Geddes, feeling their way with caution and tact. They had both learnt to fly with the Cambridge University Air Squadron, as had Jon Selway, another of our pre-war pilots, some years earlier.

Edward Crew was a small, compact man who gave one the impression of being much larger than he was. He held himself erect, with a firm dignity, and when he spoke it was in a clipped, decisive manner.

A much bigger man – big enough, in fact, to play rugby for Cambridge and for Scotland – Keith Geddes hid behind an engaging, almost sheepish smile. When he came in to ask for a gunner to fly with him it was almost apologetically, as if he were asking a favour.

Our Commanding Officer was posted to a Controller's job and Michael Anderson, the senior Flight Commander, was promoted to take his place. Michael was a typical Auxiliary officer. Keen and thrusting on the job, he had a reckless disdain for red tape and outspoken contempt for the little minds which could not rouse themselves from the dull routine of peacetime. These qualities naturally caused him to be somewhat unpopular in certain official quarters; but they endeared him to his men.

Michael was rather round-shouldered, almost with a stoop, and his walk was a shuffle. He had been on the Stock Exchange, but had not liked it. On his face there was an expression that was habitually harassed, and he affected a certain preciousness in the way he spoke. He would emerge from his office struggling into a flying-suit several sizes too big for him with what appeared to be handless arms flailing like windmills as a signal to Mick Wheadon, his Flight Sergeant, to start up.

"Hi, there," he would shout in his best Regency manner.

"Git me kerridge wound up, will you?"

There were also changes taking place in our aircraft. We had better blind-flying gear. A new Very High Frequency radio system – known simply as VHF – was introduced. This brought the voice of the controller to our headphones in the aircraft with a new and startling clarity. And most important of all, although we did not realize it at the time, was a mysterious business afoot over some other gadgets that were being fitted which had us all guessing. The most tangible part of this mystery was a collection of short, stubby aerials projecting from the wings, and another aerial, shaped like a barbed arrow, which jutted forward from the nose. Our questions about all this were turned aside with vague chatter about cutting balloon cables. But there was more to it than that. The vital part of the mystery appeared to be housed in a black metal box which sprouted various knobs and cables, and which was placed amidships inside the aircraft. And to top the whole thing there appeared to be a need for an attendant magician to prevent the whole contraption from bursting into flames.

There were rumours that this collection of plumbing would help us to locate other aircraft in the dark; but we were becoming very sceptical about all these fine ideas. We could see no further than the final free-for-all over the beaches when the Germans started their invasion, and for that we could well do without any extra dead weight.

Then suddenly we were on the move again. We were headed westward this time into the back areas of Salisbury Plain to an aerodrome having the fantastic name of Middle Wallop. That sounded crazy enough; but were we so useless that we were being banished to the rear? We knew that it was not for us to reason why. If we were destined to become nothing more than magicians playing around with strange black boxes then we should have to make the best of things and really try to make them work.

CHAPTER TWO

Unskilled Labour

WE were one of the last of the squadron to arrive on the circuit of the aerodrome at Middle Wallop. Finally we went in to land, rumbled in across the undulating grass surface, and taxied across to a couple of Nissen huts tucked away in a corner of the airfield. We switched off and climbed out, stiff and hot and sticky, into the blazing sunshine. It was the 29th of July, 1940.

The day was sultry, airless and utterly peaceful, and the profound silence of the very English countryside closed in on us as the dust settled. The smoothly rounded hills shimmered in the heat haze and snuggled drowsily in sleep, and high in the clear blue sky a skylark began to trill again after the interruption.

The road party had already arrived, and ground crews were hard at it sorting out stores and kit. I looked around and found Tommy and we set off together to find our quarters. As we stumbled across the parched, tufty grass more skylarks started up from under our feet.

Several new hangars stood up gaunt against the skyline, and behind them the still unfinished camp was rising in a jumble of bricks and scaffolding. A maze of drains and pipelines wove its way between the new buildings, and everywhere the mounds of chalk thrown up from the open trenches gleamed white under the July sun.

From the hangars we turned to look back across the airfield. Behind the south-west corner, where we had dispersed our aircraft, the ground rose steeply to the old hill fortress of Danebury. There the sentinels of ancient Britain and of the invading Romans had kept watch over the plain. And all around the windswept hills of the Hampshire-Wiltshire border lifted their tree-tufted crests to the sky and rolled spaciously away to the horizon.

It seemed inconceivable that there could be any war here; and yet we knew only too well how short was the flying time across the Channel to where the Luftwaffe was even then moving forward to its newly-won bases. It was a comforting thought that here, under the shadow of the grass-covered stronghold of Danebury Hill, the descendants of those ancient Britons were toiling like beavers to raise a new rampart against the invaders.

We began to study in detail the maps of the new sector over which we would be flying. We had been so accustomed to looking to the eastward for the enemy that it took some time for us to appreciate just how much the fall of France had extended our whole front. It soon became clear to us that our latest move was not really banishment: it was merely a change of front.

Now the sea lay to the south of us, some ten minutes flying time away.

Our job was going to be to guard the coast from the Isle of Wight to Lyme Bay. A bare twenty minutes away across the Channel, Cherbourg pointed a menacing finger at Southampton and Portland. Behind us lay Bristol, Birmingham, Coventry, Manchester and all the vital west coast seaports, dependent upon us for defence from raiders.

But this was no "soft under-belly" for the Luftwaffe to strike at. The wise planning of the staff of Fighter Command, under the direction of the Commander-in-Chief, Air Chief Marshal Sir Hugh Dowding, had seen to that. The RDF chain – "radar" as it came to be called later—had been extended in order to give more ample warning of what was happening. Many new airfields were being constructed. And the fighters stood waiting. While daylight lasted we should be able to give a good account of ourselves. But when darkness fell how should we fare? The mysterious black box in our aircraft began to occupy more and more of our thoughts and to assume a much larger place in our hopes for the future.

The magicians who operated the box were about as strangely an assorted bunch of men as one could ever hope to meet. No one seemed to know where they had come from, who they belonged to, or what they were really trying to do. At times we had a pretty strong suspicion that they were not quite sure themselves. And any inquiries from us that were perhaps too pertinent were always turned aside on the perfectly valid grounds of secrecy.

There were, first of all, the purely technical people, orthodox signals mechanics, full of a strange new double-talk and coping as well as they could with the unknown and unpredictable Thing. Instruction manuals for their guidance existed only in the heads of the scientists, known endearingly to us as "boffins", who had designed this new contraption. We soon discovered, however, that The Thing was known officially as AI, standing for Air Interception. But so high was the wall of secrecy around AI that the mystic letters were rarely uttered. It was always "The Thing," or "The Gubbins," or, more often, just "The Black Box."

The operators of the Box, the non-technical men who were to fly with it and make it work in the air, were a very different and far more varied race. Some had a completely goon-like appearance, were scarcely articulate, and were apparently solid ivory between the ears. Others looked intelligent enough but did not seem to belong to an aerodrome at all. But they all had two things in common. First, they had neither distinguishing flying badges nor NCO rank, although all aircrew had been made up to Sergeants some time before. Second, although they were expected to fly at all hours of the night and day, they hardly knew one end of the aeroplane from the other. They trod on all the wrong places; they picked up their parachute packs by the rip handle; they tried to walk into propellers. And since they were classed as aircraft-hands, neither technical tradesmen nor aircrew, they were easy prey for every Disciplinary Flight-Sergeant who might be looking for hangar sweepers, ablution cleaners or extra guards.

No wonder they wore a bewildered, harassed look. And I am afraid we gunners did not help much. We rather resented the presence of these groundlings in the aircraft, and we treated them with scant courtesy and very little respect.

But it was not long before even we began to feel that these poor unfortunates were really getting a raw deal. Slowly they won from everybody a reluctant recognition. Intelligence was rewarded with a name instead of the humiliating anonymity of "Hi Operator!", and they emerged with restored personalities.

There was Fred Larcey, tall, slow, a bit sheepish, but sound. He had started as a radio mechanic, and had applied right at the beginning for a transfer to flying. And there was Bernard Cannon, with his shock of black hair topping a dour, sallow face. Massive and tough, Bernard came from the North, where men, so he told us, "wore flat 'ats", and lifted the chickens of their neighbours as a Saturday night sport.

Another of them was Mike O'Leary, who did not strike one as being by any means as Irish as his name. But he was Irish all right, and had the genuine dash and wildness and love of a fight of his race.

And there was young John Phillipson, thoughtful, quiet, with almost girlish features. And A. G. Patston, another quiet type, not perhaps what one would call typically aircrew. Pat was small, not much taller than I was. He had a pleasant and ready smile, and an engaging wit. He had joined up at the outbreak of war, at the age of twenty-three, rather glad of the excuse to escape from the drudgery of a shipping office in the City.

O'Leary, Phillipson and Patston were all aircraftmen, and they had all had a good taste of air power from the wrong end. They had been in France as ground radar operators in the Advanced Air Striking Force, had been chased back in the retreat, and had got away by sea. Then they volunteered for air crew duties of a secret but unrevealed nature. Anything for them would have been a pleasant change. Perhaps they wanted to get some of their own back.

Life in the squadron for these newcomers was difficult. Quite apart from the constant humiliation of the kicking around they were subjected to, there was the mortification of not being able, through no fault of their own, to produce the results expected of them. They had been shown how to switch on the equipment, and what they ought to be able to see when they looked into the visor mounted on its face. Then they had been sent off to intercept other aircraft with it. There was no further instruction because there was no one to give it. They were literally the pioneers.

The Thing itself appeared to be subject to the most amazing and infuriating number of faults. The operators knew only that these fell into two categories: those which one could do something about by administrating a gentle kick in the thing's vital parts; and those which produced the Awful Smell. The latter was always followed, unless one switched off at once, by volumes of smoke and anxious inquiries from the sharp end of the aircraft.

These were the men and this was the weapon which went to make up the Magic Circle from which we, so far, were barred. But meanwhile the great struggle for the control of the air over the Channel had begun. It was a control that the Germans had to gain if they were ever to launch their invasion, and above us the battle raged on through the days of August, often coming down to seek us out where we crouched in our slit trenches. There was no place for us in the day skies: we were too slow and cumbersome, and, with our two engines and superficial resemblance to the Junkers 88, we were merely an added embarrassment to the Hurricanes and the Spitfires.

But we were not standing still. Every afternoon, whenever there was a lull, we were in the air, flying in pairs, one behind the other while the Magicians fiddled with their sets and tried their hands at intercepting the target aircraft in front. And all the time the gunners squinted up into the glare of the afternoon sun and craned their necks watching that blind spot under the tail, ready for a quick burst, at any Messerschmitt that might appear, or to fire an identifying Very light at one of our own too inquisitive fighters.

We had always made these routine afternoon flights – called night-flying tests – in order to check the aircraft which were to be used on the night programme. Now they became of even greater importance and longer duration as they offered the only chance of giving our new airborne radar operators the practice they so desperately needed.

But, for all the practice, we did not seem to be accomplishing much. Every morning those who had been flying the night before came back empty handed and sat silent and glum over breakfast, while the pilots of the day fighters, haggard of eye, went out to carry on the battle. We moved about the camp with a new, animal alertness, ears ready for the sound of a diving aircraft, eyes subconsciously measuring the distance to the nearest cover. And all the time conscience nagged at the back of our minds, ceaselessly asking what good we were in the great struggle that was being waged.

My mind was very fully occupied with this depressing thought on the last night of August as I lay in the gunners' tent at dispersal waiting for our turn to go off on patrol. It was warm and I felt smothered and uncomfortable with all my flying kit on. Following my usual practice I had changed into pyjamas before coming on duty. Over these I had a thick silk and wool aircrew vest, a roll-neck pullover, and serge battle-dress. Two pairs of thick woollen socks over a pair of my wife's east-off silk stockings filled out the flying-boots. And since we were next on the list for take-off I was wearing, on top of everything else, the fur-lined leather trousers and jacket known to us as "Goon skins". I felt uncomfortable enough, but I knew that I should need it all before we were down again. The shrill ring of the telephone in the Nissen hut nearby stilled the murmur of voices. A chair scraped on the wooden floor.

"Start up Q," came the voice of Doughy Baker, our Sergeant fitter, as he called to the ground crew.

I jumped to my feet and struggled into my Mae West, tying the tapes securely.

"You awake, Jimmy?' the Sergeant called as he came to the door of the hut.

"Yes thanks," I answered. "What's happening?"

"There're indications. Patrol Slap B."

I swung the parachute harness up across my back, caught the dangling release box between my legs, and snapped the straps into it. There were shouts and the sound of running feet in the warm darkness outside.

A quick check of my gear in the pockets of the Goon skin...torch, gen sheet giving the codes for recognition signals and beacons...pliers, screwdriver, gloves. I reached for my helmet leads securely tucked in so that they would not trail on the ground. God what a business it was getting airborne even after all these years. Now for the parachute pack...and for Pete's sake hurry!

I ran outside, got my bearings, and stumbled across the hard turf toward the vague outline of the Blenheim. There was a spurt of flame and a cough, and an engine began to chatter. The ground crew always started things up for us in advance. John was ahead of me, up on the wing, stepping in through the roof. It was usually like that.

At the back of the aircraft there was a hold-up. One of the more goonish magicians was clambering up to the rear hatch, all clutching hands and scrabbling feet. He dropped his parachute pack on my head as I came pushing up behind him. Why oh why did we have to put up with those useless clots?

Sliding down the ladder into the hull, I all but trod on the goon's fingers, then swung the hatch closed and tested the latch. Into the rack with my parachute, D-rings outward, rip handle to the left. Now for the intercom. I pulled on my helmet, felt for the socket, and rammed the plug home.

"All aboard, sir," I reported to John. "Rear hatch closed." I could hear my own breath panting into the microphone.

"OK," John replied, his voice as calm and as unhurried as ever. "'How are you receiving me?"

"Loud and clear."

The aircraft stirred as John juggled with the engines, then creaked and swayed, and I grabbed at a stanchion, checked the ammunition pans: they were all secured on their pegs. Then I turned to the oxygen bottles. I unscrewed the valve, and the little pointer flicked over to read full. Heaving myself up, I squeezed into the turret and subsided on the saddle.

I slipped the oxygen tube connection into its socket, and turned on the gunsight. Now I was all set, and only just in time for we were already swinging into the wind. I earnestly hoped that this time they would let us get away. Too often we had gone through all this rigmarole only to be recalled before we could even take off. Quickly I looked around the darkness of the down-wind skyline, and reported to John.

"All clear behind, sir."

"OK. Here we go."

This was the moment I hated. I always dreaded that first wild rush across the ground as we took off, the agonizing wait for the lift into the safety of space. I could only grin and wait for it as I had always done, just hang on and grin.

The gentle chuffing of the engines rose to a roar, the tail lifted, the turret shuddered and swayed, and the long line of flares marking the runway went racing past us. Without thinking what I was doing I started to count them. Surely it was about time we were off! The rumbling of the wheels became intermittent. There was one more gentle bump, a scarcely perceptible wriggle, and we were airborne. No longer was the aircraft an ungainly carriage trundling clumsily across the ground: she was in her element now, vibrant, living.

The tension relaxed. All the flurry and rush, the vain regrets, the useless anxieties, dropped away with the dwindling lights of the flare-path. All those things belonged to the earth, and presently we should have to go back to them. But now, for a little while, life would be shaped by the broader vision of the stars.

"Slap B" Doughy Baker had said.

That was the code name for a patrol line down near the coast, marked by a line of flares occasionally visible on the Dorset hills. "Indications" I had come to realize could mean anything from a full-scale attack to a controller's bunch. I was not feeling very optimistic about our chances of finding anything.

There was a reason for my niggling frame of mind. My wife had come down that day, and was staying the night in Salisbury. As luck would have it I was, of course, on the night-flying programme. I could have tried to get someone to take my place for the night. But how could I explain to my wife that of all the things that were not done, that was about the most rigid?

With the outbreak of war, the Civil Guard ceased to exist, just before Micki was due to go solo as a pilot. That promptly put an end to her flying, so she joined the Air Raid Precautions organization – the forerunner of Civil Defence – and was driving an ambulance in London. Having a few hours off duty, she had come down to see me. And I was flying.

Steadily we climbed from the warmth into the cold upper air. It came tearing in through the turret slot with the icy breath of the glaciers.

The misery started again as the nostrils thickened, as though from a cold in the head, and streaming eyes and snuffling nose dripped into icicles which froze the mask to the face. The skin chafed and peeled beneath it. At intervals I eased it away and squeezed the oxygen tube, crushing the ice and shaking it clear.

Slowly but surely the insidious cold worked its way through the leather and fur and sneaked through the wool and silk to strike at the shrinking flesh beneath. And with the cold came a creeping lethargy. It called for a very conscious effort just to keep up the constant sky search, to take any sort of interest in anything.

I forced myself to swing the turret around and to work the cocking-handle of the gun up and down in case there was a trace of oil left to freeze solid and jam things. I checked the oxygen and the gun sight and identified the flashing beacons on the ground, and struggled to ward off the stupefying effect of the cold.

John and I rarely spoke to each other in the air. There were times, such as this, when I wondered how he was feeling. But idle gossiping over the intercom could become a dangerous distraction. So we contented ourselves with a few words at intervals to check our microphones, and then returned to our silent vigil.

There was no sound whatsoever from the magician. I stooped down and looked back and could just see him squatting on the cold metal floor, huddled up in a cocoon of old blankets, fast asleep. I felt sorry for the poor devil: he really did not have much of a life.

The Sector Controller began to give us vectors – courses to steer – to bring us an interception with some unidentified aircraft. Was it a raider? Or was it one of our own bombers returning home? Or were we just chasing our own sound again? I had not really been concentrating on the vectors we had been given, but as far as I could judge by the stars we were heading back towards our own base. But things were livening up. The vectors came in quick succession until it seemed that we must be going around in circles. Were we really chasing our own tail again?

"Definitely hostile," the Controller stated.

The words came like a jab in the ribs. I squirmed in every direction looking for searchlight beams or bomb flashes, for any signs of activity. The blood began to course in my veins again. Oh for just one crack at a Jerry!

Down on our starboard quarter a red beacon was winking out its code, I spelt out the letters, thinking idly how strange it was that the light never seemed to reappear just where one expected it. It was our own beacon, so we must have just passed over Middle Wallop, heading again towards Salisbury.

Then came the coded instruction from the ground to switch on the radar set.

"Flash your weapon," the Controller said.

So there was something ahead of us! I stooped down again and looked at the magician. He was still asleep. Reaching out, I prodded him with my flying-boot.

"Hi…Abracadabra!" I exclaimed. "It's time to do your stuff."

He stirred and unwound himself, and thrust the blankets into an untidy heap on the floor in front of the set, and knelt on them. A familiar humming came over the intercom as he switched on. I turned back on my look out.

"Have you got anything?" John asked, eager but patient.

The only answer the operator made was a series of muffled grunts.

A vicious jar shook the aircraft, as if we had run up a concrete step. Even John was shaken.

"That was his slip-stream!" he exclaimed. "Surely you're seeing something?" There was almost an entreaty in his voice, but he kept his patience.

"It…it's very indistinct," the operator muttered. "I don't think…" The muttering died away into incoherence.

"Well keep trying," John said. Even now there was only encouragement in his voice.

I felt like getting down and putting my foot through the wretched Box. My eyes were sore with staring into the darkness, and I turned and fidgeted with frustration. Just ahead Salisbury lay helpless in its hollow, a mere phosphorescence of faintly-glowing pin points against a vaguely darker blackness.

There was another jolt as we hit the slip-stream again. I thought my eyes would pop out. Surely that Box must be able to help by now!

"There go his bombs!" John exclaimed. "We must be very close behind him."

The note in his voice of something approaching anguish made me swing around in time to see a line of white splashes leap out of the darkness below us, as though some fiendish lamplighter were striding ahead of us in seven-league boots. The splashes dropped astern, twinkling innocently, while I swung the gun around in a blind fury, trying not to remember that Micki was down there somewhere. The last of them turned into an angry red, and swelled out horribly.

But no response came from the kneeling figure amidships. I wondered if he was praying. We went blundering on impotently into the darkness, but it was no good: we found nothing at all. In a little while even the vectors gave out, and they recalled us to base. The fever of excitement died, the sweat dried cold on the skin, and all the misery and dejection came flooding back again. If we could not get this thing to work then just what were we going to do?

The magician was still kneeling on his prayer mat of blankets muttering incantations to himself. The green glow from the cathode ray tube flickered on his face. A witch doctor, I thought. A witch doctor, and black magic. And just about as useful!

We were losing height, coming in to land, down past the flashing beacon, down towards the welcome lights of the flare-path. Summer came breathing softly back into the turret, sweet with the heavy, intoxicating smell of the harvest. I tore off the clammy mask, and sucked in the blessed warm air. On the horizon an ominous red glow blinked reproachfully out of the darkness.

But Micki was all right. She was a bit peevish the next morning at being followed around by the Luftwaffe, even to this quiet haven. But that was all. I could not explain to her how I felt about it because not only were we flying in the dark but we were also working in the dark, in almost every way.

CHAPTER THREE

The Tools

A T last that memorable summer of 1940 began to fade, and the Nazi hopes of another lightning victory died in the ashes of their bomber fleets. Ahead lay the long dark nights of winter, and if perhaps the enemy bombers were not exactly ideally suited for the job and their crews insufficiently trained that did not matter a great deal. Their targets, our cities, were large enough, and they were to fly to them under the cover of darkness. The survivors of our decimated day fighter squadrons tossed the ball our way, and we knew that it was up to us to follow the example they had set.

But a chill wind was putting an edge to the golden autumn. We knew only too well how slender were our chances of success. Even if the searchlights showed a miraculous improvement, they could not shine through 10,000ft of cloud. And even if we saw an enemy aircraft illuminated, could we catch it?

John Cunningham was promoted in September to the command of B Flight, and I became senior gunner of the flight. But there was little personal satisfaction in that for me. I could not help feeling that the gunners in night fighters had had their day, and that the future belonged to the men who could make the new radar sets function as they were supposed to.

It was not merely a hunch on my part. It was something that had to come. And for the lowly magicians there was surely developing a growing respect from all ranks, from the Commanding Officer downwards. As is always the case, official recognition lagged behind, although they were classed now as Radio Operators (Air). But they were still waiting for full aircrew status and the amenities of the Sergeants' Mess. Everything that could be done by the squadron to improve their living conditions was set in motion. They had permission to stay in bed after night flying, and they had chits for late meals, and they were given some freedom from the lowlier chores. But all that, of course, only helped to curl the hair of the station disciplinary staff, and there were many bitter arguments and quarrels with them in efforts to get these concessions honoured.

There was one very necessary comfort the operators sadly lacked. The plumbing in the airmen's quarters was not yet finished and there was no way that they could get hot baths. But, to reverse the usual saying, brains can baffle bull. Phillipson and Patston found out that in the Gas Centre there was a somewhat wistful staff standing by with a constant supply of hot water eagerly waiting to decontaminate any gas victims. Armed with chits from John Cunningham, they presented themselves at the gas-proof doors and demanded that they should be decontaminated. They were received with open arms and steaming taps, and spent a luxurious half-hour in unlimited hot water.

This quick-wittedness was beginning to show in the work of the brighter operators. They seemed to be grasping the elements of air interception and, with more familiarity with their equipment, how to work out for themselves what was happening as they peered at their cathode ray tubes.

There were also renewed rumours about a new night fighter, the Bristol Beaufighter, which was going to be the answer to all our dreams. And as these rumours grew stronger, so did the prestige of the operators. Even senior pilots were behaving like talent scouts, quietly trying to snap up the services of the more promising of the newcomers.

Pat had been doing well in the practices, and one day John Cunningham approached him and asked, almost diffidently, if he would become his regular operator. Pat was very flattered. But he was also embarrassed.

"Well...er thank you very much, sir," he replied. He was finding it hard to explain. "I – I'd like to, but as a matter of fact...Mr Anderson has already asked me to operate for him."

To be asked to fly with both the Commanding Officer and the up-and-coming young Flight Commander in the same week was proof positive that he was on the way to success. But there was a cruel twist to it. A week later the squadron adjutant sent for him. He told Pat that his parents were very seriously ill, and that he was to go home at once.

Pat knew that there was more to it than that: he had only just come back from forty-eight hours' leave. And he was, by that time, quite familiar with the custom of understatement. But he had not expected the full horror of what he found when he reached that little corner of Chapham where his home had stood. It was a pile of rubble, and his mother and father and brother had all been killed by a direct hit the night he returned to Middle Wallop.

When Pat came back to us a fortnight later he was still dazed with shock. And since nearly all the pilots had by then selected their operators, he was out, in the cold again.

With autumn and winter, the night raids became more intensive and we realized that it was now up to us to stem the tide, just as the day fighters had done during the summer. But apart from a few chance encounters on the nights of bright moonlight, the enemy bombers seemed to be having things pretty much their own way.

The authorities tried all kinds of ingenious and even fantastic schemes, and a vast amount of thought and effort was expended on a fallacy. We now knew where the solution lay; but how could we, on our past showing, expect them to put all their eggs in one black and as yet unproved basket.

The fallacy lay in their deep-rooted and undesirable conviction that our failure was due simply to our inability to see another aircraft in the dark. We knew well enough that there would be no difficulty about that if – and this was the important point – we could be brought into the right position relative to the aircraft we were pursuing, going at the same speed and in the same direction. But first of all we had to be placed in the right position to make full use of our own radar.

But other schemes were brought into play and we were beset with such things as airborne searchlights, showers of magnesium flares, airsown minefields dangling on parachutes, and other menaces to our own defensive fighters. Some of these schemes were good enough in theory, but the practical difficulties were too great. And they all missed the most essential point of all: to get the fighter into a position where it could make an attack.

It was said of one very new pilot on one of his first night patrols that he suddenly saw an airborne searchlight projected horizontally out of the darkness at his own level without knowing what it was. He immediately lost all faith in his instruments and dived straight into the ground!

Another source of amusement for us was the correspondence columns of the more irresponsible newspapers. There we read of people who wanted anti-aircraft guns mounted on balloons; of the idea that bombers should fly above the raiders and drop sand into their engines; and there was even one who suggested forming up a hundred obsolete aircraft in line astern, each trailing 1,000ft of steel cable, to fly across the track of the raiders.

Fortunately for all of us the sponsors of the radar-equipped night fighters were not side-tracked. One of our staunchest supporters was Wing Commander R. G. Hart, who was at this time on the staff of the Headquarters of Fighter Command. A very young pilot in the First World War, Raymond Hart became a specialist in radar at the very earliest stages of its development; and by February 1937, he had organized the first radar training school for the RAF. As early as two years before the outbreak of war, Hart had himself operated the first airborne radar set ever to be brought into use in an aircraft. At Fighter Command he watched over the development of the radar equipment for the night fighter with a quiet but deep-rooted conviction that it would provide the answer that was being sought. It was a good thing that men such as Raymond Hart persisted with their plans; and just before the end of September we received, to our great delight, the first of our long-awaited Beaufighters.

There she stood, sturdy, powerful, fearsome, surrounded by an enthusiastic crowd. Most of us admired from the outside as only those with influence or possessed of extreme cunning got inside. Pilots, engineers, fitters, riggers, armourers and signal mechanics were in attendance, and they probed and tinkered and adjusted until they had brought her to a state of good-tempered serviceability. Then they all tiptoed quietly away for, like all young monsters in unfamiliar hands, she showed promise of being temperamental. Even Mick Wheadon, the Flight Sergeant in charge, was said to have been seen walking away backwards from the Presence.

For the gunners, however, there was a shattering disappointment. Where the turret should have been there was nothing but a plain, moulded dome of perspex. Here was our dream fighter. But where were the four free guns in the turret in the back that could fire forwards and upwards into the belly of an enemy bomber? There was not even a single free gun with which we could foster our delusion of usefulness.

Eventually I managed to elbow my way through the crowd and get to the aircraft. Just aft of the perspex dome a panel in the bottom of the fuselage hinged downwards leaving open the back entrance. I ducked down, set my feet on the steps cut in the panel, and climbed in.

Right in front of me there was a very serviceable swivel-seat, set high up under the dome, with back-rest and safety harness, and scooped out to take the one-man dinghy. That was a good start.

I squeezed past the seat, swivelling it around, and found Sandifer, one of the oldest gunners from the point of service in the squadron, red in the face, sitting on the catwalk that led forward. Stan Hawke, another of the senior gunners, was standing behind him, bent down under the curving roof, with a stop-watch in his hand.

"Where's that turret we've heard so much about?" I demanded.

Sandi was breathing hard. "We've had that," he grunted. "The only gunnery we're likely to get will be this job." He pointed at a row of 20mm ammunition drums set in racks above his head on either side of the cat-walk.

"From now on we're just powder monkeys," Stan said "We're having a go to see how long it takes to reload."

Sandi chuckled. "Wait until Tommy catches sight of this lot!" he commented. He patted something set in the floor.

It was dim in the tunnel-like fuselage, but as my eyes became accustomed to the half-light I saw them, two on each side of the cat-walk: four, solid great cannon, firmly set in place just below floor level! Their massive breeches gleamed with an evil beauty.

"Four twenties!" Sandi gloated. They ought to do a bit of no good if we ever catch anybody!"

In spite of my disappointment over the turret my gunner's heart warmed at the sight. My face must have shown it, because when I looked up Stan was smiling.

"How's the reloading going?" I asked.

Sandi was nursing one of the drums. "These things weigh 60lb each," he said. "God knows what it's going to be like hauling them out of the racks and fitting them on the cannon with all your kit on, oxygen tubes and phone cords and all...and in the dark."

"And with the pilot going into a tight turn just as you get it off the rack," Stan added. "That'll make it weigh a darn sight more."

"Probably go straight through the floor," Sandi said, "if it doesn't chop off your fingers against the breech."

I went back aft and wriggled into the seat under the dome and swung around to look out over the tail. There was a fine, unobstructed view all around above the horizon, and with a little squirming one could even see into that old Blenheim danger spot below and behind.

The radar equipment appeared to be a new version of what we had had in the Blenheim, with the Box suspended from the low roof just behind the dome. One could look into its rubber visor or keep a visual watch over the tail with only a slight movement of the head.

I looked around inside, and found that there were catches to release the whole dome in case of ditching or a belly landing. The bottom hatch, through which I had entered, was opened automatically by the slip-stream at the turn of a lever. There were an altimeter and an air-speed indicator; and – bless my frozen feet – there was a hot-air duct discharging into the lap from the starboard side.

Squeezing past the others, I went forward along the catwalk, stooping under the low roof, through a pair of armour plate doors, and into the pilot's compartment. His seat was in the centre. The windscreen was one large sheet of bullet resisting glass sloping back fairly close to the face. There would be no more mad craning and peering trying to see out, with the glow from the instruments reflecting back from half a dozen small panes. And perspex panels gave a clear view to both sides and up through the roof.

Getting out in an emergency, I found, would be a bit of a gymnastic feat for the pilot. There were parallel bars set high, one on each side, by means of which the pilot, having collapsed the back of his seat by pulling a lever, could swing himself up and back and down on to a forward escape hatch, hinged like the one at the back. When shut, this hatch formed the floor of a small well between the pilot's seat and the armour plate doors, with enough room for a passenger to stand and look out forward over the head of the pilot.

I pulled the hatch open, dropped down to the ground, and walked around to the front of the aircraft. She was good, whichever way you looked at it, sturdy and aggressive, although perhaps a bit heavy. But the two gigantic Hercules engines with which she was powered, air cooled and close cowled, with their huge propellers, sweeping through a wide arc, could surely lift anything. From the tip of that forked aerial at the nose to her shapely rudder she was a beauty. I knew that somehow, as gunner, powder-monkey, operator, or stowaway, it did not matter which, I just had to fly in her.

There was a long queue of pilots waiting to try their hands with the new aircraft. The first was naturally the CO, Michael Anderson, and he was closely followed by John Cunningham.

Wistfully I watched John as he climbed into his white flying overalls and carefully adjusted his old fawn muffler. I did not expect to go for a ride with him the very first time. Nor did I expect the bad news that came immediately afterward. The gunners were told that there was no place for them in the Beaufighter. Dejectedly we went back to the old Blenheims, wondering, now, how long even that was going to last.

Winter set in, and the mud at dispersal spread in an ever-widening arc until we were wallowing through a slippery morass that sucked the flying-boots off our feet.

Slowly more Beaufighters arrived to be groomed for replacements for the Blenheims, and as the serviceability of the new aircraft gradually improved so, one by one, the pilots mastered them. John crewed up with Phillipson as his operator, and I was left out in the cold, feeling very forlorn.

And then came the final blow. In order to boost up the performance of the remaining Blenheims – the Beaufighters were not yet being used on operations – it was decided that the gun turrets should be taken out. By then we knew that we had really had it.

But at the same time there was one ray of hope. The gunners were not just posted away, as I was afraid would happen. We were offered a choice: we could be posted as gunners to some other unit, or we could remain with the squadron and learn to become radar operators.

I was overjoyed. This was the chance to get in on the ground floor of something which I had come to feel was going to have a very great future.

CHAPTER FOUR

The Trade

S HORTLY after we received our new Beaufighters there arrived in the squadron a new Special Signals Officer, Pilot Officer K. A. B. Gilfillan, a large, forceful man who was to make his mark not only in the affairs of the squadron but also in the whole story of our radar war.

A radio engineer by profession, Gilfillan had gone through an intensive course in radar after joining the RAF, and had come straight from that to us, one of the first of these newly-appointed specialist Officers. Although the field was almost an entirely new one, Gilfillan was not the sort of man to allow difficulties to stand in his way, and he soon made his presence felt when it came to getting equipment and parts and tools. He even bearded the Air Officer Commanding the Group when it came to a showdown over getting necessary and badly needed equipment.

Through the efforts and drive Gilfillan put into his job we were probably the first to be equipped with mobile servicing gear. He also commandeered one of the married quarters and fitted it up as a workshop with a generator he bought in the Holloway Road. And then, not satisfied with getting all the ground servicing and maintenance organized in a way we had never known, he turned his attentions to matters in the air, and began to weigh up the abilities of each and every operator.

It was possibly taking on more than was laid down as part of the duties of the Special Signals Officer, but Gilfillan was interested in the overall effect rather than in doing only what he was supposed to do. Moreover, he flew regularly as an operator, and if perhaps he was not particularly good at the job, it at least gave him enough experience and authority to be able to judge for himself how the air crew were making use of his equipment.

Another new arrival – and someone who caused us considerable astonishment – came in the form of a psychologist. He promptly started asking us what seemed to be the most silly and irrelevant questions. Gunners and operators alike – magicians or not – were subjected to a series of quizzes, interviews and aptitude tests which seemed to serve only to make us all very restive.

"How much more of this pantomime are we going to get!"

Tommy complained bitterly. He had agreed, reluctantly, to continue fighting the war with a Black Box instead of his gun.

"Stick it," I suggested. "They're only trying to weed out the goons."

The next to arrive was a slim young radar specialist named Donald Parry, a Civilian Scientific Officer. He did not look a bit like our preconceived notion of a boffin. We had always rather thought of them as a queer race of long-haired crackpots. But Parry seemed, by our standards, to be quite normal and sane. It was his job to give us our first lecture on the mysterious principles of Air Interception, or AI, as it was called. That was before the name radar – an American word – had been adopted by us. At long last we were to learn what it was all about.

Inside the improvised lecture room, with the doors locked, we took our places on wooden benches. I had that tense, expectant feeling that comes over one on entering a strange country for the first time.

"AI," Parry said, "works on the same principle as an ordinary sound echo. You shout 'Boo' across a valley, and after a short interval the echo shouts 'Boo' back at you. You time the interval, and knowing the speed of sound you can work out the distance across the valley."

Pausing to let that sink in, Parry then went on: "Now if you use some sort of directional ear-trumpet, like a sound locator, you can tell the direction from which the 'Boo' is coming."

There were grins of relief going round the room, along with eager demonstrations of imaginary ear-trumpets. It was not going to be such heavy going as we had feared.

"All that AI does, then," the lecturer went on, "is to send out a series of radio 'Boos'. If there is another aircraft within range an echo bounces back from it, and the AI tells you its range and bearing."

It all sounded wonderfully simple. I could not imagine why the operators had not had more success with it. Perhaps it was because, having had no flying experience, they could not translate a series of ranges and bearings into terms of relative motion. If that was the case then the air-gunner trained to deal with relative speeds and deflection shooting should find it all very easy.

We regarded this civilian boffin with growing respect. Not only did he know his stuff, but he could put it over in language that we could all understand. Is it any wonder that we called him the Professor of Boology?

Our next visitors brought with them a touring training outfit. Again we trooped into the room and expectantly took our places on the benches. An ingenious ground trainer, a collection of metal boxes, was rigged up on a wobbly trestle table. It all looked very complicated and decidedly home-made, but it presented a face with which we were now quite familiar: the leather visor of the Black Box with its control knobs.

The demonstration of this trainer was in the hands of a young, fair-haired Corporal named Brian Cape who, like Gilfillan, was to play an important part in the work on the ground. When war broke out, Cape was studying to become an electrical engineer. In the Service he quickly got into the new field of radar, and he helped build this, the first, synthetic AI ground trainer, and then, because of the nature of his creation, he was sent off on a tour of the night-fighter squadrons to demonstrate how it worked.

He knew what he was talking about because although his job was to get on with the handling and maintenance of the equipment on the ground he had already done a little operational flying with AI.

Cape started by pulling the visor off the set, revealing the saucer-like stare of two cathode ray tubes set side by side. We watched closely as he switched on. Now we were really going to know what it was the butler saw!

A low buzzing sound came from somewhere in the depths of the equipment. On each tube there appeared a luminous green line, horizontal on one tube and vertical on the other. These, Cape explained, were what were called the time traces. He twiddled one of the knobs, and across the lines little diamonds of light came into being.

These represented the echoes – the "boos" – from the target in front, Cape went on explaining. They were commonly called "blips". The distance from one end of the trace would tell us the range of the target – the other aircraft – and their relative position athwart the lines would indicate the bearing of the target.

I glanced quickly at Tommy. He was looking as puzzled as I felt. In spite of what we had been told I had still half expected to see some kind of television picture of the aircraft we were trying to intercept. But this was something quite different. We were going to have to juggle around with a lot of blips, deducing from their appearance various ranges and bearings, and so interpret the position and movement of the target.

There was one thing we could see on the tubes and that was unexplained. One of the bolder pupils spoke up, asking:

"What's that thing like a Christmas tree across the far end of the traces?"

"That's just what we call it…a Christmas tree," Cape said. "The signals bounce back from the ground just as they do from other aircraft in the air, but they give a much stronger echo. And the lower you fly the further down the trace the Christmas tree comes. Finally, it can fill the whole tube and blot out any aircraft echoes that might be there."

That was food for thought, and we pondered over it. But not for long. Most of the raiders coming over were at heights of 15,000 to 20,000ft, so the Christmas tree should not worry us at all.

We took it in turns to sit at the Box, reading off what we saw, and giving instructions to an imaginary pilot to turn or climb or dive, to increase speed or throttle back. All the time Cape manipulated the controls which moved the blips about the tubes to simulate the effect of our manoeuvres. And each time we ended triumphantly with the blips sitting squarely across the traces in just the right position for the pilot to make a perfect attack.

I came back from my session with a feeling of elation. Sitting down next to Pat I remarked: 'Well that seems easy enough."

Pat always smiled in a quiet, knowing sort of way. Now it was more like the Mona Lisa than ever. "Yes," he said, gently. "Of course you won't find it quite the same in the air."

Getting air experience with the AI was not at all easy. We still had to continue with our stint as air-gunners in the remaining Blenheims that had turrets, and our only chance of getting any practice as operators was to fly as third man during night flying tests and try to persuade the regular crew to let us have a go.

I kept plaguing John to take me along on his trips with Phillipson. He was sympathetic but quite firm about the way things should be done.

"All in good time," he said. "We must get the more experienced people operational first."

But I was beginning to feel rather desperate. Any night now the Beaufighters would be flying on operations. I spent a lot of time in the Special Signals Section and the flight offices, cadging shamelessly in order to get information and experience. But October was nearly out before my turn came.

We went off in one of the stripped-down Blenheims with a Sergeant pilot at the wheel and one of the ex-magician operators on the prayer mat beside me. Climbing to 8,000ft, we followed visually the aircraft which was to act as our target. The operator adjusted the AI set, and made way for me. This was the big moment!

I peered into the visor, trying to accustom my eyes to the dim light. Slowly there came into view not the clear-cut picture I had seen in the ground trainer but instead a shivery confusion of waving lines. An enormous Christmas tree blotted out more than half of the cathode ray tubes, and on both sides of the wobbling traces there was a wavering, choppy fringe. Horrified at the indistinct picture I was seeing, I turned to the operator.

"What's all that stuff?" I asked.

"Grass." he replied offhandedly. "It's like the background noise of a wireless set."

We were closing in on the target aircraft. A faint, spidery blip slid down out of the Christmas tree, wobbled drunkenly from side to side, and then faded coyly into the grass.

"Any joy yet?" the pilot asked. He sounded bored, a little impatient.

I swallowed hard, and then found myself making those same non-committal noises for which I had so often derided the magicians.

"Well come on. Where is it?" the pilot demanded. He had evidently had more than enough of dim-witted operators.

My instructor took over and made some adjustments. Now and again the blip could be seen very faintly, and then it would disappear again.

"It's not very good today," he commented.

There was a snort of disgust from the front as the pilot complained: "Is it ever any good? Leave it we'd better act as target for a bit."

Thoroughly disheartened, I sat back and thought about what had happened. If this was what the operators had had to put up with, it was little wonder that we had not got anywhere.

But a few days later, on the first day of November, I had my second go in the air. This time John was flying the Blenheim, and the imperturbable Bernard Cannon was the operator and my instructor. After the previous fiasco I was feeling very nervous and anxious as I turned on the AI set and waited for things to happen.

To my great relief a fine, bonny blip edged out of the ground returns and came swinging down the trace. I took a deep breath and announced as confidently as possible: "Contact at 3,000ft. Dead ahead and 200ft up."

"Well, actually," John replied, "it's a good 300ft below us." He sounded quite friendly about it.

I looked hard at the tubes, but the picture had not altered. Then Bernard looked over my shoulder.

"It's that squint again, sir," he said to John. He looked at me and shrugged his shoulders. "You have to allow for it as you close in."

So the wretched thing was not only uncertain, coy and hard to understand: it could be a lying jade as well!

But John was very patient about it all. He opened the range again, pulling to one side. "Try bringing me in from here," he said, his voice full of encouragement. "Don't worry about the height difference. I'll look after that."

I began to give course corrections so as to bring us astern of the target. Smoothly and quickly the Blenheim slipped in and out of the turns as John implicitly followed my directions. Whenever I faltered his crisp voice easily prompting me came over the intercom.

"What range now? Is it still dead ahead?"

For some inexplicable reason I simply could not get straightened up behind the target. It seemed to be always out-turning us. The blip kept swinging from side to side and up and down the trace, and I sent John twisting after it in ever-tightening turns. Finally, we were swinging backwards and forwards like the weavers who flew at the rear of the day fighter formations to guard their tails. Then the blip took one headlong rush into the zero end of the trace and disappeared into minimum range. There was an awkward silence, and I swallowed hard.

"I'm sorry," I mumbled, utterly crestfallen. "I'm afraid I've lost it."

"Well never mind," John said briskly. "We'll try again if there's time."

If John thought that I was as stupid as I felt, he gave no sign of it. On the way back I tackled Bernard about what had happened.

"Was the target taking much evasion?" I asked.

Laughing, Bernard replied: "None at all. He was flying straight and level the whole time."

I should have found it hard to believe if I had not, as a gunner, so often seen the magicians doing exactly the same thing. When I got back to the mess I sat down with a pencil and a piece of paper and started to try to work out the reason for this weaving, for it seemed to be something from which all the operators suffered to some extent. After a while it began to dawn on me what I had been doing wrong, and I realized that I would have to stop the turn much sooner, and hold a converging course instead of blindly pointing the fighter at the target.

From this excessive weaving, perhaps the commonest fault amongst the learners, we later adopted a name for ourselves which stayed with the AI operators throughout the war: The Weavers.

That night I had a sharp and unpleasant tussle with our old enemy Isaac Newton. I was off duty, and I went into Andover to see a film. When I got back to the aerodrome I found that things were happening and that A Flight were short of a gunner. Ten minutes later, the gunner in a hastily mustered scratch crew, I was airborne in the turret of one of the few remaining unstripped Blenheims.

It was a filthy night with low cloud, a weeping drizzle, and freezing not far off the ground. We climbed up through the stuff, blind all the way, until at 17,000ft the poor old Blenheim was so solid with ice that it could stagger no higher. So down we came again, with ice flying off the airscrews and splintering off the wings in great chunks. We bucked and tossed about until I thought the wings would snap off, and we had just passed back over base at 5,000ft when, with a final, stomach-turning heave, the aircraft went out of control.

The operator and I spent the next few minutes pinned in turn against the roof and the floor, with intervals of floating between the two as weightless as spacemen. I managed to get a hand to my microphone switch and called the pilot. But there was no answer. A pan of ammunition drifted lazily past my face, hesitated, and then wandered off upwards. Bad cockpit drill, I thought, for things to be free to float around unsecured.

Down on the floor I went yet again, ground down by a brutal, irresistible force. It was a losing struggle against gravity, and sight and consciousness were beginning to fade. We must have lost a lot of height, and it could not go on much longer. I knew that I must get to the hatch, but I was gradually losing all my external senses, conscious only of my inner thoughts. It was as if I were giving in to the inevitable. There was no particular sense of fear: only a feeling of mild regret that it should all have to end like this.

And then suddenly I became aware, even as the outside world seemed to fade, of a small, intensely bright light shining somewhere deep inside me, stirring me to action as the sheer violence of the instinct of self-preservation exerted itself and forced me to get out.

Blindly I groped for the escape hatch, wrenched it off, and threw it away. I shouted and motioned to the operator to get out, but he could not or would not move. Making one last desperate effort, I clawed my way to the edge of the hatch, gathered myself into a ball, and flung myself clear of the aircraft. I must have pulled the rip handle without knowing it because the next thing I knew there was a sharp jerk and I was hanging from the parachute, swaying slowly in a vast, blissful silence, coming down through cloud. And then I was clear of it. A searchlight beam, blurred by the rain, swung dizzily across the A horizon. But it was quickly cut off by the top of an oak tree which came rushing up from below.

I was not conscious of landing, only of somersaulting backwards over the wet clay, clutching with both hands at the precious earth. For the moment I lay there gasping for breath and listening. As my ears cleared I heard the sound of hysterical laughter, and a moment later I realized that it was my own. Then I knew why I was laughing, because I heard another sound. I had been subconsciously expecting the sound of a crash. Instead I heard the even drone of the engines of the aircraft from which I had just jumped, dwindling steadily away in the darkness as the pilot headed back towards base. I could only assume that, with the aircraft relieved of my weight, he had regained control.

Making a note of the time, I carefully rolled up my faithful parachute, and then set off through the darkness to try and find a telephone. I rather felt that I had made a fool of myself, and I should probably have my leg pulled unmercifully by Tommy. But I also realized that I had had the laugh on old Isaac.

My luck was in, for after walking only a few hundred yards across some ploughed land and along a track I met an Air Raid Warden who turned out to be the Vicar of Ecchinswell, the Rev. Tom Evans, who had been called out to investigate a reported breach of the blackout. With him there was a member of the local Home Guard, who was wheeling a bicycle. I appeared before them out of the darkness with the bundle of my parachute in my arms and announced that I was a British airman and unarmed. The Home Guard promptly got behind his bicycle, but the vicar quickly understood what had happened. He took me half a mile down the hill to his home, and very kindly offered to put me up for the night.

While Mrs Evans was preparing some hot soup I 'phoned Middle Wallop and reported where I was. They told me that my pilot had landed safely, but that there was no sign of the operator. Unfortunately my message did not reach the local police, and they spent many uncomfortable hours searching for me.

I had landed on the edge of the Berkshire Downs, and I spent the night with Mr and Mrs Evans. I slept fitfully, for I seemed to spend most of the night, plunging down through dark holes in the floor of an aeroplane, and waking with a start as the parachute cracked open.

The next morning, after a long search among the fog-shrouded lanes around Newbury, a van from the squadron picked me up. They also collected the operator, who had managed to get out and had landed near a pub. He had spent a very different night to mine.

I began to worry about what sort of reception I would get when we arrived back at the station. Baling out without due cause or without orders was considered – by the gunners at any rate – as a very definite black. I had felt justified at the time, but I was not at all happy about it when I realized that the aircraft had got back safely without me. But, fortunately, John thought I was quite justified in what I had done. In any case, the pilot had, it seemed, ordered us to bale out, but as his radio plug had been jerked out of its socket we had not heard him.

After that incident I was sent off on a few days' leave, and I went home. For a Londoner that was not quite as much of a treat as it might have been, as the city was being bombed nearly every night.

I found our flat intact, though there was some cracked plaster from a near miss. Micki was on duty, so I started off for the ambulance depot where she was stationed, planning to spend the night there. As I hurried down the dark, deserted streets the guns down in the Thames estuary began to rumble, and I quickened my steps. Repeated strafing of the aerodrome had hardened me fairly well to bombing and machine-gunning, but out there in the open country one could always jump for a trench, or take to the woods. Here in these echoing black canyons of brick and concrete it was altogether different. I had a creeping horror of those menacing cliffs waiting to crash down on my head.

Three hours later I was sitting in the passenger seat of Micki's ambulance as she drove through the noisy darkness of the blackout. All I could see was the narrow strip of sky between the roofs where shell bursts twinkled and flickered among the stars. But these women ambulance drivers had apparently learnt to drive by instinct as they got very little help from the insignificant light of the masked and hooded sidelights. I was hoping that there were no craters in the road; and above the sound of our engine I could hear the crumps and thuds, the sighing whine of spent shell fragments, and the hideous, shuffling screech of falling bombs.

"Any idea where we are?" Micki asked suddenly, completely shattering my confidence in her navigation. "I can't see a thing."

A waving torch brought us to a standstill, and a Warden came to us and told us to stand by. I jumped out of the ambulance and found myself in a street of those prim and boxlike suburban houses with which the speculative builders had destroyed London's green belt between the wars. The orderly row across from where I stood was broken by a gap which jarred like a missing tooth.

The clamour of the guns was dying out as the raider that had done the damage headed away across the City. I stepped over a flattened fence, and my boots crunched on splintered wreckage. Only a few minutes before, this rubbish heap had been a neat little home surrounded by a trimly kept garden. Somewhere beneath the wreckage lay the man whose pride it had been, together with his wife and small son.

On the far side from me the rescue squads were already at work, picking a cautious way into the rubble. Then they paused, and in a lull in the gunfire they listened for sounds of life. A boy's faint voice could just be heard. All three of them were together, under what was left of the stairs. He told us that his father was dead, and he thought that his mother was dying. The rescuers shouted encouragement, and went on with their quick careful burrowing.

Then the guns started again, thudding and cracking as the next enemy aircraft came diving in. I looked up as the raider droned unscathed across the night sky, and I began to feel sick and ashamed that we should apparently be doing so little about stopping this bombing. And I was ashamed and angry with myself for not being back with the squadron, and at least trying to get at those raiders.

It was a relief to be back in the comparative safety of the aerodrome, but I was more anxious than ever to get on with my new job. The Beaufighters were coming into operational use, and if I was to regain my position in the crew with John there was no time to be lost.

During the time I had been on leave, John had been flying with Phillipson, and they had come tantalizingly close to success. They had followed one AI contact for quite a time without getting a sighting. But the turning point in our fortunes was not far off. On the night of the 20th of November, John and Phillipson went off on patrol. There were hostile aircraft about, and John was vectored after one of them. After a while he saw a concentration of searchlights on the clouds, and he headed towards it.

Phillipson was gazing intently at the cathode ray tubes. And then he got a good, firm contact. During the chase that followed he had a little trouble with his microphone freezing up, but after a short time he fixed that and he was able to bring John into close range of the target they were following.

John was searching the dark sky ahead, and for perhaps the tenth time he forced himself to look away from a cluster of stars that seemed to move in a different way from the others, and as he did so a vague dark shape formed around them, only to dissolve again as he looked directly at it. He climbed a little closer and a silhouette took definite shape.

"OK. I can see it!" he exclaimed.

At last, after all the long months of trial and error, of strain and worry and frustration, at long last he had come to grips with the enemy. A few minutes later the stricken enemy bomber – it was a Junkers 88 – was plunging to the earth, and for the first time an AI equipped Beaufighter proved its worth on routine operational flying with a squadron.

The good news was flashed immediately to Group Headquarters, to Headquarters, Fighter Command, and to Air Ministry. There was solid wreckage on the ground to justify the faith of all those who had worked for so long to bring the radar night fighter into its own. Between them they had made the magic; work and had produced the result for which it was created.

But of the magic the public, and even most of those in the Services, knew nothing; and because it was essential that it should all be kept very much of a secret they were told nothing. In order more effectively to cloak the secret a legend was created which was eagerly swallowed by the hungry Press. John Cunningham, it was said, was a pilot with night vision so miraculous that it enabled him to see in the dark as with the eyes of a cat. And so was born the stupid nickname that John and all the rest of us so heartily detested.

CHAPTER FIVE

That Elusive Echo

WHAT with the way the war was going, the weather, and the antics of old Isaac, we had found things becoming quite depressing, and the opening of the scoring with the Beaufighter and AI came as a great fillip to our morale.

Daily I became more and more impatient to get going myself. Finally, on the 11th of December 1940, my turn came when I was sent off in one of the Blenheims that had been stripped of its turret with a Sergeant pilot on a patrol at 17,000ft.

After the open, all-round vision from the gunner's turret, it gave one an eerie feeling to be buried inside the windowless hull of the aircraft; and for one who always died, as I did, a little death every time we took off, it was an even more anxious moment not to be able to see what was happening. But for perhaps the four hundredth time nothing did happen. The jolting and the rumbling stopped, the engines never faltered, and the first lethal 2,000ft of air flowed smoothly away beneath us. I relaxed and started to warm up the AI set.

It was not really very much warmer inside the unheated fuselage of the aircraft than it had been in the gunner's turret, but one was at least spared the agony of that icy blast that came squirting into the eyes from the slot of the turret. The thermometer dropped as we climbed until it stood at 57 degrees of frost. I huddled over the illusion of warmth from the glowing eyes of the cathode ray tubes, trying to find in that little world of green light some relief from the stark discomfort of the metal floor. But even through the thickness of the prayer mat of blankets upon which I was kneeling it was burning cold. Just as I was reaching that dreadful comatose state to which the cold reduces one the voice of the Sector Controller came crackling into the headphones.

"There's a bandit approaching you. Turn on to two six zero and flash your weapon."

I pressed my face into the visor. Forgotten now were the cold and the listlessness: I was alert with anticipation. The floor shifted as we swung into the turn.

"Flashing," I told the pilot. "No joy yet."

We were quite silent as he went on turning, keeping his eyes on the compass. And then it happened. A great fat blip as clear and as steady as anything the ground trainer could produce dropped out of the ground returns and came rushing down the trace.

"Contact!" I exclaimed. "Throttle back…"

I realized immediately that we must be overtaking very rapidly. Checking on the height I saw that the other aircraft was at about our level.

"Throttle right back!"

But still the blip came rushing down the trace. There was no stopping it, and I felt a surge of panic. And then, much too late, the penny dropped and I realized what was happening. I could scarcely get the words out.

"It – it must be coming head on. It's very close."

"Christ!" the pilot exploded over the intercom. "I'll say it was!"

Our aircraft bucked, jamming my face, feeling rather red by now, into the visor. The pilot was turning as tightly as he dared, and at the same time gasping out an explanation over the intercom about what had happened.

"A dirty great Heinkel skimmed just over our heads damn nearly hit it."

I was breathing heavily myself as I watched for the blip to reappear on the tubes as we came around, and impatiently I fingered the controls of the set. But it was no good. The range of the AI was too limited, and we had turned too late.

We returned to base in a gloomy silence, and during it I tried to weigh things up. I had had my first big chance; I had seen a real, live, hostile blip. Not only had I thrown it away; I had very nearly written us off. What was I going to say to Gilfillan about it.

But I was not the only one in trouble. It was happening throughout the squadron, and at both ends of the aircraft. Too many contacts were being lost, and no-one could tell why. Even when enemy aircraft were brought to battle, they showed a marked reluctance to fall out of the sky.

So far as the pilots were concerned, lost contacts meant only one thing: either the AI set or the operator was not up to the job. A lot of sorting out went on to try and determine which was to blame; and before long something in the nature of a witch-hunt was poisoning the air of the Sergeants' Mess.

Unfortunately this fear of a purge lead only to an increasing reticence amongst the operators about discussing their problems. Instead of talking freely and frankly about our difficulties, we listened sceptically to nothing but hard luck stories about enemy bombers of incredible speed and agility, about AI sets that blew up at critical moments, and about blips that just suddenly disappeared. Some of the less scrupulous operators even developed a technique of continuing the chase after an imaginary blip long after they had lost contact.

Almost as mischievous was the pilot who was too loyal to his operator. On daylight exercises he would try to cover up his operator's failings by following the target visually and making the corrections himself, instead of doing only as he was told by the operator and so giving the man on the AI set a chance to learn by his mistakes. These people were invariably beset when darkness fell by disappearing blips and unserviceable sets.

An operator who was honest with himself could nearly always tell when the pilot was cheating on his behalf. The blip would glue itself to the trace far too readily, with the fighter slowing itself down at just the right moment. From the outset I found that practice with John was never like that. He would fly exactly as the operator told him to until he could see that a mistake was developing. Then, instead of correcting the mistake himself, he would put in a timely word of warning by asking:

"How about the speed?" or "Shall I go on turning?"

Always it was the operator who had to direct things. If the practice got right out of control then John would patiently take the aircraft back and start all over again. He worked on the principle that if things were to go right at night they would have to go right first of all in daylight.

Apart from AI problems, the pilots were also having trouble with the gun-sights. A ring of light with a spot of light at the centre was projected on to a small sheet of glass just in front of the pilot. The spot gave him the aiming point. The ring helped him to judge the range and the amount of deflection that was necessary so as to allow for the target's movement relative to the fighter. The brilliance of this light was adjustable, but it was found that when the ring was dimmed enough to see through its glare to the target the spot was no longer visible. This fault had already caused a number of combats to end inconclusively.

On the 12th of December, Sandi started his scoring as an operator by bringing his pilot, Flight Lieutenant H. Speke, to a visual on a Heinkel. They were at 17,000ft over Ringwood when Speke had gone in to attack only to find that the dimmer on the gunsight would not work. And there he sat, right behind the enemy, almost blinded by the glare from the gunsight, and desperately trying to adjust the dimming switch. Nevertheless, Speke went in to close range and let fly. He got some hits: they saw the flash of the strikes. But the Heinkel roused itself and dived out of sight before they could finish it off.

A week later much the same thing happened to Peter Jackson and Patston. The impetuous Peter emptied his ammunition drums at a Junkers 88 as it dodged wildly all over the place. On the very next night, with Mike O'Leary as his operator, he found one with all its navigation lights on. This very determined young man was not going to be put off any longer. So, partly to identify the other aircraft and partly to make sure of hitting it, he closed in until he was only 30 yards behind and below it. Gunsight or no gunsight, he was going to make sure this time.

But at this point-blank range one of the gunners in the German aircraft spotted them and let fly straight down into the Beaufighter. Mike saw the tracer coming in through the roof of the fuselage and out of the back of Peter's head; and then he was hit. He saw Peter sag as the aircraft rolled over into a dive, but he managed to open the escape hatch and bale out.

Eventually he was found and carted off to hospital. One bullet had gone through one of his legs, and another had grazed his stomach.

But Peter was by no means dead, although he had had a close enough shave. He was knocked out for a few seconds, but when he came around he pulled the aircraft out of its dive and brought it back to base. He was a messy sight, covered with blood, when he walked into dispersal; but he was quite unshaken, and it was only with the greatest reluctance that he allowed himself to be led off to the sick quarters. The next morning the core of an armour-piercing bullet was extracted from between his scalp and his skull.

When we saw Mike in hospital he was cheerful enough, although a little sore.

"You must have been pretty close," I said.

"Close!" He choked back what he was about to say as a nurse walked by. "Listen! I don't mind seeing bloody great iron crosses just over my head, but when you can see the air-gunner shaking his fist at you, well damn that for a lark!"

That night I had a run of bad luck myself, without the excitement. It was my first operational trip with John in a Beaufighter. We took off three times, and each time we had to come straight back. The first return was because of a dead microphone and a faulty gun-sight; the second and third returns were because the AI set went out of commission.

Whenever a set became unserviceable in the air the code word used to notify ground control was to say that the weapon was "'bent." So unreliable were the AI sets at that time that even the youngest of the WAAF in the Operations Rooms soon gave up blushing when they heard over the loudspeaker the altogether too familiar report:

"My thing's bent!"

So, with our weapon bent, John and I had to sit on the ground fuming with rage while the radar mechanics fiddled away with their test gear trying to find the fault, and all the time the Luftwaffe streamed by overhead on their way to plaster Liverpool.

Early in November 1940, the German High Command decided to change their plan of operations. This change led to important developments in the tactics used by our night fighters, as well as in our chances of success. In some ways, I suppose, the enemy played into our hands.

It was easy enough for the Luftwaffe to make the short run across the Strait of Dover from their bases on the Continent, and up the moonlit Thames Estuary to bomb a target the size of London. But now they decided to launch attacks against Coventry, Birmingham, Wolverhampton and other places in the Midlands, and that meant crossing 70 miles of sea, followed by a long stretch of blacked-out, hostile country. They soon discovered, as our own Bomber Command found, that a large number of their aircraft failed altogether to find their targets.

To make sure of locating and marking these targets, the Luftwaffe entrusted one of their crack bomber units, the famous K Gr 100, with the task of leading the way. Flying Heinkel 111's, they were equipped with a special aid to blind bombing using radio beams known as "X-Gerät"; and their navigators could be trusted to find their targets and start the fires which the rest of the bomber force could see from afar and stoke up with ease. The destruction of any one of these pathfinders – or "firelighters", as we called them then – might pay double dividends in that it would mean the elimination of an expert crew and the possible diversion of a part of the main load of bombs.

The interception and destruction of these special Heinkels detailed to lead the way to the targets in the Midlands became our main objective. In order to get off to an early start, the Heinkels were crossing the Channel from Cherbourg while there was still some light, making a landfall between the Needles and Portland Bill. They would then continue on overland to pin point the target. We decided to meet these early birds by sending out special patrols. It was thought that by keeping below and down light the fighter might be able to see them silhouetted against the afterglow from miles away and so stalk them either visually or by AI until the light was favourable for an attack.

On the 23rd of December, John Cunningham, with John Phillipson as his operator, took off on one of the first of these dusk patrols. It was at 5 o'clock, and already getting dark on the ground. But at 15,000ft it was still broad daylight.

Everything went exactly to plan. Fifty miles out to sea, south of Lulworth, they spotted the first Heinkel coming in. After a long, cautious stalk John hit the pathfinder squarely in the bomb load. It blew up in a ghastly display of fireworks, with coloured flares and burning incendiaries showering out as the big machine lurched into a dive that was nearly vertical. The wreck, burning furiously, plunged into the cloud below and vanished from sight. Three parachute flares that had fallen out went swinging after it, garishly lighting the scene for a brief moment.

Ideas had been forming for some time in John's mind about the most suitable tactics for night attack, and this combat did a lot to confirm what he had in mind. His plan was that there should be a cautious stalk from just below the tail of the target. If identification had not been made by then a more careful check should be possible from almost vertically below the other aircraft. This would provide the broadest silhouette of the bomber with the least possibility of being seen. Then, satisfied that he was all ready for an attack, the pilot should pull up into a firing position just below and behind with the range slowly opening. On no account must there be, for John, any rushing in with hit-or-miss tactics.

It was arranged that I should fly with John on the dusk patrols for the two nights that were to follow, those of Christmas Eve and Christmas Day. Speculation was rife among those in the Services and civilians alike about the chances of an unofficial truce over the holiday. It was generally thought that the Germans would hold their hand, if only for the sake of world opinion and their own convenience; but there was no way of being sure that they would not pull a fast one and try and catch our defences with their paper hats on. Naturally I hoped for a truce in the bombing as much as anyone else, but I could not help also wishing that they might, perhaps, send over just one reconnaissance machine that we might have a go at.

All day long the weather brooded in a dull, grey overcast and on the strength of that the Christmas Eve celebrations got off to an early start. By 5 o'clock, as I changed into flying kit, everyone not on duty had caught the party spirit, and in the Sergeants' Mess things were definitely warming up. As we taxied out across the deserted airfield and roared off into the gloom, churning our way blindly up through thick cloud. I thought of what a hell of a way it was to spend a Christmas Eve. All the same, I would not have wished myself anywhere else.

And then it began to get light above us, and suddenly, like a submarine surfacing, we broke through the cloud and into a fantastic wonderland floodlit with purple light. The whole western sky was still ablaze with the glory of the afterglow. We were heading into it, and behind us the first faint stars were beginning to peep out. Below us the cloud swept to the horizon in a smooth carpet of purple snow, and in all that world we were the only living things: no reconnaissance aircraft, no firelighters, not even Father Christmas in his sleigh.

We turned and went on down towards the Channel Islands. Through an occasional gap in the cloud beneath us we saw glimpses of the small dark blurs that were Alderney and Sark. I wondered how they felt about it down there under the occupation. And what were the German sentries thinking about as they listened to the distant drone of our engines, stamping their feet to keep warm? Wondering when their invasion of our island was coming off? Or why they were not home for Christmas? Or growing sentimental, perhaps, over "Heilige Nacht?"

The light faded as we continued up and down on our patrol line, and the stars began to blaze with all that heavenly glory that can never be seen from our mist and smoke-shrouded earth. I began to watch the cathode ray tubes more intently, and to warm myself by sections from the hot air supply. Even in the new Beaufighter there were still chinks through which icy blasts sprayed into the fuselage.

Nothing came out to meet us, and we had the world to ourselves. But that did not matter: this was no night for killing. Then we were heading back for base, plunging down into the cloud. With a last swirl it closed over our heads, and we were back in the gloom again, groping our way back to base. I said goodnight to John, and went in to the lights and the noise of the party.

An overflushed Tommy pushed a spilling pint mug into my hand with the warning: "Come on you've got a lot of leeway to make up."

Mechanically I poured it down. Part of my mind was still up there with the stars. From our wing of the Mess there came the familiar sound of dustbins bouncing down stone steps. The boys were winding up in their usual fashion with a quiet session of bicycle riding down the steps with the dustbins for obstacles at each corner.

I thought of the next morning and the way we would all feel. Tommy and I would have the answer. We would wake them early to inquire what they had found in their stockings by a method known to us as "the patter of tiny feet". We had a large cabinet in our room which we called Big Bernard, and it had heavy east-iron feet. Tommy and I could just raise it to shoulder-height. When we let it go it produced in the room below, occupied by Sandi and Stan Hawke, an effect similar to that of a land-mine.

Oh well! Stille Nacht! Heilige Nacht.

CHAPTER SIX

The Prentice Hand

TWO days after the New Year, John caught another Heinkel on the dusk patrol. As luck would have it, Phillipson was with him as his operator.

They were patrolling 40 miles out in the Channel when they were given a report of a raider to the north of them. John turned, and shortly afterwards he saw a Heinkel a quarter of a mile ahead and well above him. But there was so much light on the cloud below that if they had closed in then their own silhouette would have betrayed them. So John bided his time and followed at a discreet distance, waiting for the light to fade.

Phillipson had the AI set switched on in order to make sure of holding the contact. It was just as well that he did because while John was making a final adjustment to his gun-sight he lost sight of the enemy. In spite of his microphone freezing up again at the critical moment, Phillipson managed to get over enough of his directions to give John another sighting, and they both breathed more easily.

When John finally went in to attack they were about 10 miles south of Lyme Regis. One of the cannon stopped, but he gave the Heinkel all the rest. Something heavy came back and bumped along the under surface of the Beaufighter. But there was nothing spectacular about the end of that raider. It turned gradually to the left, slowly losing height, white smoke pouring from the useless port engine. It continued turning until it was heading back to the south. But steadily it steepened its dive until it shot down into the cloud below at an angle of 50 degrees. From the scoring point of view it was rather a disappointment because John could only claim it as probably destroyed.

A few days later the Group Armament Officer came to the squadron to see why we were having so much trouble reloading the cannon in the air. He flew with John in the afternoon, and at 20,000ft I gave a faultless demonstration of how it should be done. I naturally went out of my way to explain that it was easy enough when flying straight and level in daylight, but that at night, with the aircraft twisting and turning in all directions, it was a very different story! On the other hand, I did feel rather pleased that all my zealous practising was bearing fruit. But my feeling of self-satisfaction was very shortlived. That same night I was given three hostile contacts and I lost them all through my own stupidity or, as it was put, more decisively in the Service, clottish finger trouble.

I felt pretty desperate about the way those lively echoes fooled me. Two of them had apparently run away from us with the most incredible speed. But

I had heard that story too many times already, and I still could not believe it. Thinking about it, I got the idea that we must have overtaken our target and passed below it without realizing what was happening, and we must then have run away in front. With the curly form of AI equipment we had, which could see quite well behind as well as in front, it was not always immediately apparent from the picture on the cathode ray tubes whether the echo was coming from in front of or behind the fighter. If it was behind then the faster we went the faster the range increased as the target dropped further and further behind.

When I put this theory to John he agreed to try it out during our next daylight practice. Sure enough, by coming in a little too low and too fast, we found ourselves away out in front and then running away from the target as fast as we could go. So that exploded the myth of those incredibly fast bombers which had apparently run away from so many of us. I was more impatient than ever to have another go at the real thing.

The manner in which the Luftwaffe employed K Gr 100 was the first of two new factors which did a great deal to alter in our favour the pattern of the night air fighting. The second, and far more important, of these factors was the introduction on the south coast of a new type of ground radar control station which gave our night fighters a far more accurate picture of what was happening and a much closer support.

These new ground radar stations – named Ground Controlled Interception, or, for short, GCI, stations – enabled the controller, watching the whole course of an interception on a large cathode ray tube, to direct the fighter until he had brought it into position a mile or so behind the bomber. With this close control it was hoped that the operator in the aircraft would only have to wait until the blip appeared all neatly lined up on his AI tubes and then take over the interception.

On the night of the 12th of January 1941, John and I were given a chance for me to try my hand for the first time operationally with this new system of control, which was already in use in our neighbouring sector, Tangmere.

We climbed away to the eastward, and at 3,000ft we broke through the cloud into a clear, moonlit sky. John called up the Tangmere GCI – which bore the apt code name of "Boffin" – and the controller turned us south, sending us out into the Channel. When we got to the coast we found that the cloud stopped short, hanging like a sharply trimmed ice-cap over the gleaming chalk cliffs of the Seven Sisters. I sat watching the cliffs as they receded into the moon haze on the horizon.

"Hallo, Blazer Two Four," Boffin called. "Orbit…orbit. There is a bandit coming in. Angels eleven."

"OK, Boffin," John acknowledged. "Orbiting."

The engines took on a deeper, sterner note as John opened up the throttles. Over the intercom he said to me:

"I'm going up to 15. We'd better have a bit of height in hand."

The vectors began to flow in from Boffin. One five zero...turn starboard on to two one zero...turn port on to zero six zero...

Although I was keeping my eyes fixed on the tubes of the AI set I had in my mind a picture of what this all meant. We had been turned aside so as to allow the bandit to pass. Now we were swinging around in pursuit, and heading back towards the coast.

"Flash your weapon," came the instruction from Boffin.

For about the twentieth time I adjusted the tuning control.

"No joy yet," I reported to John.

We were fairly humming along. The chase was on and we could not be far behind. Was that a bulge just beginning to form at extreme range, at the foot of the Christmas tree? I held my breath and hoped that I would not make a hash of this one. It was definitely a blip, just appearing. I gave it a few more seconds to get clearly out of the ground returns, and then I moistened my lips and found my voice.

"Contact at 15,000ft," I told John. "Slightly port and well below."

I had stuck my neck out and admitted liability for what was about to happen; now I should have to do something about it. Well, first of all to get dead astern of the target.

"Check port," I said.

The blip swung across the trace as John turned to the left and then centred again as he straightened out on the same course, having executed a neat side-step.

"Dead ahead...range 10,000." I reported. "We'd better lose some height before we get any closer."

In a manoeuvre such as this it was no good just diving. That would only have meant gathering still more speed and finally shooting over the top of the bomber. But John had already worked out a plan for this. He throttled back the engines, dropped the wheels to act as an air brake, and gently started to sink. The range went on decreasing, but at a rate that was well under control.

The blip was slowly drifting out to the left again, so we went through another side-step. While I was concentrating on this I forgot to keep an eye on the height. A timely reminder came from John as he said:

"On course. I'm still losing height, by the way."

"OK. Level out now," I replied. I hoped that it sounded as if I had thought of it myself. "Range 8,000 dead ahead and level...increase speed again."

The two Hercules engines stopped their sulky spitting and the aircraft surged forward to their happier purring as John opened up the throttles. But that blip would keep drifting to the left. We must be on a slightly diverging heading. I gave a correction:

"Turn port 10 degrees."

That ought to take care of it. We were in to 5,000ft now, and the blip was sharp and clear. But now it was drifting to the right. I had over-corrected in the last turn.

"Turn starboard 5 degrees."

"Starboard 5," John acknowledged.

That was better. We seemed to have made a lucky guess at the height too. But it was time to slow up. I increased my commentary, giving John as complete a picture as possible of what was happening.

"Range 3,000. Throttle back a bit. It's dead ahead and slightly above."

Squarely astride the trace, the blip was coming down quite well as the range decreased. But I was becoming rather excited, and with that there came a fear that we might be coming in too fast.

"Range 2,000...still ahead...15 degrees above. Throttle right back. Range 1,500..."

The blip was still moving steadily down towards minimum range, and I became really scared that we were going to overshoot.

"1,200...1,000...still ahead and 30 degrees above. 900."

The aircraft was swinging uneasily. John had cut the throttles right back, and the engines were coughing and popping. And there, at the bottom of the trace, sat the blip, fat and squat. There was a horrible moment of crisis as it hovered at minimum range. Then slowly it started to climb the trace again as our own speed dropped off.

"Increase speed again," I told John. "'It's still there, 30 degrees above."

At these close ranges quick thinking was essential. John, I knew, would be keyed up to the limit, quick to react to every call I made. His eyes would be searching where I directed, his hands and feet and brain flying the aircraft by instinct born of long experience.

As the engines picked up again I felt the aircraft settle into her normal, easy stride. And then there was a sudden, unexpected movement, followed by a short exclamation from John. The blip started moving in again, but with a new certainty of movement.

"OK. I can see it!" John said.

My heart leapt. The miracle had happened! At long last it had happened! I stifled my elation and continued to read off what I was seeing on the cathode ray tubes until the blip finally disappeared inside minimum range and I knew that I could be of no further help.

"It's all right," John said. "You can take a look now."

Covering over the visor I swung my seat around sideways. There, just where the AI had indicated, was a dark shadow, its outline blurred by the moonlight, silhouetted against the soft velvet of the night sky.

John brought the Beau in until the enemy aircraft was well above us. Then, maintaining the same position, he climbed until we were a bare 300ft beneath it. The shadow became an outline and grew a tail, and the wings took on a definite shape. A nose and engine nacelles began to fill out a well learned pattern.

"What would you say it is?" John asked.

I knew that he had already satisfied himself as to its identity, but he wanted confirmation.

"My guess is a Heinkel 111," I told him. "It's got the right sweep to the wings and the Heinie elliptical tail."

"Yes…I think it's a Heinkel all right."

We had been flying along in company with the enemy bomber for three or four minutes by now while we calmly decided on the fate of the four men just above us. It was all quite leisurely and well ordered and not at all what I had anticipated it would be like. John was taking his time as he carefully adjusted the brilliance of his gun-sight.

"All right," he said. "Here we go then."

Everything seemed to have gone deathly quiet. The only sounds I was conscious of were John's steady breathing coming over the intercom, and a pounding in my ears.

Up went our nose as John started to climb. The Heinkel seemed to sink slowly until it was in line with the top of our aircraft, shrinking into a narrow, streamlined pencil. I could see now with some satisfaction that it was quite definitely a Heinkel, with the bulbous fuselage sitting high on the wing and the engines tucked in like the talons of a bird of prey.

It sank out of sight as we came up level with it. I ducked my head inside and looked along the roof and saw it reappear just over John's head. It continued to sink into the gunsight. The Beaufighter was quivering in minute, nervous jerks as John brought the spots to bear.

Then suddenly there was a great thudding and shaking as the guns fired. Long tongues of flame as naked as gas jets came curling back from the ports, lighting every chink and cranny in the floor, and for a moment I thought we were on fire. It was as if four rowdy great giants were beating on the hull with their fists. The air was thick with acrid smoke. And then, just as suddenly as the noise had started, there was silence.

To my astonishment the Heinkel sailed on not in the least concerned that it was being attacked. This is ridiculous, I thought. It should be blowing up!

"The guns have stopped," John said.

I jumped down from my seat and had a look at them. "There's still plenty in the drums," I told him.

"All right. We'll try again."

This time I kept my eyes on the target. The pounding started, and a shower of little white flashes sparkled all over the enemy's starboard engine. And then the guns petered out again. The Heinkel still flew on, apparently quite unperturbed. It was really too absurd. Here we were barely 100 yards away in bright moonlight blazing away with four great cannon. And they just ignored us. Even though we were not using tracer, it was simply inconceivable that the German crew still did not realize that they were being fired at.

I got down to the gun controls again to have a good look around. Then I saw what was wrong: the air pressure of the firing system had failed. I was still poking around trying to find the source of the trouble when the Beau heeled over.

"Now the wretched man's shooting back at us," John said, with a slight note of irritation in his voice.

Clutching at the seat, I hauled myself to my feet and looked outside. Someone in the Heinkel had at last woken up, and a string of glowing red balls looking like hot tomatoes was floating slowly back towards us. As they got closer they seemed to swerve, and then, gathering speed, they flicked past over our starboard wing in angry red streaks.

John was turning away, diving to the left, but the angry red stream came hosing after us. I tried, with a peculiar fascination, to realize that these were incendiary bullets, and that for every one, that we could see there were three or four that we could not see. The gunner kept pumping away at us, always just a few feet behind. If only he would allow a little more deflection, I thought with a detached and rather professional interest, if he would just swing that gun a little faster! But gunners so rarely do allow enough to follow a curving path, and this one was no exception. The shooting became wilder as the distance separating us increased, and finally it stopped.

Levelling out, John turned to fly on a parallel course, keeping the Heinkel just in sight up moon. To my surprise I found myself on my feet, crouching like a boxer at the side of my seat, huddling for protection against the thin metal skin of the hull of the aircraft. I quickly shook myself out of that, feeling rather indignant and not a little foolish, and started fiddling again with the gun controls. But I could not find what was wrong. There was still not enough air pressure to fire the guns, and short of ramming the other aircraft there appeared to be nothing more we could do.

The Heinkel had slowed down a lot, and was gradually losing height. And it was also slowly turning away and heading back across the Channel. At least we had kept the German from bombing their target.

We also headed back for base. Although the result was disappointing, I had had some satisfaction out of the evening's engagement: I had at last brought a hostile echo into view and given my pilot a target to work on.

Furthermore, we had had a taste of what this close control from the ground could do. If all our customers were going to be handed to us on a plate like that when our own shop – as we had come to call the GCI – got going then we could look forward to some very lively trading.

The Shop that Brown Built

THE chief controller of the GCI station in our sector was Squadron Leader John Lawrence Brown, a big fleshy man with a roving eye and a rich, fruity voice, and that genial, well fed look that one usually associates with gentlemen farmers. But although Brownie – as he became known to all night fighters – liked the comforts of life he did not allow them to interfere with the job in which he was completely absorbed. Being a pilot himself he could discuss our problems knowledgeably and he was able to make constructive suggestions. One of the first was that we should visit his GCI and see for ourselves how he was trying to run his shop.

Small parties were made up on our nights off duty, and several of us at a time drove down to a remote field near the coast where "Starlight" – the code name of our GCI – had been set up. It was not at all easy to find, and when we did get there it was not a very impressive sight. There were a few wooden huts, with some lorries scattered about, a caravan draped in a tarpaulin, and a strange contraption which looked more like a huge, flattened bird cage than an aerial array slowly revolving on its base.

We were escorted to the caravan, and we felt our way in the darkness up the steps. Inside we found Brownie seated before the control panel which looked something like a desk, and grouped around him were several airmen and airwomen, all muffled up against the cold, and all concentrating on their various tasks. A second glance around revealed that there were apparently more airwomen than airmen, and that they were an unusually attractive lot of girls, good looking and alert.

"Just like a Sultan in his harem," Tommy whispered in my ear.

But under Brownie's guidance we soon forgot all about the beauty chorus, and we listened with the closest attention as he explained things to us. His enthusiasm was infectious, and he went carefully over everything. It was reassuring to know that our guidance from the ground was to be in the hands of such a man.

In the centre of the control desk at which Brownie sat there was a very large cathode ray tube on the face of which there had been painted the neighbouring coastline of our sector. On this tube – called the Plan Positioner Indicator, or, for short, the PPI – all aircraft coming within range of the station produced small blips which automatically marked their position on the map. The airmen and airwomen hovering around were giving readings in brisk monosyllables to others at the far end of the caravan. These, in turn, were plotting the tracks of the aircraft, juggling nimbly with navigation computers, and working out courses and speeds. Others were sitting in front of another cathode ray tube working out the height of the aircraft. The whole team was working smoothly and quietly and with an impressive absence of fuss and confusion.

In the midst of it all sat Brownie, microphone in hand, quite the genial host. Now and again he could break off from his explanations to us about what was going on to ask one of his team for a height or a speed, or to pass a vector over the radio-telephone to the fighter on patrol.

We were able to see a practice interception between two of our own squadron's aircraft, and under Brownie's seemingly casual directions we watched as he brought together the two blips on the cathode ray tube. As they merged he excused himself to give the matter his undivided attention. And then from the loudspeaker in the corner the voice of the pilot of the fighter announced:

"OK, Starlight. Contact. Thank you."

There was a smile of the proud showman on his face as Brownie turned back to us and went on with his explanations. He showed us how friend could be distinguished from foe on the PPI, something that originated in the little mystery box we had in our aircraft which we knew as IFF.

And there were the limitations with which they were faced. Low flying aircraft were very hard to track, and high ground and other obstacles had a masking effect in a way similar to the swamping of our own A.I. picture from the ground returns. By the time Brownie had finished we were only too ready to overlook the occasional blunders which had been vexing us, and even to forgive being placed in front of the target instead of behind it, as had already happened more than once.

In order to maintain a complete coverage of the sky the aerial outside had to keep sweeping around in a full circle. But by pressing a simple bell-push Brownie could quickly stop or reverse the sweep and direct the aerial to any particular part of the sky on which he wanted to concentrate.

"It's quite simple," he explained. "The bell just signals the Binders to pedal the other way."

He led us out of the caravan and across towards the aerial. And there in a shack underneath it we saw the Binders, anonymous and humble heroes. They were two airmen sitting on a contraption something like a tandem bicycle pedalling away to nowhere as they drove around the heavy structure of wire mesh above them. For them there was nothing but the sheer drudgery of pedalling: they could not even see the blips of the aircraft they were to help to pick up and destroy.

While Brownie was getting his shop in order we were far from idle. For one thing there was a great deal to learn about the best way in which we could co-operate with each other. And at the same time we continued to lay the dusk trap for the Heinkels of K Gr 100. It was not until the middle of February, however, that I had the chance to see the trap sprung.

As we headed out from Bournemouth on the start of our patrol the glowing evening sky was crystal clear right to the horizon. Ahead, on the right, the lakes and sandbanks of Poole Harbour glinted like a mirror in the twilight; behind us, on the port quarter, the tall chalk pinnacles of the Needles stood like ghosts in the vague mistiness of the encroaching tide of darkness.

Forty miles south of Lulworth, at 15,000ft, we reached our beat, and we began to plod up and down. I had the AI warmed up and tuned in: down light the visibility was deceptive and I wanted to be ready for a radar search. But for the time being I kept a visual watch outside, peering into the shining arc of the sky to the south-west.

We did not have long to wait. A few minutes after we were in position the Controller's voice came rattling into our earphones.

"Here comes the first one," he warned. "Angels twelve. You are right on his track."

Quickly John dropped to 11,500ft, so as to put us down into the misty obscurity that lay shorewards and the enemy high against the luminous backcloth. The minutes ticked by and we reached the end of our beat and turned back. Now I had the better view, and remembering my air-gunner's training I began to quarter the sky. Then I saw it.

"There he is!" I exclaimed. "High on the port quarter."

John brought the Beau wheeling around on its wing-tip. The enemy was a tiny black speck still miles away but incredibly distinct against the opal curtain of light. It must have been 1,000ft higher than we were and it was coming our way fast, growing bigger and more like a Heinkel every second. Surely, I thought, he must be able to see us.

I turned to look down light, trying to judge how far he could see in our direction. It was certainly very murky looking that way, with the sea and the sky blending into a dull grey haze. The Heinkel was soon high overhead, and John was turning in order to keep vertically beneath it. Apparently they had not seen us, and they continued serenely on their way. John held his position below them, keeping watch through the roof panel.

For a very long ten minutes we continued in company, and all the time it was getting darker. But now, all too plainly for my liking, the Dorset coast was showing up. Perhaps the German skipper thought the same thing. The Heinkel went into a slow turn to the right.

I had the horrible thought that he had spotted us against the sea and that he was going to make a run for home. But John was not to be panicked into over-hasty action. Steadily he went into a shadowing turn, glancing up and down from the bomber to his instruments. We had turned through 90 degrees and continued on to 180. Was he going to straighten up? No, he was going on around the clock. Two-seventy and then out he came at 360, straightening up on a northerly heading again. The poor devil was just waiting for it to get dark.

On we went, still keeping station, until the sweep of Lyme Bay, a dark blur by now, was close ahead. A few scattered stars began to twinkle feebly through the gathering dusk. The welcome darkness, the protecting cloak for which the German crew had been waiting, was closing around them like a shroud.

"I think it's time enough", John said.

He opened up the throttles, and the Beaufighter rose like a lift, with the bomber swelling monstrously above our heads. I was seized with a ridiculous feeling of a need for stealth, and I wanted to talk in whispers, to peer cautiously around corners, to move on tiptoe. I quickly checked the AI, the safety catches on the guns, the air pressure. Everything was in order, Then I turned and made a visual search behind and below, stretching my neck to the limit. There was nothing there: only the murky greyness of the sea. But even then there was background enough for an air-gunner who was really on the alert to spot us. Now we were in position for an attack.

"All set," I reported, making the effort to raise my voice above a stage whisper. "Nothing behind."

"Good," John said. "Here goes."

Again there came that strained silence as the Heinkel sank slowly into our sights. I waited for the hot tomatoes to come streaming back at us, and I was still waiting when our own guns started their giant pounding. For the first few noisy seconds nothing at all seemed to happen. Then through the choking haze of smoke from the guns I saw the flash of hits on the starboard engine as John shifted his aim.

The ammunition ran out, and the enemy bomber slewed around into a gentle dive. I jumped onto the cat-walk and began feverishly clawing the empty drums from the guns, tossing them up onto the racks, and gingerly easing down the heavy refills on to the hot breech blocks. The last drum was still half full, and there was a live shell jammed in the breach. Time was running short so I left it and climbed back to my seat. Gasping for breath I reported to John:

"Guns reloaded...set to fire."

But the Heinkel had disappeared. John had lost sight of it as soon as it had dived below the horizon, and the night had swallowed it up. I turned to the AI, but the picture there was as empty as the sky. It was not until then that I realized that I should have stayed on the set and kept in contact before reloading. Why did I always have to learn my lessons the hard way?

John was calling the Controller for information and fortunately they still had track of our bandit. He had turned and was heading west just inside the coast, and was steadily losing height. John opened up the engines and set off in pursuit, while I sat gazing hungrily at the empty cathode ray tubes.

Slowly but surely as we reduced height the Christmas tree of the ground returns began to swallow up the distance I could see ahead.

We were down to 3,000ft, and the things were looking pretty hopeless. The Controller's voice had faded out and we did not know which way to look next.

"We'll give it another three minutes," John said; "then we'd better turn back."

Just as he finished speaking a stick of incendiaries scored the ground a few miles ahead with a thick, unbroken line of flame, as if marking it with a jab from a red pencil.

"They were dropped from pretty low down," I commented.

Could it have been that they were jettisoning their load at the last minute? The answer came a moment later. Just beyond where the incendiaries provided a vivid pointer a sudden ugly gush of flame splashed along the ground. The Heinkel had gone in.

The radio and radar war was livening up, developing into a seesaw between weapon and counter-weapon. The Germans, although behind us in the development of radar, were not slow to realize that we were very much on the alert, and their bomber crews began to use more guile. But we held the advantages we had gained.

Gilfillan and Parry and our Special Signals people had rigged up a radar beacon – probably the first in squadron use – which we could pick up on our AI at a distance of 50 miles and more. With this we could guide our pilots back to base without cluttering up the radio channels asking for homing bearings.

And by this time when we got back to base there was greatly improved airfield lighting to welcome us home. Even if the pilot found the weather too thick there for him to make a landing, he could switch over to newly installed Standard Beam Approach and be guided to a safe landing at another airfield.

But although all these things were in our favour, we were only too well aware that any advantage they gave us might very easily be only a temporary one. Even our successes were, in a way, telling against us. The enemy's navigators took to flying with constantly changing courses and heights so as not to be sitting ducks; their air-gunners became more vigilant and much quicker on the trigger; and their pilots were ever on the alert to answer with violent evasive action any shout of warning. This all called for much swifter skill and more subtle guile on our part.

We were not lagging behind in the race for ever sharper and more reliable tools, and twice during February John and I had a glimpse of what the backroom boys were cooking up to keep us in the lead.

Early in the month John flew over to the de Havilland works at Hatfield, taking me with him, to have a look at the prototype of the new

Mosquito night fighter. The people there were anxious to have his opinion of their latest child. Geoffrey de Havilland took him around to show off its paces, and then sent him off alone. Twenty minutes later John was back, and his eyes were shining. While he went into a huddle with the team, I climbed into the cockpit and made notes about the shape of things to come.

Shortly after this there appeared one day in one of the squadron aircraft a new type of AI which was still in the experimental stage. This aimed at relaying a composite picture of what the operator was seeing on his set to the pilot, and at presenting it to him on a small, separate cathode ray tube. It provided the pilot with yet another instrument to watch, and reduced the role of the operator to that of little more than a robot machine attendant.

John and I tried it out with one of the other squadron aircraft as target, first with Gilfillan and then with Parry as instructor. Although I was intrigued with its possibilities, I was not at all convinced that it was a step in the right direction. It might well reduce the time lag that occurred when the all-too-human operator had to interpret what he was seeing and tell the pilot what was happening, as well as give corrections of course and speed. But I felt that it was going too far in transferring the burden of the problem of the interception from the operator to the already overtaxed pilot. That was all well and good with a pilot of exceptional ability. But how many such pilots could be mass produced in wartime? I felt it would be easier and quicker to take men of reasonable intelligence and train them to be efficient operators.

I advanced this argument – at the risk of being thought union minded – but it did not seem to cut much ice with the technical people. The early failures of the more dim-witted operators had left too deep an impression, and now the policy was to produce an AI set which would display its information automatically to the pilot. Until that wonder weapon arrived the purge was to be intensified, and a drive was started to recruit as operators men with intelligence and the particular ability to be able to think quickly.

Alistair Hunter had decided to have as his operator Pilot Officer T. Genny, one of the commissioned ex-gunners who had already won an MC in the First World War. It was understandable that Tommy should feel miserable about it, and with a loyalty that was almost pathetic, he shadowed Hunter like a faithful dog.

While Tommy was still changing into flying kit one night, Hunter went off on a short, belated air test, taking Genny with him. Tommy, who had been hoping to go, came rushing into the crew room, breathing fire.

"Well, stop me!" he exclaimed. "Why couldn't he wait a few minutes."

"Never mind," I said, trying to soothe his ruffled feelings. "He's only gone around the houses for ten minutes. You haven't missed much."

But I was dead wrong. Tommy missed a great deal. As we stood outside looking across at Danebury Hill, soft and round in the crisp moonlight, we heard the Beaufighter droning around the circuit. Its red and green navigation lights straightened up as the aircraft came heading in towards us. Then suddenly the red light dipped, the green one rolled over it, they both plunged out of sight beyond the boundary hedge and there was silence and darkness. We started to run. We reached the hedge and tore our way through. The fire tender was bogged down in the perimeter wire, and its crew were fighting to cut it free as we raced past. There was still no fire, so there was still a hope. All around men were running in ones and twos, cursing the wire and the unseen brambles that clawed at limbs and clothing.

The first rush was losing its momentum and direction as the searchers fanned out, and the lights of torches wandered about among the trees and bushes. Then there was a burst of shouting, and the lights closed in towards a line of tall poplars. We ran with the others, and finally we all came to a halt in a silent half-circle.

There lay the shattered aircraft, a crumpled mass on the grass. And beside it lay its crew, peacefully, as though asleep. They were both dead.

We rode back on one of the crash wagons, silent and miserable. When we got into the crew-room, Tommy gave vent to his feelings by kicking his locker door shut.

"So that jinx got him at last," he muttered. "I knew it would if he went without me."

He wondered out into the moonlight. Knowing that for once no words of mine could comfort him, I left him alone.

March, so far as I was concerned, was a terrible month. There were plenty of customers, but all I had was a long torment of fading blips and finger trouble. Several times moonlight and wandering searchlights betrayed us to the enemy, and then I was much too slow off the mark to be able to follow the panic dives of the alerted bombers. Throughout one unhappy sortie patrolling Spithead we spent the entire time trying to get a firm hold on a series of ghost echoes which could have been caused by any one of a multitude of indefinable things. And all the time a rain of bombs smashed and burned out the heart of Portsmouth. Some days later Gilfillan managed to locate an obscure fault in the set.

But it could not go on forever. Patient servicing and determined practice, I felt, must eventually pay off. And they did, one night early in April, when we had the satisfaction of seeing every cog in the complex machine working smoothly and efficiently.

We were among the last due to take off on the programme for that night, and a host of customers had already streamed in through the shop by the time we were called upon to serve them. Climbing up through a turbulent mass of cloud, we eventually broke through into the clear skies lit only by the light of the stars and a young moon. The pale glow made the ghostly cloudscape look like a lot of drifting icebergs. We headed for the coast, and John called up the GCI.

"Hallo, Starlight. This is Blazer Two Four calling. Are you receiving me?"

All formality vanished with the sound of Brownie's warm friendly voice replying: "Good evening, John." It was quite unhurried. "I think we've got a customer for you. Angels ten and stand by."

It was almost as if Brownie had just moved his stool two places along a well lighted bar and was signalling to the landlord to take our order. I thought of what it was in reality, and I could see the draughty caravan and the flapping canvas, and plotters working with chilled fingers over their computers.

Brownie began to give us vectors in his usual sure and informative way, turning us to cut off the retreat of a homeward bound bandit, what we used to call a "returned empty".

"He'll be crossing starboard to port," Brownie reported. "Range 2 miles. Turn port on to…"

It appeared on the tubes of my own set, and I cut him short as I called to John over the intercom:

"Contact…7,000ft…turn port."

We were used to jinking targets by now. This one seemed to be following no set pattern, just wandering southward in easy, haphazard curves. I cut the corners in order to close in faster, and had just slowed down for the final stalk when I had to leave the set to make an adjustment to the IFF. During the few seconds I was away John caught a glimpse of the engine exhausts of the bomber drifting across at fairly close range. But they quickly disappeared, and he throttled back and waited for me to take up the story again where I had left off.

The blip was still there, only 2,000ft away. We closed in to half that range. And then John said:

"OK. You can have a look."

I swivelled around and I saw our bird, already taking the familiar shape of a Heinkel as John cautiously moved in below it. But that was not what caught my attention. What took my breath away was the fantastic setting of the scene. All around us there towered great mountains of billowing cumulo-nimbus cloud, and the Heinkel was winding its way between their snowy, moonlit crests. We were sneaking along behind and below it in the darkened valleys between what looked like mighty cliffs of ice. Now I understood the reason for those erratic curves. That German pilot was not going to endure the discomfort of flying through a turbulent cumulo-nimbus cloud when he could go around it.

A violent thunderstorm was raging in the depths of that heaving turmoil of cloud, and every few seconds the lightning flashed across, lighting the whole scene with a horrible, steel-blue clarity. We could see clear-cut every detail of the Heinkel.

Surely, I thought, their gunners must be able to see us just as plainly as we could see them. We were barely 100 yards away. As we crept in, each flash of lightning was a stab at the nerves, and as the darkness leapt back over us I sighed with relief. The Heinkel rode on, beautiful, serene and unheeding. Finally we were right below it, ready to attack.

"OK?" John asked.

"Yes," I replied. "Hold your hat on."

"Right. In we go!"

Slowly, very slowly, the Heinkel sank towards our sights. This was their gunner's chance, just before we could bring our cannon to bear. We were a sitting duck, only 80 yards away, and in moonlight. Pale-blue exhaust flames licked along the engine cowlings of the bomber, and John, in his calm, detached way, noticed that the outboard flames were on a lower level than those inboard.

Our aircraft wriggled nervously as John brought the gunsight on to his target. Then he opened fire, and almost at once the whole sky ahead of us seemed to dissolve in flame. My knees caved in as the floor heaved underfoot. Every slot and chink in the hull was lit by the lurid glow of the sea of fire from the exploding Heinkel as we ploughed on through it. Things bumped and scraped along outside. And then we were through it all and out into the darkness. My eardrums and breathing relaxed, and I became conscious again of the reassuring roar of our own engines. We still seemed to be flying.

"Are we all in one piece?" I asked.

"Yes...I think so," John replied. His voice was still quite calm as he took stock, methodically checking over his instruments. "Let's see now. Oil pressures...temperatures...yes...everything seems to be all right."

There had come back into our Beaufighter the typical smell of a burning German aircraft, a smell that was to make a deep and most unpleasant impression on me. It was sweet and sickly, and came, I understood from the light alloy used in the airframe as it burned. Others had remarked on that smell and we all found it rather nauseating.

I looked out quickly over our starboard quarter, and there I saw a terrible sight. The shattered Heinkel, with only one wing left, was spinning down vertically, spewing out as it went a helix of burning petrol. It looked like a gigantic Catherine Wheel, and I watched until it plunged into the floor of the cloud below. The snows flurried and glowed from within for a few seconds, and then it was all swallowed up by the cloud. The severed wing fluttered slowly down, a falling leaf spilling out drops of flame. Then that, too, disappeared into the cloud, and we sailed on alone. Two miles below us the icy black water of the Channel would be quenching that dreadful fire.

CHAPTER EIGHT

Customers!

THE business partnership that Starlight Blazer had entered into was getting into its stride. We did not know then that fifty customers would be dealt with most satisfactorily by the squadron in the course of the next few months, but we were all becoming imbued with a very keen business sense. Every afternoon the night flying programme would be eagerly scanned by the duty crews, and up would go the cry:

"You lucky dog…first for Starlight again!"

With experience the crews began to meet with successes, and these, in turn, built the reputation of the squadron. We began to get a stream of visitors: staff officers, boffins, wistful crews from squadrons in the backwaters, all wanting to know the form. Even in the Sergeants' Mess we became aware that the official ear was a great deal readier to listen to and be sympathetic towards what we had to say. We were in the money, and the morale of the squadron was soaring.

The successes were by no means confined to a few favoured crews. As with all good squadrons, we had no use for the "ace" system; in fact, the word "ace" was used only in derision. Even pilots who lacked natural ability but who had sufficient determination and a good operator soon found themselves signing combat reports.

We had long since lost our pre-war, exclusively Auxiliary character; now we were to lose our Commanding Officer, Michael Anderson, who had led us through our days and nights of early trials and doubts and successes. He was posted to a staff job. Our new CO was Wing Commander Charles H. Appleton, every inch a Regular officer in spite of the swagger stick under his arm. He had that razor-sharp look of a man who habitually drove himself hard, and who expected those under his Command to do the same thing. But Charles Appleton was no mere parade-ground martinet. Within a very short time of his arrival he was up in a Beaufighter and painstakingly getting the feel of things, although he never completely mastered all the difficulties of the job. Not the least of his problems was getting the hang of the strange patter poured into his ear over the intercom by a diffident radar operator.

It was while Appleton was making up his mind about who should fly with him as his regular operator that one of the strangest creatures we had yet seen arrived on the squadron strength. He was a Pilot Officer, and he was wearing an airgunner's flying badge. When I first saw him he was glaring out of bloodshot eyes at Chiefy Wheadon, who had just told him that the aircraft in which he was to fly was parked at the far end of the airfield.

"No, surely not, Flight-Sergeant!" he spluttered querulously.

"You're just teasing me, aren't you?"

He waddled out, ungainly and splay-footed, and a gust of laughter swept the room.

"Where the hell do they find them?" Wheadon growled.

But we very soon discovered what a mistake we had made in laughing at this extraordinary character. His name was Derek Jackson, and he was a University professor, a physicist of world-wide repute, and a hard-riding amateur jockey who had risked his neck in the Grand National. He had been rescued from what he called "the Hell of Loughborough", an elementary training establishment for officers, and filched from the air-gunner's trade, to become an operator. He was one of the prize finds in the great drive to recruit master brains for our new trade.

Jackson had the mind of the first-rate scientist, detached and objective in his approach to his job, and his interceptions became polished and balanced exercises. To him, an enemy aircraft bristling with lethal weapons was merely an object in the sky whose relative position and movement were to be determined by an exact and precise use of the cathode ray tubes with which he was so familiar. It may all have been a trade to us: to Jackson it was a science and, because of the complex nature of the man, perhaps in some ways an art. In selecting his operator, our new CO decided that this was the man for him.

It was at this time that another forceful character in the squadron began to make his presence felt. Rory Chisholm, a Flight Lieutenant, was a tall, spare man who had first joined the squadron as a pilot back in the early 1930s. On the outbreak of war he had returned from the oilfields of Persia where he had been working for some years, bringing with him the mature judgment of an experienced engineer and the clear thinking, as with Jackson, of the scientist. Having refurbished his flying skill – in order to bring himself up-to-date he had to start almost all over again – he managed to get back to his old squadron.

Mastering the new technique of radar controlled tactics had not been easy for Chisholm. Eternally restless in his search for perfection, and never satisfied with himself or his operator, he forged ahead in uneasy partnership with a happy-go-lucky and somewhat bucolic Sergeant by the name of W. G. Ripley. Although Ripley had anything but the scientific approach toward things, they were nevertheless successful, and together they destroyed several enemy aircraft at this time.

Chisholm was too tormented by some inner struggle ever to be an easy man to work with. It was a battle, perhaps, between the limitations of the ordinary man and some sense of vocation that made him strive so hard for perfection.

There was something of the same quality about Edward Crew. Trim, compact, a parcel of restrained energy, Crew had as his operator his former gunner, Sergeant Norman Guthrie, known as "Gus", one of our pre-war Auxiliaries. He set about hunting down his victims with a ferocity that was in strange contrast to his quietly spoken manner, almost patrician in its dignity, and always imperturbable.

But it was to John Cunningham that we all turned to be shown the way. It was not that it had been at all easy for John to find the right way to do things. It did seem, to watch him, that he had the natural touch and the exacting sense of balance and judgment that made it all look so simple and effortless. But nobody worked harder than John did to achieve that mastery. An example of that was in his attitude towards his landings. If he ever made a landing, day or night, that was not to his satisfaction, he would always take off immediately and try it again.

The others watched him closely, some with delight, some with envy, and in imitating his style they followed him with pride and affection. With blood and sweat, not to mention tears, they strove to acquire his easy mastery, and in doing so many of them, over the years ahead, fought their way to future leadership.

The public, fed by the Press on chatter about heroes, summed it all up in one word – courage. As if that were enough! On the other hand, what could they know of the torments and the doubts and the endless experiments, of the infinite patience that was required, of the untiring, meticulous attention that had to be paid to a hundred details, of the sheer, hard, slogging drudgery that all went to make up success in this new form of air fighting?

At the start it had been our squadron motto that had summed up things for us. Now we were learning to live more by the motto of the Service to which we belonged.

With the Luftwaffe all but driven from the skies by day, life on the ground became less harassing and a great deal more comfortable. We moved from the mud of the dispersal point and the discomfort of the Nissen huts into the luxury of heated crew rooms in one of the hangars. Between sorties and on quiet nights we could relax in blissful ease, dozing in the semi-darkness, which preserved our night vision.

But the Luftwaffe Intelligence knew who were inflicting their casualties over our part of the country, and they knew where we lived. Now and again they would send a lone intruder to come sneaking in by night. He would fling out a few bombs, spray the place with his machine-guns, and then run for it, having done surprisingly little damage. But it added a spice to life, and over one period he made such regular visits that they took on quite a personal touch. Our airmen referred to him, almost affectionately as "Von Plonk".

One of these intrusions took place late one night. The evening's activities had died down, and we were lying half asleep on our beds. And then we heard the familiar sound of Von Plonk's engines as he came diving in towards the aerodrome. With the reflex action of bomb-hardened veterans we rolled as one man off and under the beds. There was a shriek and a crump as the first bomb ploughed up the grass between the Officers' Mess and the hangars. Then came three more, each one a little closer, shaking the ground and the building. There was a snarl from his engines as he passed overhead, and the stutter of a machine-gun, followed by a long-drawn swish as his load of incendiaries spread out across the far boundary; and then a dwindling drone as he climbed away.

We started to crawl from under the beds, grinning or cursing according to the way we had landed on the floor. Von Plonk was in his usual form: a neat straddle, with no damage except to the turf. I sat up, and found myself facing a furious glare from the CO, who had come rushing in to use the telephone.

"What the devil are you doing down there, Sergeant?" he snapped. "Get up at once!"

I climbed to my feet, feeling very angry. There was nothing I could say that would explain away a total difference of temperament. Charles Appleton would never have understood any sort of compromise with danger. His was the kind of courage that induced infantry officers to stand on the parapet to direct the fire of their men. I was just as anxious as he was to get at the enemy, but I felt it could be done far more efficiently without a face full of broken glass.

But we all reacted in different ways. On the morning after another of Von Plonk's visits I found the squadron storekeeper sweeping the glass out of his office. It was the second time that month that his windows had been blown in, and he was more than a little peevish.

"When the hell is that fellow going to learn to aim straight?" he complained. "Twenty yards further this way and I could have written off two years' deficiencies."

Although by that spring of 1941 the battle by day had dwindled considerably there was no lessening of enemy activity by night. Brownie's shop just could not serve the customers fast enough. Another radar beacon had been set up near the GCI to act as a holding point so that we could keep ourselves in position until we were wanted. Starlight always had one fighter on patrol. At the first sign of a raid developing, Sector would order off further aircraft to fly to the holding beacon and wait there for instructions.

As soon as the first patrol had been brought into contact with a raider the Starlight controller had only to call up the next fighter from the cab rank of the holding beacon nearby to keep the trade flowing. When the fighter had either dealt with his customer or lost contact altogether, he would return to the rank and wait his turn for the next one. It all worked very smoothly just so long as a nice balance was maintained between discipline and opportunism. But there was a great temptation to go after any unmarked target that offered itself to a fighter not already put on to one, and all initiative had to be tempered by the need to keep the rank manned.

One of our most difficult problems was that of identification, and experience had taught us the need for visual recognition before making an attack. With the sky to ourselves and plenty of time to spare, there was no real excuse for any mistake. But more and more fighters were being thrown into the air. This admittedly made it possible for a greater number of raiders to be engaged. But it also made the problem of identification more acute because there was less time in which to take action. Some tragic mistakes had already been made.

At one time we had welcomed the light of the moon to help us in our search. But now it could also betray us to the raiders' more vigilant gunners, and instead of delivering quick stabs in the dark, as we had been doing, we now faced the prospect of some ding-dong battles.

On the night of the 11th of April the moon was nearly full, but we saw little of it as we followed our first contact up through a thick layer of cloud.

Our target was well above us, and we had to climb in steps in order to avoid being left behind, alternating between picking up speed and gaining height. By the time we had reduced the range to 1,000ft we were well into the cloud and flying blind, and things were becoming a little tricky.

"1,000ft...throttle back more," I told John. "900. Still ahead and 20 degrees above."

But we were still in thick cloud with no earthly chance of getting a visual. The blip was only just visible at minimum range, and my spine was beginning to tingle.

"800, 30 degrees above," I went on. "I shall lose it if we get any closer."

"We're still in cloud," John reported. "Hold on for a minute and we'll see if it clears."

I was sweating by then. We ran on in silence for some minutes. Our target held steadily on its course with the blip hovering at the very bottom of the trace.

"I can't believe the man's deliberately flying in this stuff," John said. "I'm going to drop back and then go up a bit."

The range increased to 1,200ft, and the horrible feeling of touch-and-go receded with the blip. The Beaufighter surged forward as we started to climb. And almost at once John said:

"Ah...that's better...it's clearing. There he is sitting just on top!"

Quickly I looked around. We were rushing, breast-high, through a dazzling sea of cloud, line upon line of silver-crested rollers flashing past at 240 miles an hour. And there was our Heinkel, less than 400 yards away, skimming through the waves and tossing back shining swirls of mist as his propellers clipped the crests. There was only time for one quick look at it before John pushed the stick forward and we submerged again.

"We'll get a bit closer first," he said.

I turned back to the AI set, and we began to edge in, just below periscope height. Nine hundred feet...800...700. With the contact squarely ahead and everything set, we prepared to surface.

Above us the mists began to lighten, and then they parted and the moonlight streamed down through the roof panel. The cloud still swirled back past the side windows, and for a few more seconds they blinded the windscreen. Then they were swept away and we could clearly see our target ahead of us.

Surging in through the flying spray, we were about 250 yards behind when John opened fire. A shower of pieces came flying back from the starboard engine of the bomber, and it plunged down into the cloud. John thrust our nose down into the next wave and we went hurtling down after it, holding contact on the AI at less than 1,000ft. It was still there when we broke out below cloud, and John started firing again as we rocketed down in pursuit. At the sound of the guns I looked out again. The Heinkel was diving fast, one propeller windmilling uselessly, oil or smoke, or both, streaming from the engine.

Our guns stopped as the ammunition ran out. For a second I hesitated about leaving the AI as I had been caught like that before. But visibility was good, and the bomber could not do much in the way of aerobatics on one engine.

"Can you hold him while I reload?" I asked John.

"Yes," he replied. "I think so."

"OK. Rock the wings if you want me."

I took a deep draught of oxygen, shed the hampering helmet, and dropped to my knees between the guns. It meant working in complete darkness, and as the Beaufighter was picking up speed in the dive she began to lurch and jolt like a runaway bus. The floor bucked in unpredictable leaps and then dropped away as I snatched off the empty drums. I dared not leave them loose in the racks and it took up precious seconds as I fiddled the locking pins into place. Now came the heavier work of getting on the refills. It was going to take all of two hands. I supported myself as best I could, bracing myself with feet and knees and shoulders and head against anything that felt solid. Out came the first pin, and the 60lb drum leapt up from the rack as wanton gravity poured vicious life into the dead weight of metal. It came crashing down, doubly heavy, and I grabbed at it and clutched it in my arms and eased it on to the breech-block. In order to fit properly it had to go on at just the right angle, and with the fingers of my right hand gripped around the first shell I fought to slide it into position. My left hand was busy trying to ease the weight. With every leap of its wild dance the drum gouged a few more bits from my fingers. I had not realized that an aircraft had so many sharp corners. At last I got the front pins entered, and snapped the locking-catch home.

Blinded with sweat, I groped for my helmet and took another gulp of oxygen. It was very heavy going without it, but if I had been cluttered up with tubes and cords around my neck reloading would have been just about impossible. Now to get on the second drum, with two more to go after that. Again I went through the frantic wrestling, followed by the blind fumbling, and then the triumphant snap of the catch.

It seemed to me that I had taken a devil of a time about things. As I reached for my helmet for more oxygen I felt John rocking the aircraft to recall me. Gasping for breath, I reported:

"I've done two…just about puffed…have you still got him?"

"Yes, but he's pulling away," John replied. "I'll have a go with two."

Setting the two guns to fire, I struggled back into the seat. The Heinkel was away out in front, in a dive that was steeper than ever. Our own engines were howling as we chased after him, and the bumps were solid and vicious. We were 300 yards behind when John fired again, struggling to keep the madly dancing sight on the target.

The banging of the cannon sounded thin even for two guns. Some more pieces flew off the Heinkel, but still it continued on its way more or less in one piece. After three or four bursts our refills were finished. By then the target was a good quarter of a mile ahead, going down in a dive that was steeper and faster than ever. The Beaufighter was shaking all over in the most horrible way.

"It's no good," John said. "The controls are getting just about solid."

Very gently and carefully he began to level out. Below us, at a height of about 1,500ft, there was a solid layer of cloud. The Heinkel went hurtling on down and finally disappeared into it.

"I very much doubt if he'll ever pull out of that," John remarked as we regained an even keel. "Keep watching. We might see him hit."

We held on our course for some minutes, anxiously scanning the cloud below us for a tell-tale flash. But there was no sign of it. They might have gone straight in. On the other hand, they might have managed to pull out and limp home to relate yet another horror story of British night fighters that popped up out of cloud right on your tail. All John could claim was another Heinkel probably destroyed. Reluctantly we turned homeward to rearm.

I found to my disgust when we got back that in spite of all my efforts I had muffed the reloading of one of the two guns, and our second attack had been delivered with only one of them firing. I was very disappointed with myself because the extra weight of metal with two guns firing might have made all the difference in the result.

But there was no time to spare for vain regrets. Almost as soon as we had finished rearming and refuelling we were off again on a second sortie. This time we did not even have to wait on the cab rank. While we were still on the way to the holding beacon, Starlight called:

"Hullo, Two Four. There's a customer for you just coming into the shop."

We had to move quickly. We had already turned out into the Channel, and then we re-crossed the coast flying north, and we were approaching Sherborne before John had the target in sight. It was another Heinkel. We were below a thick ceiling of cloud, which sheltered us from the moon, and John went right in to 80 yards and gave it one short burst. There was a shower of debris, and as smoothly and as slickly as if it were in a flying display the big Heinkel rolled over to the right into an absolutely vertical dive. As I pressed my face against the perspex of the dome I gave John a running commentary of what was happening.

"It's going straight down on the right. Can you drop the wing a bit that's better it's still going straight down it's gone in!"

It had all happened with a horrible swiftness, and the Heinkel was splattered over the ground like hot clinkers thrown from a boilerman's shovel.

"It's spread all over the place!" I exclaimed. "The bits are burning."

I felt a little sick. Perhaps John detected the over-emotional note in my voice. In an even, conversational way he replied:

"Good. That'll teach 'em to crack nuts in church."

On the way back to the cab rank I reloaded the cannon as John regained height. We were up in the brilliant moonlight again, waiting our turn. We knew that customers were still coming in, and we were patrolling our beat just inside the coast. And then, clearly visible from over a mile away, we saw a Heinkel approaching on the beam.

John turned to cut it off. The German pilot must have been able to see us just as clearly as we could see him. He was several hundred feet above us, and he was quick to make the most of this initial advantage. He held on his course and climbed as steeply as he could towards the cover of some broken cloud above. We were vertically below him, almost at the stalling point, as John struggled to climb into a position for an attack.

The Heinkel reached the cloud, but it was not continuous enough to give satisfactory cover. The German pilot continued to stagger up, just off the point of stalling himself. While John tried all the tricks he knew in an effort to out-climb the other aircraft, I was on the AI set maintaining radar contact. For ten minutes we hung on our props. From his vantage point 300ft above our defenceless heads the enemy gunner poured down a stream of tracer every time there was a gap in the cloud. It seemed to me that all I saw each time I glanced out was a shower of hot tomatoes coming down past the dome. I felt a great longing for that missing gun turret with which I could have answered back.

"There's no future in this," John said at last.

"How about pulling off to one side while we climb?" I suggested.

We tried that, holding AI contact out on the beam. But I had to be careful not to get too far away as we could not afford to risk losing contact altogether. But every time we swung back, the Heinkel was still high above us. Both John and I were becoming very tired, and finally we had to give up the chase and turn back.

It was a disappointing end to a pretty full night's work. We had destroyed one, probably destroyed another, and had a skirmish with a third who had done all the shooting himself.

Shortly after this I was awarded a DFM. John had already, in March, received a DFC. He now added to that a DSO. And shortly after that he was awarded a bar to his DFC.

CHAPTER NINE

The Open Market

IT was not long before it was realized by us that the numbers of aircraft the Germans were sending over at night were beginning to crowd our ground control system, and that there was too much congestion for efficient handling of the number of fighters needed to take care of the raiders. If we, the fighters, were to take care of these raiders satisfactorily then we would have to extend our activities and go in for a little freelancing, although still within the limits of our sector. The GCI would continue to control as many fighters as possible; the rest would do the best they could with any contacts that came their way.

On the night of the 9th of April, John and I sat at 15,000ft over base fuming in idleness while enemy aircraft streamed in thick and fast across the western edge of the sector. The GCI already had on the job all the fighters that they could handle, and we were waiting for our turn to come around to be called up.

But John was not the man to sit there cooling his heels. He called up Sector control and got permission to go freelancing, and off we went to the westward to look for our own trade, working out our tactics as we climbed to 20,000ft.

"We're heading west and they're going north," John said, "so they'll be crossing us from left to right."

I was visualizing what it would all look like on the cathode ray tubes. "If I get contact on the right we'll turn right at once and go after it," I replied. "If the contact shows up on the left, we'll wait for it to cross to the right and then turn after it."

For ten minutes we flew on in silence. Then John said:

"There're some searchlights waving about down on the coast. It looks like something coming in now."

I turned away from the AI set to watch the tell-tale fingers of light groping out across the sea. They steepened and shortened over the coast into a tight cone, like an Indian teepee. Then the tip of the cone started moving steadily inland, and the fingers, growing longer and thinner as they were depressed, swept down, and stretched yearningly after it, pointing hopefully across our path. I felt the old tingle of excitement as I turned back to the AI set.

"No joy yet," I reported to John.

We held on our course in silence. The German crew would be breathing easier now that they had cleared the coastal searchlights, even relaxing a little, perhaps, as they set course for their target. How could they know that they were converging at 5 miles a minute on to that great arc of magic vision that was pulsing out from the nose of our Beaufighter? And then they reached it.

"Contact!" I exclaimed. "Coming in from the left."

"Good," John said. "Do you want me to turn yet?"

"No…hold it. It's well below. Range 8,000ft."

Because of the difference in our heights there was no need to worry about a collision. The blip came quickly down the trace, and at 5,000ft it began to slide most conveniently across to the right.

"It's crossing now," I told John. "Turn starboard and dive."

We went curving down in pursuit, and then levelled out at 12,000ft, rapidly overhauling our target. We were about 20 miles south of Bristol by then, and still half a mile from the other aircraft when John caught sight of it, another Heinkel. We closed in and John gave it a short burst; but it was not until his second burst had splashed all over the centre section that the enemy made any response. Then it slowed down abruptly, and the left wing dropped. Tracer came streaking up from their guns as we went shooting over the top, but that was the last we saw of it. I spent too long with my face pressed against the perspex of the dome waiting for the Heinkel to reappear behind our wing, and when I turned back to the AI set the picture was a blank.

But there was no time to spare regretting mistakes as there were still other raiders about. The Sector Controller advised us to make for the south, but John decided to get a little closer to base first, and he turned eastward. Again we worked out tactics in advance.

"Anything coming in will be crossing from right to left John said. "But we might get one going home now."

"I'll wait to see which way it's crossing before we do anything," I replied, feeling a little more confident.

We did not have long to wait before a contact appeared coming in from the left. In a matter of seconds it rushed down the time trace and drifted across, just as the first one had done. It was almost certainly a raider scurrying homeward.

Everything went quite smoothly and to plan. We caught up with the contact over Bournemouth and it turned out to be yet another Heinkel. This time John closed in to 80 yards before opening fire. A great flash came from its belly, and again we whistled just over the top as John pulled clear.

Later we were told of the report of some Air Raid wardens who had been standing at the entrance to their shelter looking out across the bay towards the Needles. They heard the heavy drone of the Heinkel's engines, and the more sonorous hum of our Hercules as we closed in. Then came the sudden roar of our cannon, which gave way to the rising flame of the stricken Heinkel as it fell out of the sky. They saw it crash into the sea.

We had plied our trade in the open market, and the evening had not been unprofitable. We began to feel that perhaps searchlights might after all provide one of the answers. They could be used to track the raider so that a patrolling fighter could get into a position to get AI contact. There was nothing new about the idea of course: some of John's earliest combats had come from following the indications provided by the searchlight beams.

But now we were working towards a different conception of their usefulness. We had more confidence in our ability to hold contact on a target crossing our path, or even coming head on, so long as we had some warning of its line of approach. We no longer asked that the target should be illuminated: in some ways it was better that it should not be as an illuminated bomber crew became, somewhat, naturally, nervous and alert and took too much evasive action. All we wanted was a good, firm indication from three or four lights coming steadily and reasonably close to the target and not wandering back on to the fighter as it closed in.

But this last and vital requirement was the most difficult of all to obtain. Too often we had been betrayed by a lagging beam, holding us blinded and helpless as our target dived away to safety. It was all infuriating, and it had been the cause of a great deal of friction between us and the Army. Our criticisms had been, perhaps, more outspoken than constructive; but the Army, in turn, had accused us of being non-cooperative.

During the early days of working up to the right relationship with Starlight we had found that personal contact gave the answer. The same thing was true now of our relationship with the Army. Over a pint of beer, "Useless Pongos" and "Brylcreem Boys" became transformed in each other's eyes into ordinary, friendly beings anxious only to help one another. We went down to the searchlight sites and tried our hands – without a great deal of success – at operating the lights. Army officers came riding with us at night, and were dismayed at what they saw, or, rather, at what they did not see.

On one of these trips we took our passenger on a Cupertino exercise. We sailed up and down under Sector control waiting for the lights to pick us up. Our passenger stood in the well behind John, craning his neck to see what was happening, which was precious little. Control was slowly but surely losing all patience.

"How many beams on you now?" they asked.

"None at the moment," John replied.

There was a brooding silence for a little while, and then, with mounting irritation, came the demand:

"Well, how many can you see?"

All three of us took a good look around. Breaking it as gently as he could, John answered:

"There're one or two a long way away."

"But there must be more!" the Controller demanded indignantly, almost snorting with disbelief. "They're all exposed!"

"No, I'm sorry," John replied equably. "Oh now those have gone out."

Our passenger all but climbed out of the window in his efforts to see what was happening, and when he saw that there was complete darkness he could not get to the ground quickly enough. We heard no more talk about non-cooperation because he happened to be the Brigadier in command of all the searchlights in our area.

By the time Mike O'Leary returned to the squadron from his sojourn in hospital he found that his place with Peter Jackson – who had just received his commission – was being filled by Stan Hawke and Sandi, taking it in turns. Mike, however, from his early days as a magician, had been used to flying with all comers.

Shortly after he got back he went off on patrol one night with Flying Officer I. K. Joll in the aircraft in which he had been wounded while flying with Peter. In a very short time they were close behind another Junkers 88, and with mounting uneasiness he watched his pilot allowing himself to get into the same fatal position too high and much too close to the enemy. And then there came the same burst of fire from the belly of the bomber, with the same fiery streaks tearing down through the roof of the Beaufighter.

Five bullets hit Mike in the leg. Fortunately, Joll was not hit, and he tagged along after the zig-zagging bomber and hacked it down. When they were able to take stock of what had happened they found that the radio had been shot out and along with it the intercom. Mike dragged himself along the catwalk and by shouts and gestures he and Joll arranged a code of signals that they could exchange on the emergency buzzer. Then Mike dragged himself back again, hoisted himself up into the seat, and guided his pilot by radar back to base.

"This is getting monotonous," he said as they carted him off to hospital.

Tommy was also still having his troubles. Since Alistair Hunter's death he had been flying with one of the Sergeant pilots. John and I got back to base one night right behind them to find that the flarepath had become obstructed through some slight mishap.

As we waited, orbiting the airfield, we could see the navigation lights of Tommy's aircraft going around just below us. Down on the ground the headlights of the crash tender stabbed through the blackout, and the lesser beams of cars and hand-torches wandered all over the place.

They eventually got things clear on the flarepath, with all the stray lights out, and I watched as the other aircraft circled Danebury Hill and straightened up for the final approach. But just at that moment the driver of the crash tender switched on his headlights again and started charging down the airfield straight towards the aircraft coming in to land. I looked back quickly and saw that the navigation lights of the Beaufighter had reached the perimeter hedge. Then suddenly a shower of sparks trailed out behind them, the lights snapped out, and there was darkness, utter darkness, thank God, and no fire.

We continued on the circuit, waiting for a chance to get in to land, and with a sinking heart I remembered the argument I had had with Tommy only that morning. It was an argument that was always cropping up with all of us: should one use the safety harness attached to the seat? Tommy had held the not unusual view that using it was a bit faint-hearted and liable, in any case, to trap one in a crash. I had tried to persuade him that it would at least prevent one from being thrown about in a heavy landing. As usual, we had left the argument unfinished.

At last we got down, and we found that Tommy and his pilot were unhurt except for lumps as big as eggs on their foreheads. Tommy told me that he also thought of our argument while they were orbiting, and for once he had strapped himself tightly in his seat. Dazzled by the headlights of the crash tender as he was making his final approach, the pilot had undershot and hit a dispersal pen. The Beaufighter had shed quite a lot of itself before it slithered to a stop on its belly. So violent had been the deceleration of the landing that Tommy's harness had stretched the full 18in between his head and the front rim of the dome, only barely holding him back from having his face smashed in. We agreed to call the argument settled.

The month of April continued to be one of heavy night raids, and Brownie and his assistant, John McGrath, served the customers as fast as they could, with the eager fighters queueing on the cab rank, nosing around the searchlights, or freelancing as best as they could.

It was a combination of all three of these, aided by good liaison with the Army at Sector Control, that enabled John during the night of the 15th to get his hat trick.

We were returning from the western edge of the sector, and still out of range for Starlight, when the searchlights gave indication of a raider coming in. Again they had not managed to illuminate the bomber. But judging his course shrewdly, John got into a position as the cone converged on us which gave me a contact as the enemy crossed our path. We turned north after it and caught up with it, a Heinkel, over Monmouthshire.

John fired only forty rounds, straight into the fuselage. There was a flash and some smoke, and pieces came flying back over us. The metal of the skin of the Heinkel began to burn as it sank into a long, shallow dive, and the trail it left, white and molten, caught the eyes of the searchlight crews. Triumphantly the beams held the wretched bomber until it shone like silver in the cone of a dozen lights. It dived out of sight beneath us, still dripping white fire, as though melting in the intensity of the searchlight beams.

We returned to base, but very soon we were sent off on a second sortie, to reinforce the cab rank. While we were waiting for instructions, John saw a searchlight cone well to the north, somewhere towards Marlborough. It was obviously indicating the course a customer was following on his way home. Starlight was still too busy to be able to use us and they readily gave us permission to go and investigate.

Again John timed to a nicety his turn to the southward drifting cone. But the difference in headings was rather more than I had bargained for, and, as John wheeled around, the blip rushed on and off the tube before I could hold it. But we knew the direction in which the bomber was heading. John pushed the nose down and opened the throttles wide, and we soon had the contact sliding down towards visual range.

Just as I was thinking that it was about time John saw the other aircraft, a host of long, straggly blips came swarming out of the Christmas tree at the top of the trace. For one stupefied moment I thought that we must have run into the rest of the Luftwaffe. With an effort I kept my eye fixed on our own private blip and continued to pour out the patter, while in a spare corner of my mind I searched for an explanation for the other blips. Then suddenly I had it.

"We're just approaching the Southampton balloons," I said. The floor of the aircraft heaved slightly. "But they're all well below us," I added somewhat hastily.

"I'm glad of that," John commented, and then almost in the same breath he said: "I think I can see him."

Southampton was a notoriously trigger-happy gun zone, and as we closed in I wondered who would shoot first: John, the Heinkel, or our ack-ack. There was a good half moon ahead of us. That could be the trickiest of all light, with the target neither wholly illuminated nor sharply silhouetted.

There were no flashes from the ground, and no sign from the Heinkel that they knew that we were behind them. John was closing in quickly…150 yards…100…he was making sure this time…80 yards…and he beat the others to the draw. With the flash of his hits, the Heinkel flicked over to the left.

We went diving after it, but at 9,000ft John decided that the balloons were quite close enough and he levelled out. A great red flash came up from the ground as the bomber smacked down into the town. It lingered on, and in the ruddy glow I saw for a horrified second walls and gaping windows all around. It lasted just long enough for me to make out that the walls were empty shells, and to confirm that we had added no fresh disaster to the already heavily bombed city.

Marvelling at the restraint shown by the gunners, we hurriedly climbed out of the zone. We headed back for base, and arrived over Middle Wallop at 17,000ft. John had come to the conclusion that in dealing with "returned empties", which were running light and often diving fast for home, it was always a good thing to have some height in hand.

Starlight had just run out of fighters, and they had their eye on an outward-bound customer following almost the same track as our last victim. Taking us over, they sent us to the north-west, and then swung us back in their usual masterly style right on to the tail of the bandit. But our precaution about having sufficient height in hand proved this time to be an embarrassment, as we were about 6,000ft too high. I maintained contact while John nursed the Beaufighter down. It took time, and we were on the outskirts of Southampton again before John saw the moonlight glinting on the perspex of another Heinkel.

Again we were on tenterhooks about whether the gunners would open fire. And again John ran right in to 80 yards. The moonlight shone all along the Heinkel's port side, softening the lines and blurring the silhouette. The crew must have been either very tired or very lax because they showed no sign of being on the alert until the very last moment, when there was a sudden flicker of reflected light as the dorsal gunner swung his gun around. But the brief flash of his gun was instantly engulfed in flames as our shells ripped into the fuselage. Burning wreckage bounced off our nose as John jerked us up and away to the left. There was another orange flash from somewhere beneath us, and I was back on the AI set watching the blip race away up the trace. It was quickly swallowed up in the ground echoes as John's third victim that night sprinkled the earth with its fragments somewhere near Lymington.

CHAPTER TEN

Command Performance

EARLY in May it was announced, without a great deal of warning, that His Majesty the King was coming to visit us; and there was a sudden scrubbing and polishing to make everything, including us, look as presentable as possible.

All the aircrews were paraded for inspection in the evening. There were two other units on the station with us, and their crews all turned out in their flying kit, looking very operational. Our CO gave us orders that we were all to parade in our best blue; and by the time we lined up we were feeling very self-conscious and rather like a lot of unemployed bandsmen. It was at a time of the day when we normally went to readiness, dressed in a motley and far more practical rig of battle-dress and pullovers and scarves.

The parade was outside one of the hangars, and we waited with an anxious eye on the light and the clock as the dusk crept up Danebury Hill. John and I were due for the first patrol with Starlight, and we were not going to have much time to spare.

"Here he comes!" somebody exclaimed.

There was a flurry of excitement as the cars rolled on to the tarmac. The King, who had dined in the Mess, walked along the ranks, accompanied by the Air Officer Commanding-in-Chief, Fighter Command, Air Marshal Sir Sholto Douglas, who had himself been a fighter pilot in the war of 1914-1918, and who later became Marshal of the Royal Air Force Lord Douglas of Kirtleside. Here and there His Majesty stopped for a few words with the pilots. When he reached the operators he stopped short opposite some of the wingless ex-magicians.

"Why aren't these men wearing flying badges?" he asked.

Hurried explanations were produced to explain the difference between ex-gunners and magicians, and the lack of any flying badge to cover the new trade. The King made some comment to the C-in-C which was passed quickly down the ranks of the retinue from Great Rings to Many Rings to Fewer and Lesser Rings until finally it reached the tail end, where it was furiously scribbled into The Notebook.

His Majesty continued down the line, until he faced me. He asked me what my score was.

"Er—nine, sir," I replied, a bit dazed after some hasty mental arithmetic.

"Nine, eh? Will you get another one tonight for me?"

I must confess that that sent me a bit goggle-eyed. A Command Performance was rather a tall order. On the other hand, we could fairly claim that our trade was very definitely under Royal Patronage.

"Well, sir," I said, "I'll do my best."

After the inspection was over His Majesty got into his car and was driven off down to Starlight to be shown how the GCI worked. We all made a wild rush to the Mess to change, and then back to the airfield. Panting and slightly behind time, the first patrols climbed into their aircraft and headed for the Channel with the throttles wide open.

When we were at the right height and in the right position John called Brownie on the radio, and he sounded rather relieved to have us there. His distinguished visitor had arrived and the stage was all set for the show to begin. The only member of the cast not yet present was the duty customer. But with a punctuality that led someone to declare that Brownie must have had a direct connection with the Luftwaffe GHQ, the missing player entered on cue and the show was on.

The enemy raider was well out to sea, heading in towards the Royal Box, and Brownie had plenty of time to arrange things quite neatly. Cautiously he began to edge us in from the wings.

"Vector three three zero," he instructed, and then: "Three one zero."

Intently I watched the cathode ray tubes. It was a fine, healthy picture, for which I was thankful, but there was no sign of any contact.

"Three six zero." And then, as we turned on to this final vector, Brownie added: "You're 3 miles behind now."

The note of our engines changed as John speeded up. The time was rapidly approaching when we would have to play our piece.

Down in the dimness of the caravan at Starlight the visitors stood looking over Brownie's shoulder at the glowing tube of the PPI. The time-trace swept around the face of the tube with a remorseless, hypnotic rhythm; and with each sweep of the great aerial the two little blobs of light which represented the players came closer together, snail-tracking their way across the tube. Only the harsh background noise of mush from the loud-speaker broke the silence as they finally merged into one. The audience waited...and went on waiting. Surely Two Four must have contact by now? But still they were kept waiting.

Then I had my cue. Onto the tubes came a blip, 2 miles ahead, and well below us.

"Contact, thank you," John reported to the ground.

The words crackled out of the loudspeaker in the caravan, breaking the tension. Brownie's expression relaxed into a smile as the burden of the interception was lifted from his shoulders. Now they could only watch and wait for the report that would tell of success or failure.

I knew that it was up to me, and that it was no good feeling nervous. I must treat it like any other interception, as a job to be done. And the first thing to do was to take care of the difference in height. Skilfully John eased the Beaufighter down, and the 2 miles that separated us began to shrink.

We were still over the sea and 4,000 ft behind when John's welcome exclamation lifted the burden, in turn, from me. I raised my head from the visor and thankfully took my bow. Now it was up to John. He was taking his time about closing in, carefully considering the best angle of approach. The stage lighting was really far too bright, with the moon glaring down on our back and, below us, the sea a shimmering backcloth of silver.

"I reckon they'll spot us against the sea," I said. "How about coming in just below? It's fairly hazy around the horizon."

"Yes," John replied, dubiously, "perhaps. But I think we'll wait for a while."

He had a better idea. Just ahead he could see the coast-line, and overland there would be no shining back-cloth to give us away.

Brownie suggested to the visitors that they should go outside as they might be able to hear, if not see, something of what was going to happen. His Majesty and the C-in-C left the caravan and went down the steps and out into the cold moonlight. From the south came the sound of aircraft engines.

The unsuspecting Heinkel was stooging on ahead of us. Keep going, you poor devil, I thought, you have a star part to play. I turned and watched the coast receding behind us. The glistening sea was giving way to a hazy, mottled landscape.

"It's all right behind now," I told John.

"Good," he replied. "In we go then."

We were right below our target, a great fat prima-donna of a Heinkel. John started pulling up behind it, and the long, long wait was even more agonizing than usual. But the enemy crew showed no reaction. We were right behind, and there came the final moment of tension with the sharp little lurches as John brought the sight to bear. Still there was no response from the Heinkel.

Then came the blessed relief of the crash of the guns, and the sudden surge upwards to get out of the way of the hurtling wreckage. A wicked orange glow appeared inside the fuselage of the Heinkel, and the wheels fell down in the most forlorn way. As we flew alongside, the glow burst through the skin and the flames took over. The whole aircraft trembled and broke into a violent pitching, and with a plume of flames streaming out behind it the Heinkel went down in a headlong plunge to earth. The show was over.

We got back to base shortly after midnight, and John immediately had an enthusiastic telephone call from Brownie. He reported that His Majesty and the C-in-C had heard the combat, and that they had seen the burning Heinkel fall from the sky. No showman could have wished for better timing or a better setting.

But for another of the players who had taken part in the performance the night was to end in tragedy. I went to the aircraft to collect my parachute, and I found the ground crew busily checking her over for any possible damage. The rigger jerked a thumb towards the eleven swastikas painted on the tail fin.

"That'll make the round dozen," he said, grinning happily.

I gave our faithful R for Robert a friendly pat, and then I walked away and went to bed. It was an early night for us because John had to get some sleep before going off to a conference the next day.

In the small hours of the morning another crew was ordered off, and they took our R for Robert. They made a successful attack on another Heinkel; but the return fire from the enemy aircraft took the top off one of the pilot's fingers and clouted the port engine of the Beaufighter rather hard. They tried desperately hard to bring the aircraft back, but a few miles from the base the damaged engine burst into flames and the crew had to bale out. R for Robert's thirteenth victim was her last.

The operator, fortunately, was quite unhurt, although he was killed in a crash a few months later, and the pilot scarcely seemed to notice the loss of a finger. What worried him was the thought of having to tell his Flight Commander that he had lost that very special aeroplane.

By this time I had come to feel that it would be a good idea if all the operators pooled the stories of their experiences so that we might try to work from all information some formula for more effective operating. I suggested to Gilfillan that everybody who had had combats should jot down a few notes on them as well as on the contacts that had eluded them.

In the middle of May I had a week's leave, and I joined my wife at a quiet spot in Sussex. The weather was perfect, and I spent a lot of my time up in the Rewell Wood, a lovely, beech covered ridge of the Downs, quietly scribbling away. John and I had had twelve combats in just over a month, and I was feeling tired and in the mood for a little peace.

But when I got back I found that our idea did not work out quite the way I had hoped. Most people were apparently too shy to talk about their successes – or loath to admit their failures – and my small effort and some notes by Gilfillan and by some of the people from 219 Squadron were, I believe, the only ones to appear on paper. I heard nothing more about mine for a long time. But word about what I had called my comic screed must eventually have penetrated to the outer world because something was made out of it, along with the material from the others, and the notes were circulated to all night fighter squadrons. About three years later these notes were used in the preparation of the first official and complete, and most secret, handbook on night fighter tactics and the use of AI.

After I got back there came a period during which, for us, nothing would go right. We knew well enough that it always took time to groom a new aircraft, and to work it up to a state which would satisfy a conscientious pilot, and our ground crew worked loyally and hard at the job. But to John, being a perfectionist, the snags that cropped up seemed to be unending. So far as my side of things was concerned, the AI squinted, went off tune, or became just plain sulky.

Even the weather turned sour, and the spring flowers wept beneath the drizzling clouds. And so it continued on until towards the end of May, when we reached a sort of climax.

We returned late one afternoon from an air test with trouble in the blind-flying instruments. By the time the faulty panel had been changed darkness had fallen, and the cloud hung low across the fields. But John was not going to risk taking an untried aircraft on patrol, so we took off for a very quick test.

The moment we were off the ground, and just as we were about to enter cloud, John remarked:

"Well you'll no doubt be interested to know that we are 200ft below the ground and going backwards."

Someone had made a mistake in connecting up the instruments of the new blind flying panel, and all their readings were the wrong way around.

It seemed to me that I could hear the beat of Isaac's wings; but John could fly by feel and the turn-and-bank indicator, and we got back quite safely. It was a clear case of that combination of skill and good judgment which was so often mistakenly called luck.

For some of the others, that luck did not always hold. One afternoon at this time Edward Crew and Peter Jackson set off in their aircraft to fire their guns at splash targets at Chesil Beach. Although Stan Hawke and Sandi had been taking it in turns to fly with Peter, they decided that afternoon to go along together just for the ride. They were all dressed and getting into the aircraft when the Flight Commander brought a new Australian pilot to the Beaufighter and gave instructions that he should go with Peter to watch the form on air-to-sea firing. Stan and Sandi tossed up to decide which of them should go along as operator: Stan won and went off with the others, leaving Sandi behind.

Cloud started creeping in from the sea, and before long the Dorset hills were shrouded in it. Their task completed, the two pilots turned for home. But by then the cloud was pretty thick. Edward Crew climbed up through the murk, and homed on the Middle Wallop beacon. But Peter was east in a different mould. He had always been quite confident that he could thumb his way home through anything.

John and I had been on a night flying test during this time. When we landed Chiefy Fitzgibbon was there to meet us, and the look on his face was not good to see.

"Have you heard about Stan?" he asked.

His words struck a chill in my heart. Peter's luck had at last given out, and Isaac had been ready. They had flown into a stuffed cloud, and all of them were killed. I turned away to hide my distress as I wandered off to find Sandi.

Their deaths did not go unavenged for long. On the last night of May the mists were gathering in the valleys as we climbed into a clear, starlit sky. The forecast had threatened us with fog; but there was trade about, and conditions for stalking were ideal.

About 15 miles west of base, Starlight put us on to an outgoing raider. We made a quick approach, and John spotted the Heinkel across from the left. He fired only forty-three rounds, and set it ablaze in the starboard centre section.

We flew in formation on the port side watching the flames spread, the bomber standing out in sharp relief against its own pyre. I noticed the square windows of the ventral gunner's station outlined against the fire, but there was no sign of the gunner. The fire spread, and the bomber lurched into a shallow dive. It hit the ground somewhere near Blandford. John had broken the spell: it was his thirteenth enemy destroyed.

But now we had to face the problem of the fog. Middle Wallop was already enveloped in it, and one by one the other airfields open for use in an emergency diversion were being swallowed up. Only Colerne remained open, perched as it was high on a hill above Bath. And all the other stray aircraft shut out from their own bases were converging on that last haven. We queued up in the circuit, waiting for our turn to land.

As we milled around that dwindling island of safety the sinister grey tide of the fog crept steadily up from the surrounding valleys. We were the last on the stack, and it looked like being a pretty close thing. One by one the landmarks in the surrounding gloom were engulfed until only the airfield lights remained.

There was a Defiant, a "cat's-eye" fighter – the name given to single-engined night fighters not equipped with radar – immediately ahead of us, and at last we saw its navigation lights run along the flare-path and turn off. John was already turning in to make his approach, and as we lined up and flattened out I saw the fog rolling in over the hedge behind us. By the time we were walking away from our aircraft it had closed in over our heads.

When we got to the crew room we found another of our own crews already there. They had had a successful battle with a raider which they had shot down, and then they also had had to make for Colerne, and had got in just before us.

Colerne was the home at that time of another Auxiliary unit, No. 600 (City of London) Squadron, also on night fighting. They had been neighbours of ours at Hendon before the war, and they made us welcome even though they looked a little rueful. They had cast their nets all night and had caught nothing, and it must have been a little galling to have a neighbour's successes thrust upon them. After a very late supper we all settled down in the dispersal hut to wait for morning.

Waking up in a strange room or a strange place was an experience to which we had all become quite accustomed, and when I surfaced the next morning and found myself greeted by the sight of a diminutive Sergeant air-gunner sitting on the foot of the bed there was no cause for wonder, even though the face was unfamiliar. On the other hand, one did have the right to expect the face to be human. The face that stared into my sleep-heavy eyes were brown and hairy, the little, beady eyes were much too close together, and the mouth yammered at me like that of a monkey.

I shut my eyes and counted to three, waiting for the dream to fade and trying to get my bearings. Then I opened them again. The face was still there. By heavens…it was a monkey! I sat up with a jerk, and found my bed surrounded by a circle of grinning and chortling aircrew. Some of those from 600 had planted their mascot, dressed in his best blue, complete with Sergeant's stripes and flying badge, on the rail of my bed, and then they had all waited for results. Judging by the expressions on their faces, I had not disappointed them.

The weather early in the morning was still unsuitable for flying, so motor transport was provided, and soon after 7 o'clock we set off by road to return to Middle Wallop, driving through the freshness of a glorious spring morning. The mist was still clinging to the valleys and dripping from the trees and the hedgerows, but as the car climbed up the winding hills and rattled between the grey stone walls of the slumbering villages the sun began to break through. It glistened upon the dewdrops on the new-born foliage, and struck warmly through the keen air, and I felt that it was a wonderful day to be alive.

We passed an old lady dressed in her Sunday best, Prayer Book in hand, hurrying along to an early church service; and suddenly I remembered that it was Whit Sunday. It seemed to me that we were terribly out of place in our battledress and flying kit. And then I started remembering other things: that blazing Heinkel of only a few hours before; and Stan lying dead on the Purbeck Hills. This was a glorious first of June. But somehow the morning had lost something of its glory, and I knew that spring would never be quite the same again.

As it happened, quite a lot of things were about to change for us. Up until this time our little group of pre-war Auxiliary gunners had managed somehow to hold together. But postings were beginning to strike hard, and within month all the old guard disappeared. Some went to pass on their knowledge as instructors at Operational Training Units, some to serve overseas, some revert to their old trade as air-gunners.

Among the last to go were Sandi, Sid Shirley, Tommy, and his great chum Nobby Kennedy. Sandi, Tommy and Nobby went, with secret misgivings, to No. 109 Squadron, a hush-hush outfit part of whose activities was the early tracking down of the German bombing beams. It was the start of what became the mysterious No. 100 Group in Bomber Command.

With all my intimate friends of such long standing gone, the buoyant craziness of the life we had led in the Sergeants' Mess seemed to abate. But for a little while longer trade with the enemy went on much the same as before. The first phase of the night battle was nearly over, and if we had not achieved successes as spectacular as those of the day fighters, we nevertheless had not done too badly. The Luftwaffe's losses in night raids had risen from a total of 3 during January and 4 in February to 22 in March, 48 in April and 96 in May. We felt, perhaps justifiably, that the radar equipped night fighter was proving its worth.

And then came time, for me to readjust myself to a wider outlook on Service life. I had just received a bar to my DFM and had only just been promoted to Flight Sergeant when I was commissioned. Pat received his at the same time, but he was posted away soon afterwards to an operational Training Unit at Church Fenton. I stayed on with the squadron.

I knew that I had to grow up at some time or other, and that I had put off the painful process long enough. But before I could proceed any further with that my fellow Sergeants gave me a party in the village of Middle Wallop. Borne on the stalwart shoulders of Fred Larcey, I was given a public baptism in the stream that runs through the village. In the middle of the ceremony we found ourselves under the scandalized eye of the Station Warrant Officer. But he was human enough – or perhaps discreet enough, for the boys were in a baptismal mood – to look the other way.

CHAPTER ELEVEN

Our Big Friends

WHEN Hitler went to war with Russia in June, 1941, it meant that the Luftwaffe – already severely strained in its efforts to cope with the demands of the German High Command in the Mediterranean – had to supply large numbers of all types of aircraft for this new, eastern, front. Bombers had to be withdrawn from France for these new operations, which meant that the intensive night raids over our own country ceased. And that, in turn, made things easier for those concerned with the problems of our own night defences.

While I was still trying to get used to less hectic nights as well as to my new status as a Pilot Officer, John was given command of the squadron and promoted to the rank of Wing Commander. His place as B Flight Commander was taken by Rory Chisholm.

For me, however, the problems of readjustment were eased by a complete change of scene. The inaugural beer stains were scarcely dry on my new Uniform when B Flight was sent off to spend a little time at Coltishall, an aerodrome in Norfolk. The squadron, No. 255, which was to take over this sector had just changed over from "cat's-eye," fighting in Defiants to working with AI Beaufighters powered with Merlin engines, and until they had settled in with their new radar equipped aircraft we were to act for them.

By all accounts it looked like being a busy and tricky assignment. There was a fairly steady trade with bombers running in across the mouth of the Wash on their way to raid the industrial towns of the Midlands; and there were minelayers which were flying low around the Humber and other east coast ports. We had already had some experience of these low flying raiders, and we knew how hard they were to get at. But, more difficult still to cope with were the enemy intruders, roving night fighters which mingled with our own returning bombers to spread confusion and destruction among the closely spaced aerodromes of East Anglia.

But if this pleasant countryside of rich soil and quiet waterways was an intruder's paradise, at least Isaac had few allies here, for when the sea fog crept in there was nothing higher than the church tower to hit. As an incurable lover of mountains I found it rather depressing after the rolling hills of the West Country. John Selway summed it up neatly with:

"What, flat as your hat? No, flatter than that!"

In the crowded pubs of Norwich, the natural hub of life in those parts, we rubbed shoulders with bomber crews from half a dozen stations. Well versed though we were in the ways of the Air Force, there was something different about these men. It was as if they were trying to hide behind a still mask the signs of what was happening to them. But they could not help showing the inner strain, any more than they could help revealing things in the snatches of careless talk that filtered through the bedlam of laughter and chinking glasses.

"...the third CO in succession..."

"...went through the whole strength of the squadron in three weeks."

Surrounded by this grim and desperate gaiety, I began to feel a little guilty about my own comparative safe existence. I knew quite well that I was doing the job I had been given to do, and that it was just the luck of the game as to which Command one served in. But in the presence of the bomber boys I felt uncomfortable and rather like an interloper. It was all well and good being a fighter; but ours was a defensive role, whereas they were going out on the offensive. I used to come away from those sessions feeling very humbled.

One big difficulty beset the defences of the sector in which we were now working, and we very quickly ran into it. When Bomber Command was out in force it was almost impossible for Seacut, the local GCI, to pick out, from the swarm on their cathode ray tube, their own fighters or any customers that might be about. And finding oneself crossing the main stream of heavy bombers was, for us, a somewhat unnerving experience. We were used to much less traffic-laden highways. Control would do all they could to keep us out in the clear, but if that became impossible they would blandly come up with the warning:

"There are many Big Friends near you."

When that happened the operator in the night fighter could only gaze in horror at the pock-marked tubes of his AI set and reflect that a Big Friend could be just as unfriendly in a collision as an enemy. He could either get to hell out of it, which meant leaving the field clear for any possible intruders, or he could try to avoid a collision by rapid changes of height as each contact crossed his path. Or he could trust to the law of averages, switch everything off, and let his pilot fly on in a blind if not blissful ignorance.

It was under these conditions that our freelance experience came in very handy as blips, hostile and otherwise, arrived on our AI tubes more often than not quite unannounced. The GCI Controller had so much on his tube that it was difficult for him to give us any warning at all. The only chance of success lay in getting on the tail of these contacts first and asking questions afterwards.

Our first success came late in August. Seacut had brought us in on a fruitless chase from our off-shore patrol line without being able to give us contact. We were returning to our beat at 9,000ft when suddenly a contact appeared on the set without warning and started rushing down the trace.

"Contact...head on...port about," I gabbled. "Hard as you can...it's well below us."

The words came out in one exploding breath; but without a second's hesitation John hurled the Beaufighter around on its wing-tip. My face was flattened against the visor, and the tubes began to grow dim with the onset of a blackout. The blip slewed over to the right, slowed up, and then began to recede. With an effort I managed to focus my eyes, and I saw that it was sliding back towards the centre.

"Ease off," I warned John. "You're holding him at 6,000ft. Steady!"

As we came out of the turn, the pressure eased, and I could see that we had the other aircraft cold. John's handling of the Beaufighter had clinched that. Closing head-on at nearly 7 miles a minute on a dark, hazy night with no moon and no horizon, he had started to wheel a heavy and rather unstable aircraft around when only a mile away, and yet he had pulled out of that turn little more than that distance behind.

When John got his visual he found that it was a bandit all right. It was another Heinkel, weaving gently and ineffectively from side to side. His first shots started a fire inside the bomb-bay. We pulled clear and flew along on the port quarter, watching it burn. The enemy crew had plenty of time to bale out as the Heinkel went flying steadily on its course for some minutes while the fire ate its way along the fuselage. The flames began to engulf the tail, and plumed out behind. Then slowly the bomber nosed over and went down like a rocket into the Wash.

I took a fix while John orbited, reporting to control. We were 35 miles north-west of base, and the time was six minutes past ten. Seacut had no more trade to offer so we went out to sea again to cool our heels for an hour off Cromer.

But nothing more showed up, and when we had finished our stint we were ordered back to base. We were back on the circuit and down to 1,000ft and I had switched everything off at my end when suddenly Sector told us to call Seacut again. The Controller at the GCI had picked up another customer for us, outward bound at 6,000ft.

We scurried around and got everything working again. It was a short chase, and we were quickly on the tail of another Heinkel. And then our troubles started. The night was darker than ever. From below the outline of the bomber was reasonably distinct; but when John pulled up to get into a position to fire the silhouette all but disappeared. I could just make out the four groups of fluttering blue exhaust flames, spreading wider apart as we closed in.

Our shells were striking their tinder and flint sparks along the top of the fuselage. That did not look at all right. At the same time the silhouette was becoming more distinct and the tail bigger. In fact, it was much too big, and we were almost into it before John realized that he had got into a fatal position and was coming in above instead of below his target, and was having to dive in order to keep the sight on.

With an ugly jerk, John yanked us up and over the fin, and in the same instant the enemy dorsal gunner fired straight up and into us. I heard the crack of his gun as we whooshed by a few feet above his head. Our aircraft yawed drunkenly as the port engine cut out. Quickly I turned to look at it, and what I saw made my heart jump: little wisps of flame were licking out behind the engine cowling.

The drill I had rehearsed came into play. Mechanically I switched the IFF set to distress coding, reached for my parachute, and clipped my dinghy to my harness. We had seen it happen to plenty of others: now it was our turn.

"You'd better put your 'chute on," John said.

His voice was calm, and that reminded me that I should try to get a fix before the power failed altogether. By then John had readjusted the trim of the aircraft to counteract the effect of the dead engine, operated the fire extinguisher, and was easing around on to a heading for the coast.

"Emergency homing, please," he called on the radio, passing on the bearing and distance as I gave them to him.

I looked out and wondered if it was my imagination that made the flames appear to be dying down. We were 60 miles from base. That meant that it was about 35 miles to the nearest landfall at Lowestoft. It was not far to fly, but it would be a devil of a long swim.

Suddenly there was more banging and spluttering, and the aircraft swung helplessly for a moment.

"Oh...now that's a pity!" John remarked. "Now the other engine seems to be packing up."

My throat went dry. Becoming scared, and scared stiff, is a humiliating business, and I tried very hard to reason with myself. We were by this time only about 20 miles from land. The rescue launches would pick us up...if they found us. That is if the parachute and the dinghy drill worked out all right...and if we got out safely. But suppose a petrol tank went up with a woof? I remembered that firelighter we had caught, and the way it had fallen like a Catherine Wheel out of the sky.

And then the starboard engine started up again, just as I had reached my lowest ebb. I caught myself going into one of those wretched, whining, please-God-get-me-out-of-this-and-I-will-always-be-a-good-boy so-called prayers. I felt ashamed of myself, but fortunately my sense of humour began to stir and exert itself.

Here we were, loaded to the gills with the most inflammable and explosive stuff imaginable. Our one object was the destruction of our fellow men. If, in pursuing that object, we got into a jam, was it fair – or logical, for that matter – to start crying to the Creator to get us out of it?

But I did not have a great deal of time to waste on these thoughts as it was not long before we were crossing the coast, and I could see the lights of the aerodrome, a fairy ring charming us home to safety. I unclipped my dinghy. There was nothing scaring about baling out over land, particularly when it was friendly land. I knew the drill for that all right.

Smoothly we slid in to the circuit, turning right-handed against the good engine. John made a faultless touchdown, swung clear at the end of the flarepath, and we rolled to a standstill. In the blessed silence I took off my parachute and then my helmet and wiped the sweat from my forehead as I stood beside my seat for a moment before getting out of the aircraft and into the sweet night air. Then suddenly John shouted:

"Get out...quickly! I've an idea that engine's still burning."

Galvanized into action, I flung back the catches of the top hatch and pushed at the dome, but it would not budge. I had complained once too often of the draught, and some well-meaning rigger had sealed things up a little too well. Just as I made a grab at the release wire of the floor hatch John shouted again:

"I can't open my hatch!"

Heaving myself up, I went racing up the cat-walk towards the front to try and help him. But I was stopped dead by a stunning blow on the head. A new signal gun had been fitted in the roof, and some genius had left two long bolts projecting downwards.

With blood streaming down my face from a slight gash in my scalp, and still rather dazed, I staggered up to the front. John had already managed to barge his way out. The fire tender, an ambulance and two or three cars had reached us by then, and they were standing in a semi-circle around the nose of the aircraft as I came staggering out into the glare of their headlights.

And then everything became pure farce. Before I could explain that I was no wounded hero – merely a victim of my own bad cockpit drill – stalwart arms were supporting me and sympathetic voices were trying to coax me on to a waiting stretcher.

By the time we got to the crew-room I had straightened things out, and we started working on a crate of beer that had appeared. That started my bleeding again, and they had to pull the poor, wretched doctor out of bed to sew me up. He, naturally, did not see the funny side of it. His sleep had been broken, it was 3 o'clock in the morning, and my beery breath smelt to high heaven. Was it any wonder that he jumped to the conclusion that I had been salvaged from some tavern brawl? I did not spoil the joke by telling him what had really happened.

The night fighter squadron which was to take over this sector made rather an inauspicious arrival. First of all one of their aircraft had an engine failure coming in to land, dropped a wing, and crashed just outside the airfield. A few days later their Commanding Officer was killed, also following an engine failure. These misfortunes were a serious set-back for them, and as a result we were ordered to stay on at Coltishall for a few more weeks.

It was obvious by then that one of the main tasks in this sector would be coping with the intruders. One night, as we were sitting in our dispersal hut, we had a vivid demonstration of what they were up to. There was a normal sound of aircraft engines about; but suddenly it was interrupted by the roar of cannon fire overhead. We all rushed outside, and we saw a Wellington with its navigation lights on flying low across the airfield. And right behind it there was a Junkers 88, plainly visible in the bright moonlight.

As we watched, sick with helplessness, another burst of tracer leapt in a tight bundle from the nose of the German intruder and raked our bomber, which was already going down in a shallow dive. Its tail behind the distant trees, and then a red glow lit the horizon as it crashed. Cascades of coloured stars flared up as the Very cartridges went off, and there came back to us through the still woods the crackle of exploding ammunition.

Our standing patrols were already after the killer, but they stood little chance of finding it with their AI at that height. The cathode ray tubes would be swamped with echoes from the ground, and the operator would be almost helpless. And ground control would not be of much more help. Trying to pick out a single raider dodging among so many of our own bombers was about as easy as trying to pick out a pickpocket in a football crowd. It was yet more proof to us that we were certainly going to need an AI that would read low down, unhampered by ground returns.

On the 1st September we had our last encounter with the enemy in flying from Coltishall. Seacut were at the top of their form. They snapped up a homeward bound raider that was foolish enough to cross out at 10,000ft, and handed him neatly over to us as he passed through our off-shore trap. Their controlling was so accurate that we bumped through the slip-stream of the other aircraft as we turned on to their final vector.

There was a glaring moon on our starboard bow as we started the chase across the North Sea, heading to the south-eastward. Everything went quite smoothly until we had closed in to 3,000ft, and then our target started a diving turn to the right. For a moment we thought that he might have spotted us, although that did not seem likely at that range. The Station Commander of Coltishall, Group Captain R. B. Lees, was along with us for the ride, which gave us two pairs of eyes looking out ahead. We went on diving and turning. Below, at 8,000ft, there was a layer of broken cloud. Had the intruder become suspicious and started diving for cover? He had turned right around, and now we were heading back towards the coast of England.

"I'm still turning," John remarked, an edge of suspicion in his voice.

"OK. Keep turning and diving," I replied. "He's still there at 4,000ft."

"All right. But hang on to him. He must be doing a complete orbit."

Out of the corner of my eye I could see that the moonlight was not as sharp as it had been, and I imagined that we were going down through the cloud layer that I had seen earlier.

"Ease off your turn," I warned John. "Steady now…and level out."

"Steady," John acknowledged. "He's back on his old heading."

On we went again, with the range steadily closing. But why that orbit, I wondered. Was it just a routine precaution? Maybe it made them feel better, and now they were settling down in their seats and grinning at each other and thinking about getting back to their base.

It was Lees who first sighted the other aircraft 2,000ft away. We were possibly a pretty expensive crew – a Group Captain, a Wing Commander, and an Acting Pilot Officer on Probation! – but it was paying a dividend.

We went rushing in at 230mph, and I quickly saw the reason for it. The moon, diffuse and pale, was riding hard for a clear patch of sky, and John was trying to get in while the shadow still lasted.

But the moon beat him to it. The intruder was in the clear light again, and I got my first really good look at a Junkers 88. As we shot out into that cold, clear light, John edged over to the left so as to keep us down moon. We had 300 yards to go, and we raced in, taut, expectant, and anxious to finish things off before we were spotted.

We were 30 miles out from the coast of England by now, and down to 5,000ft; and the Germans were probably approaching that fatal moment of feeling that they were well out of harm's way. But at that moment we were in to 150 yards, and John had started firing.

The Junkers dived out of sight, but I still had contact with it. The blips showed that he was still line ahead, but that he was going down rapidly. John levelled out, waiting to see what was going to happen. It was an anxious pause for me because I was not sure that I would ever be able to close in again if we followed him down. And then, right under our nose, a streak of flame splashed along the surface of the sea. It spread out, but as we turned away it was drowned in steam and oily smoke.

The time was just five minutes short of midnight.

CHAPTER TWELVE

Stock-taking

O N the way back from Coltishall to Middle Wallop we called at the de Havilland works at Hatfield to have another look at the new Mosquito night fighter. Compared with the Beaufighter it was very sleek and trim; but I noticed with some inward misgiving that the liquid-cooled Merlin engines called for a wide and vulnerable area of radiator in each centre-section. On the other hand, the thoroughbred showed up in every line of the aircraft.

To my dismay, however, I found that the Mosquito was being fitted, as standard equipment, with the new Mark V, pilot-indicator, AI. For a junior officer I was not good at keeping my mouth shut, and my rather outspoken comments about this type of AI were not very well received. I tried to console myself with the thought that perhaps we had been unlucky every time we had tried out this new gear; but I could not help wishing that all the effort that had gone into bringing this quite unnecessary modification into existence could have been put into a concentrated effort to develop a system for seeing really low down.

It was good to be back with the rest of the squadron at Middle Wallop, although we were sorry to have to leave behind us all the activity of the east coast. The tempo of things in our own sector had slowed down a lot. With the main weight of the Luftwaffe's striking force now switched to their eastern front, we had time to look around and take stock of what had happened, and to plan more carefully for what might be ahead.

There were newcomers to the squadron, one of whom, Flying Officer F. S. Gonsalves, I had heard about before the war. He had started his flying career at the de Havilland Technical School at about the same time that John had been there. He had then learnt to fly, and had been one of my wife's flying instructors at Hatfield at the flying club run by de Havillands. From that he had gone on to commercial flying. "Gon", as he was known to everybody, was more mature than most of the newcomers; and although his sense of humour was sardonic it was also very English, contrasting rather strangely with the southern fire of his background and appearance.

By this time the position, or aircrew status, of the operators had been properly defined, and the Sergeants of the new trade were known officially as Observers (Radio). The new flying badge, however, bore the letters R O, which we now wore in place of the air-gunner's half wing with the A G. Why the letters should have been twisted around like that I do not know. If it was meant to cloak our trade in secrecy it was a failure because it only led to a lot of curiosity which in turn caused us to become enmeshed in the most fantastic explanations. And this trade of ours was, naturally, of the utmost secrecy.

Hitherto I had had only the vaguest ideas about the background to the story of airborne radar and of the route by which our equipment and replacement crews reached us. But John had always taken an intense interest in every new development, and with his successes the boffins and the staff officers were only too anxious to have his opinion; and I soon found myself going with him to various conferences, to trials and demonstrations, and to the remote hideouts of the backroom boys. Life at Middle Wallop was quieter, but I found it much fuller and richer.

It was all somewhat like a jigsaw puzzle with the various pieces now beginning to fall into place. I had heard very vaguely of the three main mystery outfits with which we were linked – TRE, TFU, and FIU – but now they ceased to be mere alphabetical conundrums. They became real places with real people, essential links in the long production line which was hammering out the tools for us to work with.

The very fountain-head of boffinry was TRE – the Telecommunications Research Establishment. Here it was that the requirements of Air Ministry were dreamt into practical shape by some of the best scientific brains in the country. In order to protect them from a possible commando raid, they were housed in the seclusion of Malvern College, tucked into a fold of the Worcester Beacon. It was only a short trip for us from Middle Wallop, and we would skim over Bredon Hill and slip down on to the aerodrome at Defford, where the latest experimental gadgets were tried out in the air by TFU – the Telecommunications Flying Unit. From there a short trip by car took us to the barbed wire surrounding Malvern, and after a great show of identity cards and passes we would be sitting spellbound as we listened to the great brains expounding their ideas and shattering one another's theories.

The enthusiasm of these scientists was a great tonic for our rather jaded minds. They had few of the restraints and inhibitions in discussion to which Service life had accustomed us, and they pulled no punches. One of them would energetically work up a case for ten minutes, covering a blackboard with diagrams and mathematical symbols while his fellow boffins sat fidgeting and muttering to themselves until one of them could stand it no longer. Then onto his feet he would leap and, snatching the piece of chalk, he would begin to tear the arguments apart. This was usually accompanied by the opening comment:

"But surely it must be clear to the very meanest intelligence that…"

When things got to that stage we were glad that we had Derek Jackson with us. He could talk their language, and more often than not beat them on their own ground.

But to me the most impressive thing about these stalwart characters was their total absorption in their work, often they would arrive late in the evening on a visit to us after a most wearisome journey. Without thought of rest or refreshment, they would plunge straight into a discussion that might go on until the small hours of the morning. If an air test had to be made they would plague the pilot into taking off, quite regardless of the weather. Fog…low cloud…ice? They were not interested in those things so they paid no attention to them.

There was a story told about one of their pilots at TFU who allowed himself to be talked into making some urgently needed test. As he was flying through the most hair-raising weather, just clear of the trees and with his heart in his mouth, he heard the voice of the boffin in the back exclaim:

"I say, pilot, would you mind doing that run again a bit lower? And could you do it upside-down?"

The impersonal "I say, pilot" they used was one of their more maddening habits. It used to infuriate John, who always said that it made him feel like a taxi-driver with a querulous fare tapping him on the shoulder.

But it was through our contacts with TRE that we were given encouraging glimpses of the way in which efforts were being made to shape new tools for our use. Work was well along with ultra-high frequency radar which, with the use of strange, dish-like scanners, flung the pulses out in narrow beams. Here was deliverance from the restrictions of ground returns, and the means of flying low down and seeing well ahead. Here was the answer to the sneaking intruder and the very low flying minelayer.

After TRE and TFU had got their experimental sets into working condition they were sent for operational trials to the Fighter Interception Unit – FIU – which was based on the aerodrome at Ford, down on the Sussex coast.

FIU was made up of a number of highly qualified technical men and handpicked night fighter crews nominally on a rest from operational flying; and in their work they combined the analytical judgment of the scientist, the hard-headedness of the practical engineer, and the urgency and wear and tear of an operational squadron. They tested and assessed the values of the prototypes and made suggestions for alterations and improvements. And since so much depended on their findings they readily welcomed the opinions of experienced outsiders to weigh against their own conclusions.

John was a frequent visitor to Ford, and I, also, had already been down there with him to see a pathetically futile demonstration in daylight of the pilot indicating AI. We had found that even the experts at FIU could be fooled in handling the equipment, and could, in fact, through its inherent faults, be led very badly astray. I had a difficult time choking back my own comments when the interception we witnessed was a complete failure.

Postings from squadrons to FIU were highly prized. Not only was it a happy unit on a happy station but it also offered to those really keen on flying a great variety of new and interesting jobs, as well as better chances of combats than many squadron crews could hope for. It was no place for the playboy or the operationally tired. Service with the unit was supposed to be a rest between tours of operational flying; but the definition of a rest depended very largely on the individual. Guy Gibson, for instance, undertook a tour of flying with a night-fighter squadron as a rest between two of his various bomber tours.

It was an aircraft from FIU that had the record of being the very first radar equipped fighter in the history of air warfare to shoot down one of the enemy as a direct result of an AI interception. On the night of the 22nd of July 1940, one of their Blenheims with a specialist crew made up of Flying Officer G. Ashfield as pilot, Pilot Officer G. E. Morris as observer, and Sergeant R. H. Leyland as radar operator made a successful radar interception and destroyed a Dornier 17.

Enemy activity had by now come almost to a standstill, and raiders were few and far between. But that did not mean to say that we slackened off at all with our flying. It was, in fact, a time when we were able to do a great deal in working out new and more involved tactics, and in standardizing our methods. We stepped up the difficulties of our exercises, making our evasion more tricky and more violent, looking all the time for our own weaknesses. We worked in pairs and each did his utmost to outmanoeuvre the other.

This was also a time when we had an opportunity to get to know each other better. The old Auxiliary nature of the squadron had almost completely disappeared, and in its place there was a blending of individual characters – along with their strengths and weaknesses – of an almost amazing diversity.

They came from here at home, from the Dominions, and from the various countries of our Allies, bringing with them the tang of the New World to blend with the tempered steel of those of the older countries of Europe. Men from Canada and the United States of America, from Australia and New Zealand, from Poland and Norway all found their way into this new form of warfare, and they all worked with a reassuring smoothness in the common cause. One could not escape the thought that we could just as easily have absorbed a few Germans, shorn of their Nazi bluster and cant, except that so many of that tormented race seem to draw on with their jackboots another and more sinister personality.

One of the newcomers who will always remain firmly in my memory was a bright, fair-haired youngster named John Quinton. From the outset he promised well. Although he had a devastatingly shy stammer, it vanished completely at the first sight of a blip on his cathode ray tubes, and his words flowed as surely and as effectively as the way in which he thought.

John Quinton was crewed up with a long-haired, unkempt, strangely mystical being, a Flight Lieutenant named Michael Maxwell, whose views about the way things should be done were, to say the least, individualistic.

By some strange, unaccountable process, Maxwell and Quinton, although so entirely different in every way, managed to get along quite well together. I would not then have suspected that Maxwell was destined one day to command the squadron, although I would certainly have backed John Quinton as a future leader.

Of all the embarrassing and tiresome chores that we were asked to undertake, the worst the propaganda people threw our way was that of visiting factories to give pep talks to the factory workers. It was embarrassing for obvious reasons; it was tiresome because at the time I felt that the factory workers did not need pepping up, and, in any case, they were not going to be spurred on by seeing us stumbling around. Later, however, I came to feel that perhaps it was of interest to them to meet the people who were actually using the equipment and the aircraft they were making.

John was persuaded to make just one of these visits to a factory which was making our AI sets. The tour of the works was, in itself, most interesting, and the ordeal of the few kind words was mercifully dulled, for us, by an excellent lunch. But there was one awkward moment. John was presented to a large and rather comatose cat, an animal of which he was never very fond, and whose alleged powers of seeing in the dark had already caused him a great deal of embarrassment.

This story of John's alleged miraculous night vision, which the propaganda people had sown so well, died very hard. It did not matter so much outside the Service because we knew that a large section of the public, especially in wartime, revelled in sensational, cheap-jack nicknames and the more revolting forms of hero worship. The difficulty was that it produced an understandable feeling of nausea in the other, less publicized branches of the Service, who considered, rightly enough, that the so-called "fighter boy" was already surrounded with too much glamour.

The experts, the doctors and the boffins all came and talked to John about the problems of seeing in the dark. He never failed to emphasize that, in his view, it was of relative unimportance. He told them that what was needed was a good AI set and the ability to use it – which meant a good team spirit from the crew – and then a sound tactical approach and accurate shooting. Those were the things that he always stressed were the first essentials.

But I always felt that either through his own natural modesty or because of his sheer inability to realize how outstandingly skilful he was, John was never quite fair to himself. It was quite true that night vision played only a very small part in his successes. There were other factors, of more importance, such as his superb mastery of the aircraft, his ability to fly with only a minimum of concentration, even under the worst conditions, leaving himself free to pay attention to what his operator was saying and to what was happening outside, and to searching for the target. Where other pilots would be sweating blood to keep their aircraft flying, John would be sitting relaxed and cool, concentrating on the interception, swinging instantly into smooth, tight, turns long after the instruments had all gone haywire and the blind flying panel had given up trying to keep pace with him.

John always maintained that his night vision was no better than average, a fact substantiated by various special tests. Certainly I never had any difficulty in spotting any target by the time he had freed me to look around, but how distinct it had been at his first sighting I could not judge. On the other hand, in daylight his sight was remarkably acute, both for extreme range and awareness, as I often noticed during our daylight trips.

It was the medical people who finally set the matter at rest – not that that meant anything to the Press? – by publishing a pamphlet in which all the facts were set out simply and clearly in a non-technical way. It made plain that neither cats nor men can see in the dark, not in real, total darkness; but it was shown how we might make the most of the smallest amount of light even on the blackest of nights. We had already learnt by experience to make the fullest use of oxygen, and how to search from the side of the eye and not by trying to look straight at the target.

Another of the fanciful theories that died hard was the one about carrots being good for night vision. It had its origin in the half-truth that a deficiency of certain vitamins could cause night blindness. Since the normal aircrew diet contained enough vitamins to stock a laboratory, as we well knew, the story about carrots so far as we were concerned fell rather flat.

Vitamin tablets were always on tap on the tables at every meal. Most of us consumed them in place of sweets, knowing that they were really quite unnecessary. Some of our more dashing youngsters, however, stoked up with them before going on leave under the mistaken impression that the pleasures of the night, no less than their vision, might thereby be enhanced.

One of the cynics with us once likened a night fighter sortie to the affairs of a married couple: once the door had slammed behind them no one quite knew what went on except that one of the partners had a virtual monopoly of speech and the other of action.

It was this sort of story that appealed to the robust sense of humour of another of the new operators who joined us in the autumn, Flying Officer Robert Wright. I did not know then, of course, that it was the beginning of a friendship that, fifteen years later, would result in the two of us putting our heads together in the writing of this book.

Born in England, Bob had grown up in Africa and Australia. For some time he lived in New Zealand, and then for eleven years before the war he was in the United States, the latter part of it in Hollywood, working as a journalist and script writer for broadcasting and films.

On the outbreak of war, Bob returned to England after an absence of twenty-five years. He joined the RAF, and almost overnight he found himself at Fighter Command Headquarters, deep underground in the holy of holies, the Filter Room, where all the vital information from the coastal radar stations was sorted out and passed on to the fighter stations.

After a few months of that, Bob was made Personal Assistant to the Air Officer Commanding-in-Chief, Air Chief Marshal Sir Hugh (later Lord) Dowding; and when Air Marshal Sholto Douglas was appointed to take over Fighter Command, Bob had stayed on as his Personal Assistant for another year. Then, after a short course of training in radar at Prestwick, he came to us, and he was crewed up with Flight Lieutenant George McLannahan, an ex-civil pilot of very great experience who was later to become B Flight Commander in place of Rory Chisholm.

For some time I was sent up at intervals to give talks at the Radio School at Prestwick. It was there that the newly trained navigators finished off with a course in AI. From the school at Prestwick the fledgling operator was sent to an OUT – Operational Training Unit – where he was crewed up with a pilot and learnt to work in harmony with him, and so became part of a crew ready to go to a squadron.

But we were finding by then that no two instructors spoke with the same voice. By the time the sorely perplexed pupil arrived at a squadron he was pretty thoroughly confused; and on top of that he was then told that he might as well forget all that he had been taught and learn whatever technique the particular squadron happened to be using. Although we had come a long way in a short time, each squadron, and to some extent each crew, had followed its own way to success or failure.

Finally it was realized that we would really have to pool our knowledge, and so, early in November, we were called to a conference at Headquarters, Fighter Command. John Selway, Derek Jackson and I went along with John Cunningham to speak for our squadron. There were also representatives from the training schools, all eager for information, but even more eager to defend their methods.

It was not really a wide enough selection to represent all views, but it was quite wide enough, as it turned out, to threaten to prolong the meeting interminably. It very soon became a heated wrangle between the operators with all the others patiently listening. But in the end we were able to evolve an elementary standard technique. It was far from perfect, but it served its purpose as it meant that an operator could be sure that the patter he learnt in his training would be understood when he reached a squadron, no matter how many different pilots he might fly with.

By the autumn of 1941 we had several crews in the squadron that had developed into closely knit and very effective teams. We had learnt by then that perhaps the greatest factor contributing to the effectiveness of such teams was understanding between the pilot and operator. A good example of that was the way in which John Selway and Derek Jackson worked together.

After Appleton left the squadron Derek flew with various pilots until finally he crewed up with Selway, who had been away on the sick list for a few months. They made a team that was not only effective, but also a source of not a little enjoyment and amusement to the rest of us, mainly, I think, because of the eccentricities that were so much a part of the character of Derek Jackson, and the geniality of John Selway.

One of my warmest memories of them was the way in which they played chess. They frequently had to leave a game unfinished in order to go off on patrol. On their return to the crew room, there was no satisfying Derek, no matter how exhausted they might be, until they had completed the game. He would walk in, and while still in flying kit, even, at times, with his parachute still in one hand, he would make the next move. He nearly always won, and as victory came in sight he would remark:

"Brains will tell, y'know, John."

And, in Derek's case, brains did tell. He was not with us for very long before he went to a staff job at Fighter Command.

John Selway then crewed up with a young airman radar mechanic from the Special Signals Section named Norman Bamford, who was trained by us as an operator. He was a budding architect by profession, and from the start he showed signs of becoming an outstanding operator. He and Selway flew together, except for a few months off during which Selway went to a staff job at Group, for the next two years.

One of the highlights of that winter of 1941–42, and one of the happiest events in the life of the squadron, was the arrival of the Norwegians. We were the first to receive Norwegian crews trained for night fighters, and from that time on we made a speciality of them, always having a few of them with us.

The first to come to us were four Lieutenants of the Royal Norwegian Air Force by the names of Per Bugge, Johan Räd, Leif Lövestad and Claus Björn.

Per and Johan had both been engineering students in Norway when war broke out, Per in mining, Johan in electricity. They had started, in their spare time, being trained as pilots in the Reserve of the Air Force, but the occupation of Norway had put a stop to that. They went into the underground movement in Trondheim, and started planning their escape. Six months later they managed to buy a small fishing boat, and with eleven others on board they set out across the North Sea, following for reasons of safety the longest route, from the Lofoten Islands to the Shetlands.

The journey took them nine days. They missed the Shetlands, and went sailing out into the Atlantic; but finally they decided to turn back and they landed on the north-west corner of Scotland. For a couple of days they rested in the shelter of a small bay, and then they sailed on to Thurso, where they made their official landing, only to be informed that it had been very naughty of them to go ashore without permission and clearance from the customs.

As they were the only two Norwegians in this country at that time who had had some training as pilots, they were allowed to complete their instruction in England, rather than having to follow the usual course of going to Canada. And from that they were sent to us.

A flaxen haired giant whose rare words emerged reluctantly in a series of scarcely audible grunts, Per Bugge appeared to be unshakable, and was always pleasant and most courteous. He soon made a name for himself as an exceptionally capable pilot. Claus Björn, who was Bugge's operator, had escaped from Norway through Sweden, and had then made his way through Russia and Japan and on to America. He was trained as an observer in Canada.

The liveliest of the four Norwegians was Johan Räd. Tall and slim, Johan was nearly always laughing; but despite his cheerfulness, I felt that he, like Rory Chisholm, was tormented by some demon of self-criticism, always wondering whether he should not be doing better than he was. But in contrast to the reserved Rory, whose humour was dry and subtle, Johan was openly gay and amusing.

Johan was very well served by his operator, Leif Lövestad, a man with massive hands and broad shoulders, a cheerful smile lighting a rugged, homely face, who tagged along after his pilot like a shaggy, faithful dog behind his master. Though he stood no more than shoulder high to Johan, Leif had tremendous strength, and had been known to change with ease a car wheel without using a jack. Sometimes in the evening he would smile slowly at Johan and say in a coaxing way of a nursemaid:

"Now, Johan...you must be tired. Why don't you sit down."

And then, without any apparent effort and in spite of Johan's struggles, he would lift him at arm's length as gently as a baby and deposit him on the counter of the bar.

Using that same strength, Leif, shortly after they joined us, battered his way through the side of their crashed Beaufighter, and lifted the unconscious Johan clear of the wreckage as the flames sprang up around them.

We were unanimous in our admiration and our fondness for those Norwegians: they were a very gallant band of men.

CHAPTER THIRTEEN

Stalemate

WITH the arrival of Christmas 1941, austerity was relaxed for a little while; but although we enjoyed our full scale of festivities there nevertheless hung over everything a somewhat dead pall of stalemate. We were not geared to inactivity, and although to the country as a whole the falling off of enemy activity came as a very great relief, to us, whose sole purpose was the waging of war, it was galling to have nothing to do but wait.

We had learnt right at the beginning of the war to thrust aside all thoughts of the future. At that time, if the precedent of the First World War was anything to go by, we felt that our chances of survival were negligible. We had willingly accepted what seemed to be inevitable, and we lived happily enough for the moment. At the time of Dunkirk and the Battle of Britain that happiness had been dimmed by the fear that we might die in vain, but we had at least been too busy to have time to brood about things.

But after those battles were over we were rather like someone struggling back to consciousness after a desperate operation, scarcely able to believe that he was alive. But we were alive, and, like convalescents, we now had time to look to the future and to try and judge the possible length of the struggle that lay ahead. Having come through so far we could not overlook the possibility that we might yet see it all the way through. For the first time there came to life a sneaking regard for one's own life, an almost furtive hope that one might survive, and, with that, a lurking fear that one might not.

The officers of the squadron were moved out of the Mess on the station and installed in a fine old coaching inn some 6 miles away on the road to Salisbury. The Pheasant, or Winterslow Hut, to give it its old coaching name, had been modernized with central heating and adequate plumbing without spoiling its quiet, mellowed charm with chromium plate and juke-boxes. We were there all by ourselves, with no neighbours nearer than the little hamlet of Winterslow, over the brow of the hill to the east. Behind us, to the west, the Porton bombing ranges rolled away for miles across Salisbury Plain. It was just the place for either quiet relaxation or a little gentle screeching, as we felt inclined, without being a nuisance to anyone.

We quickly settled down to a quiet life, however, and when we were not flying it took a very special occasion to coax us away from the congenial company around the log fire. That sinister expression, "…a few quiet drinks in the Mess", came to mean just that rather than beer in the piano and the sooty footprints of Abominable Airmen across the ante-room ceiling.

It was noticeable about this time that the pilots and operators that were coming to us as replacements were younger than those we had been receiving in the past. One of them, whose father was an Admiral, was H. C. Phillips, known to everybody as Micky, who had joined the Air Force straight from school. He came to us as a Sergeant pilot, and shortly afterwards was commissioned. His operator, Derek Smith, was only about my size, and was somewhat suitably nicknamed "The Gremlin" by his lanky pilot.

Micky always had his long hair hanging down over one eye. It was as if he had a fixed aversion to having it cut. John would notice it, and he would look steadfastly at Micky for a while without saying a word. Then he would firmly press sixpence into Micky's hand and issue a quiet reminder to have his hair cut by merely saying:

"The next time you are in town."

Among our Sergeant operators there was one, Freddie French, who had a narrow escape that winter. He was flying with a pilot who had only recently joined us. They hit a hill near the aerodrome one night and the aircraft – a Beaufighter – broke up. The pilot was killed, but Freddie was trapped in a part of the fuselage that had broken off. Luckily this was clear of the flames which consumed the rest of the wreckage. He was in there, badly injured, for some time before the rescue party arrived and hacked him out. Freddie was on the sick list for a long time, but eventually, although still shaken, he returned to operational flying.

But we were also still receiving from time to time some of the older and more mature men selected to become operators. One of these was Flying Officer Basil G. Duckett. An architect by profession, married, with one child, a son, Basil had been trained as a navigator, and had finished that off with a course in AI at Prestwick. He was a quiet, gentle man who could always be relied upon for pleasant, interesting companionship. Always unobtrusively in the background, generally listening rather than talking, Basil became known affectionately to all of us as "The Distinguished Stranger".

It took me a little time to readjust my life to the ways of the Officers' Mess. In spite of wartime austerity, there still lingered on a little of the traditional way of life associated with the Auxiliary Air Force, with its richness of experience, liveliness of wit, and fine appreciation of the good things of life. To this many of the newcomers made their contributions, and I became aware of a wider vision and a deeper stirring of the imagination. It was a fuller and more colourful – and much less noisy – life than the one I had been used to.

I still treasured very highly the comradeship of the rankers with whom I had worked and played for so long. Among them I had found many with the same keenness of wit and tastes just as cultured as those. I was finding now in the Officers' Mess. Many of my friends from my days as an airman and later in the Sergeants' Mess were now officers themselves. But before there had been the fear of ridicule, and exaggerated care had been taken not to appear to be putting on airs, and that had, with most of us, kept the finer things submerged beneath a veneer of a coarser banter and a wilder horseplay. In the Officers' Mess the finer things were discussed openly and easily, and without affectation. There were discussions and even strenuous arguments, but seldom, if ever, any shouting down; and I quickly realized that not only was every man allowed to have opinions of his own: he was also expected to defend them should that become necessary.

Many a night, until the small hours of the morning, I sat and listened to these opinions being expressed in a fascinating variety of ways. When the possibility of enemy activity had all but vanished, and three-quarters of the duty crews for the night had been released from immediate readiness, we would go back to the Mess for the so-called night flying supper. After the precious fried egg – the jealously guarded privilege of the duty crews – the conversation would begin to flow along with the black coffee. Sometimes it would be nothing but shop. Battles would be fought over again, theories discussed, mistakes thrashed out, and new ideas put forward. At other times the talk would range from ballet to boiler-making. I sat once until 4 o'clock in the morning, nodding over my coffee but too fascinated to go to bed, listening to Derek Jackson as he wound up a brisk discussion on space travel by scribbling a few hieroglyphics on the tablecloth and then announcing the acceleration and escape velocity of his suggested rocket to the moon.

One of those always to the fore in these discussions was Rory Chisholm, particularly when it came to talking shop. Rory's active brain kept him constantly searching for perfection; and his over-developed sense of self-criticism would not allow him to let things rest. He it was who had taken the lead in the drive for the better gun-sight, his arguments putting the armament boffins on the right road to producing one. On Rory's initiative we had built an optical trainer in the crew-room, a sort of Punch and Judy show in which model aircraft could be hung in various conditions of lighting for recognition practice, and manipulated in a way to simulate the right angle of approach for spotting and attack.

But it was this same driving fever of impatience that led Rory to distrust so much of the work of his operators – at times rather unfairly – as he seemed to despair of ever attaining with them the degree of perfection which he was for ever seeking. He had worked out a system of his own whereby he conducted the whole interception himself, and all he would take from his operator was a non-stop series of ranges and bearings; the rest he would work out in his own mind along with flying the aeroplane and planning the attack. He was, of course, a very strong advocate for the pilot-indicator AI which John and I, and quite a few others, disliked. Rory hoped that it would do the job far quicker and more accurately for him than the all too human operator. I was distressed to find that other pilots were beginning to take a fancy to what I began to call the

Chisholm heresy. One of them was Michael Maxwell, and that I found quite unwarranted in that his operator, John Quinton, was so very good.

Every afternoon the duty flight climbed into the Bedford van and rattled away over the hill to the aerodrome. They made their night flying tests, had tea in the Mess on the Station, and at dusk went to readiness. Those not flying slept peacefully at the Pheasant.

Sometimes there were brief flurries of activity as a few enemy bombers appeared, or an intruder started poking around, or a mine-layer or two crawled up the Bristol Channel. We always maintained standing patrols which did some good work trying out co-operation with the searchlights, or did practice interceptions on each other under the guidance of Starlight or one of the other new GCI stations that had been set up around the sector. But without the urgent spur of hostile activity it called for a constant effort to keep up the standard of AI operating: it was all too easy to relax into a comfortable routine of slap-dash tests and of lazy interceptions of targets doing nothing more than flying straight and level.

Early in the New Year this became more than a purely personal problem for me. I was given the job of Navigator Leader of the squadron, and with it promoted to Flight Lieutenant. I fully realized that from now on the easy friendliness of my relationship with the other operators would be much more difficult to maintain as it was going to be my job to watch over them with a much more critical eye. I would also have to train the newcomers, coaxing the stubborn, encouraging the diffident, and chasing the lazy. And since above all else a leader must lead, I would have to keep my own work on the top line.

I started out by flying with each of the crews in turn, standing behind the pilot during their night flying tests. In this way I could watch an interception pre-arranged with the target, listen to the patter, and compare different methods. It was a very revealing experience. I knew from the outset that I would have to make allowances for the nervousness of those working under observation – I had been through all that myself – but I never had to make excuses for the crews who got results. Their methods might vary, but there was always the same smooth co-operation between the pilot and the operator, with quick, clear directions and ready, exact responses. And it was just as easy to see why the others had failed at night. Hesitant mutterings would come from the back with the pilot taking sly peeps out of the window and following the target visually, easing into turns that were not asked for, acting on information that was never given. I realized that they were doing it out of a mistaken sense of crew loyalty, but I always wondered whom they thought they were fooling, apart from themselves. They were certainly not leading any Germans up the garden path.

Very touching in more ways than one, were the reactions of some of the more junior pilots when they had me on board. Knowing that I had flown for so long with the CO, they would be unnecessarily nervous. But if they were timid with me, their reactions were far more pronounced when they flew with John. He made a practice of taking every new crew for a demonstration flight in his own aircraft when they first arrived at the squadron, in order to dispel the erroneous idea prevalent at some of the OTUs that the Beaufighter was a death trap and an engine failure inevitably fatal. The new pilot would stand up behind John in the front, and the operator would squeeze in beside me in the back.

With the load of the four of us on board, John would start off to show the newcomers what could be done. Just as we cleared the boundary hedge he would chop one throttle right back, and we would stagger around the circuit on one engine. With our landing made quite safely with one of the propellers still idly windmilling, the colour would return to the faces of our passengers. After that we would take off in company with another aircraft and give a demonstration of an interception and an attack. John always finished off the show with one of his masterly approaches in that steep curve, with power in hand, which enabled him to keep a look out even below and behind him before flattening out to land. Those approaches always rather horrified the unenlightened, but John had the final word to say on that.

"It's better to step out of the wreckage at the far end of the flare-path," he would say, "than to be dug out at the near end."

Those approaches would be followed by the lightest of touch-downs and the shortest of runs. And then the passengers would climb out, smiling and a little dazed, with entirely different views about their expectation of life and a much greater eagerness to get on with their own flying.

With the approach of spring we ran into long spells of the doldrums, and it was becoming more of a battle against the corroding effects of inactivity, apart from routine practice patrols, than against the enemy. It called for a different, humdrum fortitude, particularly when it came to counting the deadly hours of the last, dreary, pre-dawn patrol.

Somewhere south of the Needles our engines hummed a drugging lullaby as we turned north for the fifth – or was it the sixth? – time. Much as I fought against it, my eyelids were drooping and my head was nodding. In order to shake myself out of it I went through yet another cockpit check. My eyes and my fingers made the familiar round: the oxygen still showed half-full, the generators were charging and the air pressure was normal.

Would the dawn never come? How about the beacon? There it was: 20 miles ahead. We droned on without speaking. In a little while a faint blur showed up against the grey of the sea, and we knew that England was just ahead. Would they send us home this time?

"Hallo, Blazer Two Four," came the Controller's voice over the radio. "Vector one eight zero."

Oh hell! We were being turned to the south again. Out we went, 40 miles out to sea, and I was beginning to loathe the whole business. Only 40 miles, and those Coastal chaps were pushing out across the Atlantic for hundreds of miles and thinking nothing of it. Only 40 miles; but of late I had begun to hate flying over the sea. In fact, it was all becoming more and more of an effort. But over land, if one did have to bale out, it was usually simply a matter of walking home. Floating gently down to earth was a very different matter to dropping into that cold and hungry sea…Oh…come on…snap out of it!

The stars were swinging around as we headed out yet again towards France. Were they really a shade paler, or was it nothing more than my wishful thinking?

"Vector zero one zero," the Controller ordered.

The stars swung back again, and there was the beacon, 40 miles ahead. Now, surely, there was a lighter patch of grey in the sky to the eastward, forcing the darkness slowly to loosen its grip. The night watch was nearly over

"Vector zero three zero for base," the Controller told us. "D Dog and call Harlequin. Good morning."

That time he had really said base! The aerodrome and a bath and breakfast and wonderful, wonderful bed!

We crossed the coast, and all the time the light was becoming stronger. Then we were passing Salisbury, already stirring uneasily, the smoke of the early fires curling up slowly through the mist which clung to the river and hung heavy over the roof tops. Above it the balloons glistened like airborne dew-drops in the first rays of the sun.

John picked up the black ribbon of the Andover road and held down the Beaufighter in a long, shallow dive.

"Let's see if there's anyone up yet at the Pheasant," he said.

There was mischief in his voice. The flight off duty had had a party there last night, and they would probably be sleeping late.

The aircraft was gathering speed as the road came closer. The fork of Lobscombe corner was ahead and the roof of the Pheasant was in the gun-sight. Down…down…down, we went, and the telegraph poles were flashing past just below the window. This was the Beaufighter that the Japanese later came to call The Whispering Death.

"I can't see anyone about," John said. "It must have been a good party."

With a tile-lifting roar we skimmed over the roof, zoomed over the crest of the hill, and dived for the circuit of the aerodrome; and as we did so I thought of a dozen hangovers in the Pheasant leaping from the pillows and then painfully subsiding.

Three Cornered Contest

WE were all very conscious of the fact that our greatest enemy was really the dreaded Isaac Newton, and that the moment we left the ground he was there waiting for us. There were times, however, when even he could be enlisted as an ally, unwilling though he might be to take sides.

By the spring of 1942 the hair raising art of intruding was being practised quite extensively by the RAF as well as by the Luftwaffe. Whenever the weathermen were able to give an appropriate forecast, aircraft would take off from either side to try and make the greatest possible use of the cloud cover in attacking the opposition. It was usually quite pointless sending up day fighters under these weather conditions as they rarely found the raiders and move often than not finished themselves off in a loud heap of smoke.

Our night fighter pilots were generally more experienced in blind flying than the day fighters. They also had better homing and blind approach aids, and longer range with which they could reach, if necessary, some other airfield; and with AI they could follow the enemy whenever he tried to slip into cloud cover. It soon became the custom at fighter stations, whenever the weather became too thick for the effective use of day fighters, for a section of Beaufighters, manned by the more experienced pilots and operators, to be called to readiness. This was the origin of what later became known as the "all-weather" fighter.

By this time it was known that our old opponents K Gr 100 had been equipped with a new system of blind bombing. This, it was said, would enable them to fly to their target, release their bombs, and return to their base without once emerging from cloud, and they were only waiting for suitable weather conditions to try out this new equipment on operations.

On the 4th of April, low cloud with drizzling rain and a straggling mist over our part of the country brought visibility down to less than 1,000 yards. Everyone expected that the night flying programme would be cancelled. But John was taking no chances, and he decided in the afternoon to make a quick test below the weather.

No sooner were we airborne than the Sector Controller asked us to go 40 miles to the south-west. There had apparently been an attack on the Gloster aircraft factory at Brockworth. Now the raiders were on their way out, and Starlight were waiting to try and cut them off. No. 600 Squadron had some Beaufighters in the air, and we could also hear Fearsome One Nine – Edward Crew and Basil Duckett – talking on the radio to control.

Soon we were flying in unbroken cloud of varying density. It was the baffling, tenuous sort of cloud that fell walkers know so well. Enough daylight filtered through from above to turn our world into a dazzling, white void with neither top nor bottom and without direction. Visibility might be anything from 100 yards to a mile: there was no way of judging. At 9,000ft the windscreen was opaque with a coating of ice.

We could hear Starlight vectoring Edward Crew on to one of the raiders, and then they took us over. But no sooner had they done so than our AI, which had been looking rather sick at the indignity of getting only a rearward contact, gave up the ghost with a last, tired flicker. I switched off quickly as the familiar Awful Smell came stealing out of the set, and I went back to a sky search, blinking painfully at the blinding whiteness, just as the interception reached a climax.

"He's crossing you now, starboard to port," Starlight reported.

Out of the void, not 300 yards away, popped a Heinkel, crossing close below our tail.

"There she goes," I shouted. "Turn hard port and dive…behind and below!"

John wasted no time and brought the Beaufighter wheeling around on its wing-tip before even I had finished speaking.

"OK. I've got it," he said.

He dived in on the starboard quarter of the other aircraft and pulled up 400 yards astern. But his windscreen was still iced over and the target was nothing more than a mere blur behind the gun-sight. Also, the German gunners had spotted us.

For some minutes we chased on southwards across the unseen Channel towards Cap de la Hague, closing in very slowly with John waiting for his windscreen to clear. Through the top panel, and from my dome at the back, the Heinkel was clearly visible, and we closely studied the details of the aircraft. There was an unusual projection under the nose, and from the port wing there trailed several long whip aerials. I wished that I had brought my camera with me as a photograph of that aircraft would have provided some excitement for the boffins.

When we were in to 300 yards the enemy gunners evidently thought that it was time for them to do something about it. The Heinkel began to weave, and there came from the dorsal gun a few bursts of fire which went wide of us.

John pulled up and had a crack back at them, but the screen was still not clear enough for accurate deflection shooting. He tried a longer second burst, waving the nose of the aircraft around a little, and he saw some hits on the starboard wing of the Heinkel. It was not long before the ammunition drums ran out, and while I was reloading the Heinkel slipped out of John's clouded sight. When I had finished I jumped up and had a look around. I found the Heinkel trying to creep up under our tail. John whipped around again and made another attack, but it was the same story as before. All he could do was take long, uncertain bursts at a twisting target that could only be dimly seen. The return fire from the enemy gunners was equally ineffective. It was maddening, but we just could not close in for a really lethal, point-blank burst.

Finally our second lot of ammunition ran out. We were by then some 50 miles out to sea with a windscreen still iced up and our ammunition racks empty. There was nothing else we could do but turn away and watch our target disappear into the mist. Glumly we headed back towards base, letting down through the cloud on homing vectors from our Sector Controller.

When we landed we found that Edward Crew had been involved in two combats with no more success than we had had. He, too, put off by evasion and icing, had only managed to get in wing hits on his second target. He had, however, managed to collect quite a lot of German lead in his own aircraft. He had finally lost contact, while Basil Duckett was reloading.

It could scarcely be said of our first all weather operation that it had ended at all conclusively. And yet, I thought, if any German Intelligence Officers had been rash enough to promise the crews of K Gr 100 immunity from attack under these weather conditions they must have received some pretty sharp answers from those crews when they got back.

Some weeks later, on the 23rd of May, the Germans looked at their weather reports and decided to have another try. It was as dank and as horrible a day as it was possible for the English spring to produce, with weeping clouds dragging right down over the hills and layered above right up to 20,000ft.

At 4 o'clock in the afternoon we scraped off after them into the drizzle and set course for Swanage. The earth was gone in a flash, and we were alone in the centre of a ball of white emptiness. Only the needles of their instruments of the blind-flying panel could tell us what was happening: air speed, height, rate of climb, altitude, direction. Without them we were anywhere and nowhere, and we had to believe them or perish. We were still, floating motionless in a void, going neither up nor down, until we looked at the instruments.

Calling Starlight, John received an answer in the reassuring voice of Keith Geddes, who was now on a rest from operational flying and acting as a controller at the GCI. Keith gave us a lead to a quick and easy stern chase, and very soon John had a Heinkel in sight 1,000 yards ahead. And almost immediately it was obvious to us that the crew of that aircraft were not going to be caught napping.

The Heinkel banked steeply over to the left and came running back at us, the gunners firing broadsides as they flashed past only 100 yards away on the beam. John had the Beaufighter already staggering around after them, the force of the turn pressing me down outrageously into my seat. But this German pilot knew what he was about, and he had already faded into the mist before we were around. I pushed my head down into the visor, but my eyes had been so dazzled by the glare outside that nearly a minute, passed before I could make out anything on the face of the cathode ray tubes; and by that time there was nothing worth seeing.

"More help, please," John appealed to Starlight.

It was acutely embarrassing to hear my failure broadcast in such a way, but Starlight were still coping with things, and they had our customer tracked to the north of us, near Shaftesbury. They passed to us more vectors, and another chase followed. Our luck was in, and again John caught sight of the Heinkel. I tried resolutely to keep my head down on the AI set, but sitting in a ring-side seat with champions in the lists and not watching what was happening was more than I could endure. And the pilot of that Heinkel was a champion. Then suddenly I remembered the sunglasses I always carried for daylight practices. The pull of gravity was viciously building up again as I groped in my pockets, but finally I got the glasses on. I looked out just in time to see the Heinkel flash past, heeling over at a staggering angle, with the gunners still blazing away, wasting their ammunition. John was holding his fire, saving his ammunition until he could be sure of getting in a lethal shot.

I twisted quickly back on to the set, and this time the blip showed up clearly as soon as I whipped off the glasses. The other aircraft had straightened up, apparently thinking he had thrown us off. I wondered what his feelings were and if he was beginning to despair when we reappeared behind him a few minutes later. He certainly showed no signs of any panic for he immediately repeated his sound tactics of turning in to our attack.

But this time John was already turning inside him, determined not to be thrown off. The turns steepened until the Heinkel appeared to be almost upside down over our heads. The effects of the "G" were becoming intolerable as the duel developed into a grim winding match, a term John always used to describe two aircraft trying to out-turn each other. My eyeballs were dragging at their sockets, and my neck muscles were aching with the sheer effort it took to try and hold up my head. Over the intercom I could hear John's breathing becoming laboured as he relentlessly lugged those tons of flying metal around the sky.

Finding that he could not out-turn us, the German began to twist and dive. I kept losing sight of him under the wing, and then he would reappear on the opposite track, flashing past at seemingly impossible angles. It was a contest between masters of flying, but the pace was becoming too hot to last. I began to wonder which of the two would be the first man to crack, and whether it would be machine or man.

But a third champion had slipped by now into the lists. That sinister

Black Knight Sir Isaac was standing quietly waiting for one of his human adversaries to over-reach himself so that he, too, could join in and make it a three-cornered contest. And the way things were going he would not have long to wait.

The whole fuselage of the Beaufighter was shaking and the engines were howling as the airspeed steadily climbed. The needles of the altimeter raced backwards around the dial as we ran out of feet; and the blind-flying panel had long since gone crazy. The artificial horizon had given up trying and was sulking in one corner. Things were happening altogether too fast.

"Hm…this isn't good enough," John said very quietly, talking half to himself. He went through a little soliloquy as he calmly and deliberately sorted out the outrageous story that the instruments were trying to tell him. "Now…let me see…left bank…that's better."

The Beaufighter lurched over drunkenly, and peculiar things happened to its trim. The floor re-established itself in a position that was totally different from where I had supposed it should be. But now things began to quieten down, and as we swung back on to what must have been an even keel I had a clear picture of the Heinkel as it flashed past in full plain view, heading straight downwards.

"If I'd only brought my camera," I commented.

"'A fine time to start worrying about cameras!" John snapped with justifiable asperity.

It needed only a quick glance at the AI set for me to see how horribly close we were to the ground, and I did not need to look at the altimeter to see what it was showing. We were over high ground rising in places to 900ft. As I watched the blip from the other aircraft it raced swiftly up the shortened trace and was swallowed in those menacing ground returns.

"More help, please," John appealed again.

But Starlight could not give us any further help as the blip from the customer had faded from their tube.

I was feeling quite exhausted as I searched for our homing beacon on the AI set and guided John back to Middle Wallop. He felt his way down through the cloud and finally broke out into the welcome reality of a dripping landscape, thankful for the relief after two and a half hours of argument with the staring – and often angrily glaring – dials of his instrument panels.

And then we were told that our adversary had also seen the blessed earth again, although it could only have been for a brief, horrifying moment. The German was still diving almost vertically in a last desperate bid for escape when he broke cloud a few hundred feet above that unexpectedly high ground of the sodden slopes of Cranbourne Chase. He must have failed by only a few feet to pull out in time; and close to the lonely crossroads of Alvediston there was found the wreckage of the Heinkel with what was left of that spirited pilot and his crew.

Our Intelligence people discovered that the pilot – Hauptmann Langer – was the Commanding Officer of the proving, or development, unit of the famous K Gr 100. Since John had not fired a single shot, it had indeed been a match between champions. John later confirmed that his air speed indicator was reading 340 miles an hour when he broke off, a speed that was decidedly high for the Beaufighter and under those conditions.

The squadron had three aircraft airborne at that time, and we all reported contacts. Per Bugge had had much the same experience that we had been through, and when he broke off the chase the Heinkel he was after was also going vertically downwards very low over the sea, and had disappeared into cloud.

It would seem that the Black Knight had made quite a day of it.

CHAPTER FIFTEEN

Under the Counter

THE standard of AI operating in the squadron had by now reached a fairly proficient level. We were members of a fully recognized trade; and at this time all the various observers, navigators and operators at work in the different commands of the RAF were grouped together under the general name of Navigator with, in parentheses, a word qualifying the particular type of navigator one happened to be. In our case we were now known as Navigator (Radio), and in place of the RO in our half wing flying badge we now had N. Most of the operators who had had no previous training in navigation were sent off on a special course, and gradually we came to be known as navigators rather than operators.

But although we were most diligent about practising, and all the navigators worked very hard to keep their skill in the finest shape possible, we could still only barely meet the demands made upon us. Stung to retaliation by the growing weight of the raids made by Bomber Command, the Luftwaffe began to step up the tempo of their own night attack. But they had learnt a lesson from the past, and there were to be no more night-long processions ambling confidently through the shop. Now we had to face a series of stealthy smash-and-grab raids, swiftly executed by some pretty wary customers.

For some time the Germans had been probing away at our defences, feeling for our weaknesses, and now they started exploiting them to the full. The worst of these – which they evidently quite understood – was our difficulty in dealing with low-flying aircraft. We knew all about that and we had been trying for a long time to overcome the weakness; but the minelayers and the intruders were still coming and going with comparative impunity while our navigators searched desperately among the ground echoes that were hopelessly swamping their tubes.

Making the most of this weakness, the Luftwaffe put in a series of sharp, concentrated attacks against coastal targets. They crossed the sea flying low, climbed quickly for a short bombing run as they neared the coast, dropped their loads, and then dived out again. The fighter had to snap up these under-the-counter customers very quickly or he would find the door of the shop slammed in his face almost before the bell had stopped ringing.

On top of all this, to add to our difficulties, a strange, new phenomenon had lately been appearing on our AI tubes. This was a dancing, confusing mass of grass that swamped our blips out of existence whenever we ventured out towards the enemy coastline. It was the beginning of that back-room war of jamming and counter-jamming which only the boffins could win for us.

One of the first places to suffer from these new attacks was Exeter, which was bombed disastrously in April. This was in a neighbouring sector to ours, manned by No. 307 (Polish) Squadron, whose crews had raged impotently about the night sky. Although John and I were allowed to poach, we met with no better success. It was a dark night, and I followed one contact almost into minimum range.

Finally, John said: "I believe I can see it."

We were so close that the blip hovered on the brink of disappearing. And then suddenly it seemed to split into two, and one part rushed away from us "Dive!" I shouted. "He's diving away!"

John rammed the nose down, but the contact was dropping away at an incredible speed. As we rushed down after it I noticed that the other half of the blip was also receding, but it was well above us. Then I realized what a mistake I had made. I was trying to intercept the bombs that had just been dropped by the raider. By the time we had flattened out and climbed again our customer was on his way out.

Early in June the same type of attack was made in our own sector when a military target at the back of Poole Harbour was bombed. Again the enemy came in so low that Starlight could not pick them up until they began to climb for their bombing run a few miles from the coast. That meant that we had only a very short distance in which to be vectored into position, to get our contact, and to close in.

It was no consolation to learn that the Luftwaffe had unloaded nearly all their bombs that night on a magnificent decoy fire on Brownsea Island. I knew that they would come again, that they would use the same tactics, and that as yet we had no effective answer. I knew that new GCI stations were being built and that they would see farther and lower across the sea, and so give us a longer run at our targets. But it was becoming imperative that we should have a new AI that could see low down. We knew it was on the way because we had seen what progress had been made in the TRE workshops. Given that, we might, perhaps, regain our old mastery.

Emboldened by their low-flying successes, the Luftwaffe started coming in higher again and roaming farther afield. This time they were not in any great numbers, and they concentrated their attacks on small inland towns in what became known as the notorious reprisal, or Baedeker, raids. Quite often they achieved damage out of all proportion to the effort because of the smallness of the target and the absence of any effective static defences.

Business was brisk but not very profitable as the fast and manoeuvrable Dornier 217 the Luftwaffe were now using was hard to catch and their crews were on the alert. But even then we had some successes. The unrelenting Edward Crew had found in Basil Duckett, an operator with a quiet persistence to match his own, and early in May they shot down Dorniers on two nights in succession.

From the first of these encounters, Crew came back with his victim's trailing aerial wrapped around his starboard aircrew. The second battle developed into quite a protracted affair. He was given a contact by an inland GCI rejoicing in the delightful name of "Moonglow", and the chase went on until they were well out to sea. The Dornier twisted and dived and fought hard to get away, but Crew was not to be shaken off. He ran out of ammunition, but he still held on to the frantic bomber while Basil Duckett struggled to reload two of the guns. With his next burst Edward set the Dornier on fire and slowed it up. Even then the enemy gunners were staunchly firing back as the Beaufighter overshot. But he managed to keep it in sight while Basil reloaded the other guns. They were down to 2,000ft when he saw the enemy aircraft hit the sea in a flurry of smoke and steam.

With customers such as this about we could not afford to take any chances of being caught sitting on the ground. At the slightest sign of any possible activity, standing patrols were maintained regardless of the weather. It was June, but with the English climate that was no indication as to what the flying conditions might be. To the ice-bound night fighter stooging up and down through unbroken cloud it could all very easily have been November.

If the weather conditions were at all doubtful, John always insisted on going off first so as to have a look at things for himself. Then he would call control and tell them who might or might not follow him into the air if required. He knew whom he could trust to do a useful job under the adverse conditions of bad weather without killing themselves or breaking an aircraft.

Early in June we ran into a foul night. We took off into the filth on the strength of some more of the well-known "indications", meaning almost anything. Whatever they were, they must have been both strong and persistent because control were most reluctant to allow us to return, even though it was quite obvious from the outset that we were wasting our time.

The cloud through which we climbed was dense all the way up, and rain swilled from the windscreen in a solid bow wave. It drummed upon the hull of the aircraft and even blotted out the navigation lights on our wing-tips. John resigned himself to an hour or two of practice in instrument flying, and we started plodding up and down just off the coast.

It was not long before the Glowgremlins found us and came clambering on board. The ignorant mariner misnamed them "St. Elmo's Fire", but he did not understand the jolly little creatures. They made themselves thoroughly at home with us, swarming all over the aircraft, clinging in dense clusters to the aerials and the rudder, riding their roundabouts on the tips of the airscrews. They blushed furiously in the blue fashion that was their custom, making the air around us glow uncannily with a chilly radiance. And our headphones sizzled and crackled with their elfin chatter.

Some claim that these little chaps gather electricity from the air on the tips of their tiny umbrellas. Others hold that it is merely the perishing cold that makes their noses glow so vividly with a blue light. In any case, they are harmless enough, although it can be very disconcerting when one of them perhaps more mischievous than the rest flicks veins of light across the windscreen.

"We might just as well be on the Underground," John commented.

To complete the illusion, I switched on a few shaded lights along the cat-walk between the cannon. The little pools of yellow light shining along the metal hull, the rattling on the roof, and the blue flickering and flashing all added up to just the right effect.

"Leicester Square…change for the Piccadilly Line," I started chanting. "Mind the doors…ri-i-ght!"

The cold sanity of the voice of the controller brought me back to reality as he called us with instructions to return to base. John turned into a shallow dive, and as he did so the King Glowgremlin rose to his feet astride the rudder, solemnly raised his top hat, and stepped off. One by one, as the rising pressure became too much for them, his followers opened their parachute umbrellas and were whisked off by the slip-stream. I waved to them, took a good lung full of oxygen, and set about tuning in to the homing beacon.

At last the new low-looking AI arrived, known as Mark VII. It was still scarcely out of the development stage, and it was beset with plenty of teething troubles; but it was ours to play with, to tinker with, and to master. With the first of the new Beaufighters fitted with the new equipment we had the double task of keeping the business going with the old gear while learning to use the new.

The first thing one noticed about the new aircraft was the absence of any external wire-cutter aerials. Both the booing and the harking were now done within a new plastic nose to the. Beaufighter inside which a scanner shaped like a dish whirled around at high speed.

In addition to the new equipment inside the aircraft, we also discovered, to our unbounded relief, that the ammunition for the cannon was now stored in tanks spaced across the cat-walk. Although this made progress from back to front of the aircraft something, of an obstacle it meant that we no longer had the task of reloading, and the slight added constriction of movement was well worth paying for.

Before any of us tried using the new AI, Basil Duckett, "Chalky" White – one of our most promising Sergeants who was killed a few months later – and I went to FIU at Ford for a few days' instruction from the people who had been doing the operational trials with the stuff. First of all we had lectures and demonstrations in the workshop; and then we flew with Ken Davison, a Flight Lieutenant, and two navigators, who showed us how to interpret the picture and what to look out for in the way of pitfalls.

The presentation of this new AI, we found, was entirely different from what we had been used to. For one thing, all the information was displayed on one tube. The ground echoes, although they now kept at a respectable distance, could still be seen when flying low, surging up down at the bottom of the tube as the scanner revolved; but they did not interfere nearly as much, with the overall picture. This thing, we soon discovered, could see with great accuracy within a strictly limited beam not unlike that of a sharply-focused headlight of a car. A really first-rate man should be able to work wonders with it; but it was obvious that the slow thinker who allowed his target to slip out of that narrow beam was going to be worse off than ever.

Bulging with information and advice, we returned to the squadron and set to work converting to the new AI. We all had very high hopes, and we felt that now, perhaps, we would be able to deal with our more awkward – not to mention low down – customers. There was no doubt that the stuff would work low down, and it became the fashion for us to follow each other down on the AI after night flying tests until we were almost on the ground. The long-suffering local inhabitants must have thought that some new and suicidal spirit had come over us as we chased around their chimney pots.

One of the difficulties we soon ran into with the new gear was in the matter of the servicing, and that became quite a problem. Trained radio engineers found that their previous experience was not of a great deal of use to them as the technique of these ultra-high frequencies which we were now using was still very much in the research stage. It seemed that quite often a fresh mind, given a sound scientific training, could cope better with the problems of this new form of radar.

We had with us for a while a likeable civilian boffin named Michael Callan, a Scientific Officer from TRE, whose job it was to help with the servicing of the new AI. Callan and I were gossiping together one day and I casually asked him what he had been doing before the war.

"My last job was on the Island of Capri," he said.

Curiosity overcame good manners, and I could not help demanding: "But surely they weren't developing radar down there?"

He was not at all put out, and he laughed at that idea. "No," he said. "I'm a biologist really. My job there was to interfere with the sex life of the octopus."

I never heard how the octopus got on, but under his care our new AI certainly began to thrive.

And all the time we went on with learning to master it, making our practice interceptions stiffer and stiffer. Finally, we felt that we were ready for business. A new shop, planned to deal exclusively with under-the-counter trade, had opened its doors in the Isle of Wight.

By this time I knew that I was going to have to start facing another enemy, one that I had been forcing myself to disregard for some time. It was nothing more nor less than that insidious, soul-destroying decay which the kindly authorities called "operational tiredness", and which the more honest aircrew described as "the twitch".

I had seen too many others wrestling with it not to recognize the symptoms in myself: the constant weariness, and the carefully concealed relief at finding oneself off duty for the night; the equally carefully feigned eagerness at finding that after all there was the first patrol to do with Starlight. I considered all this in myself as dispassionately as I had studied it in others, looking for the cause and the cure. It was not usually any hectic moments in the air that started the thing. I felt that it was more the cumulative, wearing effect of prolonged nervous tension, broken nights, and a very shrewd working knowledge of the law of averages. But it also needed some other factor to trigger the whole thing off: personal problems – including love affairs! – and domestic troubles; some niggling doubt about something or other; or continued failure at the job one was doing.

It was this last factor, I felt, that was beginning to nag at me. I was becoming haunted by the idea that I had let the team down, that I was not big enough for my boots as the Navigator Leader, that I had had my big chance and had thrown it away.

But I did not have long to worry about all these things. Three weeks later John and I were suddenly told the shattering news that we were both to go on a rest.

It had been arranged that John would take over from Rory Chisholm the job of directing the work of all the night Operational Training Units in Fighter Command. I was to have gone to No. 62 OTU, at Usworth, near Newcastle-upon-Tyne, but John waved a few magic wands and instead I went with him into exile at Headquarters, No. 81 Group, the Training Group of Fighter Command.

We said our goodbyes to our ground crews who had served us so very well. The Mess gave us a farewell dinner at the Pheasant. When it was all over John and I walked outside together for a breath of air before turning in. A Beaufighter droned by overhead on its way out to Bournemouth and the old beat. We listened in silence to the sweet music of its Hercules engines as it died away on the soft night air.

"Well...that's that," John said quietly. "There'll never be another three years quite like it."

We had had a good innings together: three years of preparation, and three years of war. In that time we had seen the whole fabric of night defence built up. It had been three years of hard work and good fun, of long dreary nights of boredom, of nights of frustration and nights of triumph, of nights of fear and of tragedy, and of nights of sweet content under the glory of the stars. It had been three years of happy companionship in a worthwhile job. I knew that the break was not going to be an easy one.

My thoughts turned to the freshness of the dawn, and I remembered the larks getting up from under our feet, the dew dripping from shrouded aircraft as heavy-eyed fitters pulled off the engine covers, the hush of evening as we sat outside the crew room on a warm summer night and Johan lazily tossed up pebbles to fool the twisting bats. And I saw again the razor-sharp silhouette of the first patrol climbing away into the gathering dusk.

I recalled the unforgettable smells: the sweet, nostalgic and quite incongruous mixture of wet grass and warm tarmac, of new mown hay and high octane petrol, and the whiff of dope thinners in the clean night air.

I looked back at the old Pheasant, standing silent and lightness in the moonlight, and I thought of the many faces that had come and gone, so many of them never to come back. We had all of us learnt our night flying the hard way, and we had made the most of our time.

"I suppose we'd better finish packing," John said.

That was all that passed between us, but I knew that in that understanding silence he also had been back over the years during which we had worked so closely together.

The following day it was announced that John had been awarded a bar to his DSO. The squadron lost no time in using that as an excuse for a continuation of our farewell party for yet another day.

CHAPTER SIXTEEN

The Dreaded Rest

T HE headquarters of No. 81 Group were located in a mellow old manor house on the outskirts of the village of Avening, a remote and tiny hamlet tucked away in a fold in the Cotswolds. To look at it was a time-weathered idyll of lichen covered grey stone, isolated in a countryside denuded of signposts and public transport. In its own peculiar way the house was a masterpiece: a straggling place of great age, with the startling additions and renovations which had been made from time to time struggling for mastery.

John and I drove to Avening from Middle Wallop. We arrived late in the afternoon. The debris of a garden party was being cleared from the lawns, and a few exhausted survivors were reclining on the steps. We were greeted by an individual who, but for his RAF officer's uniform, might have been all unfrocked parson or a shady clerk or perhaps even a superior type of bookie's runner.

"Ah…good afternoon!" he exclaimed. "Welcome to Avening."

He led the way to the open french windows with a flourish that conferred upon us the freedom of the place, and followed us into an oak panelled ante-room. He regarded us, and there was a dramatic pause before he asked:

"By the way…" His eyes managed to focus and take in John's rank. "Sir…are you saved?"

John looked a little puzzled, but he rose to the occasion. "No," he said; "not noticeably so."

"Good!" came the answer. "Then, sir, have a drink?"

We took stock of the place and met various people who came wandering in. Despite the sunshine outside, it all looked rather gloomy and dismal, and we both began to feel even more depressed about this whole wretched business of being on a rest.

For the first couple of weeks, however, I revelled in being able to get to bed every night and all night. But that was about the only thing I did enjoy. And as the tiredness began to wear off I found the evenings began to drag; and the long days shut in by office walls took on the aspect and the dreariness of a prison sentence.

My family life had really ceased to exist two years before. My wife had now joined the ATS, and although we caught up with one another at rare intervals – she was at first a driving instructor at Camberley – she was now on a signals course up in Scotland, which meant that we saw even less of each other.

Co-author
Flight Sergeant C.F. "Jimmy" Rawnsley

King George VI talking to Flt Sgt C.F. Rawnsley while visiting No. 604 Squadron
at Middle Wallop, May 1941

Test flight of the Bristol Beaufighter, September 1941

II

The Beaufighter was fitted with two Bristol Hercules engines, armed with four cannon guns in the fuselage and six machine guns on the wings. It had a nominal range of 1,500 miles and a speed of over 330mph at 14,000ft.

Group Captain John Cunningham

In addition to being on a rest, which we hated from the start, John was also going through what he described, with his usual reticence, as a rather difficult and unhappy time. The endless paper work was a torment, and he was rapidly stifling in an atmosphere where the nicely-turned phrase, the correct minute and the neatly kept file all seem to be so much more important than the realities they dealt with.

John's office was at the opposite end of the building to mine, and whenever I rushed to the window at the sound of a passing aircraft I would usually see his head thrust out of his window and gazing skywards. We would grin at one another a little ruefully and go back to our desks.

It was not long, fortunately, before we found that the Senior Air Staff Officer, Group Captain M. S. W. Robinson, was not only a very able man but also a most understanding one. He had fought with distinction in the Battle of Britain, and he knew well enough what John was feeling, and that it was all too easy to waste his time keeping him stuck in an office, John could do more good in half an hour's personal contact with instructors and pupils than he could in days of pining behind a desk. So when John suggested that he should spend more of his time visiting Operational Training Units, Robinson agreed with good humour, and life took on a slightly rosier tinge.

From then on I never quite knew when John's head would appear round the door of my office and, with a gleam in his eye, he would say:

"Ready for a trip? I've sent for a car."

Then I would joyfully shoot my little pile of files into the "Out" tray. We would slip quietly away over the hill to the aerodrome at Aston Down, where the Group's communication aircraft were kept, and sail off happily into the fresher, more familiar air of the training airfields.

These night-fighter Operational Training Units were scattered all over the country, and flying was the only practical way of getting to them. At first John flew around in a somewhat sedate fashion, in the Group's Oxford, finding his way during bad weather – it had no navigational aids – by following the railway lines. It was a dual-control aircraft, and at times I was allowed to try my hand at flying it. I felt that I became quite reasonably proficient at what John called "flying straight or level". But he soon tired of this slow and limited flying, and he arranged for a long-term loan from the squadron of his old Beaufighter. It was all most irregular, and the curse of the lives of the ground engineers wherever we went. They would lift the cowlings and look at those mighty engines, whistle and shake their heads, slip the cowlings back into place, and then hastily sign the servicing book as illegibly as possible, keeping their fingers crossed until we were safely off the ground and on our way. But we were happy, and once again we were flying confidently above the weather, making our way from one radar beacon to the next. And at the OTUs, instructors and pupils alike watched with awe John's faultless touch-downs and impossibly short landing runs, and listened with even greater respect to his suggestions and advice.

After a time I began to gain a more complete understanding of the whole training programme, and to appreciate some of the many difficulties which beset it. The main one was that in the past it had been bedevilled by a vicious circle of bad faith. All too often an unscrupulous squadron CO, called upon to send one of his crews due for a rest to act as instructors at one of the OTUs, would joyfully unload any incapable or ill-disciplined men he happened to have on his hands. The news got around, and to be sent to an OTU came to be regarded as a disgrace, an indication of failure. Those at the OTUs who took their jobs seriously and genuinely tried to run the training programme as it was planned, battled on with this sort of misfit material, often despairing, and clinging to such good men as they had until even they began to falter and wonder if they would ever see a squadron again.

At one of the OTUs at Cranfield I found my old friend Pat Patston. He had been there for over a year, caught up in the machine and thoroughly discouraged. Listening to his hair-raising stories of flying in worn out Blenheims – "clapped-out" was our expression for their condition – with inexperienced pupils and instructors who could not have cared less about what they were doing, I began to understand why so many of our replacement crews at the squadron had arrived in rather a perplexed and twitch-ridden state.

Rory Chisholm had already gone a long way towards changing the unhappy state of affairs at the OTUs John carried on with what he had done by bringing about with all those concerned a gentleman's agreement with respect to instructors. If the squadrons wanted good crews then they would have to supply good instructors. In return, the instructors supplied to the OTUs would be guaranteed a return to operational flying with their squadrons at the end of six months, provided that they really pulled their weight.

As the months went by we found the vicious circle beginning to unwind, and new vigour came to life in the training programme as instructors arrived who knew their jobs and had up-to-date experience. All the ground work that had gone in before and that had been urged on by Rory and John began to show results. The instructors had something to work for; and the squadrons found the difference reflected in the standard of the crews they received. But there always seemed to remain two things about which we could do nothing: the amount of flying done, and the weather. For want of flying, the training programmes dropped badly behind. It was due to the aircraft standing idle on the tarmac, there not being enough skilled technical men available to service them. As for the weather: it continued to do its foul worst. And as winter closed in life became pretty grim, particularly at those widely dispersed, Nissen-hutted aerodromes among the bleak Scottish hills.

The determined efforts made to keep the training programme up to schedule in spite of the foul weather did not help at all to improve the accident rate, and one of the pupils who met his death during that grim January was Richard Hillary, the talented young author of *The Last Enemy*.

Hillary was a man who apparently had every kind of courage but the sort needed to go to his Commanding Officer and admit that night flying was too much for him. Terribly burnt after being shot down during the Battle of Britain, he had endured the long torment suffered by so many who came to call themselves "Guinea Pigs". It was during that period of mental and physical agony that he wrote his book, as fine a piece of writing as anything that appeared on the Second World War. Then, driven by some inner torment, or perhaps by some taunt, he had forced himself, against his better judgment, to go back to flying. Unfortunately, he made the not uncommon mistake of imagining that night flying and night fighting would come to him more easily than the split second reaction that he knew was essential for the day fighter. Just after midnight on the 7th of January his aircraft, a Blenheim, which had been orbiting a flashing beacon, was seen to spiral down and crash, and Hillary was killed. And Walter Fison, his loyal and promising young navigator, who had been so fond of music, died with him.

Of particular interest to me – perhaps because of the way I had had to grope around in my own elementary AI training – was the work being done at the OTU at Usworth. Up to the time of the establishment of the AI school there, after its move from Prestwick, those who had had the job of introducing the newcomers to AI had been badly starved of facilities. They had done their best against some rather overwhelming odds. But now things were better, with more reliable aircraft, efficient ground trainers, and more enthusiastic instructors.

The aircraft used were Ansons, which were fitted up as flying "class rooms", with a staff pilot, an instructor, and two pupils. They had duplicate AI indicators so that the instructor could monitor the pupil's interpretation of what was being seen on the cathode ray tubes while the second pupil watched the target's behaviour visually from the front seat as he listened to the commentary over the intercom. With two three-hour flights a day everybody was getting in plenty of flying time. When the turn came to act as the target aircraft, the pupils took the chance to keep their pilot on track between two radar beacons, a boring but very useful exercise known as "beacon bashing".

I spent a week at the school flying with the pupils and I was astonished, and delighted, when I saw how much the standard of operating had improved. With good instructors and suitable aircraft – the Ansons were very easy to maintain – and more reliable AI, the pupils were progressing much more rapidly to a state of proficiency that many a squadron navigator would have envied.

As all those who served in the RAF know, the Anson was a slow and stately aircraft, characteristics which could produce on the AI some misleading and very surprising effects. It was quite easy for the aircraft when acting as target to turn right around in its tracks at a range of only a mile and come rushing back at the perplexed pupil without indicating more than a few degrees of deviation on the AI picture. The usual reaction when that happened was for the pupil to think that he was overtaking too fast, whereupon he would call urgently for the throttles to be chopped right back, and, when that failed to cut down the rate of closing, glance involuntarily out of the window. It was then, to his horror, that he saw that what had been a chase had turned into a head-on contact. Whenever I heard of that happening I thought of my first hostile contact, and I could not help grinning sympathetically.

After six weeks of carefully graduated exercises, the navigator, if he had it in him at all, had gained such a sound grasp of the principles involved that he was soon able to adapt himself to the higher speeds of the operational aircraft. From Usworth he then went to one of the advanced Operational Training Units where he was crewed up with his future pilot. There the team was moulded and finally prepared for service with a squadron.

At the other end of the scale there was the matter of the squadron Navigator Leaders. The standard of the Leaders was being reviewed by Headquarters, Fighter Command, with the object of improving it. Nearly all the existing Leaders had fallen into their jobs by chance, either through sheer seniority or just because they happened to fly with the CO. Now it was decided to set up a school under the auspices of FIU for short post-graduate courses. It was intended that this should serve the double purpose of ensuring that the present Leaders were up to the job, and of giving a final polish to candidates selected to become Leaders in the future.

It was clear that the man who was going to take charge of the new school would have to be, above all things, a pretty strong-minded individual. The officer finally selected was Flight Lieutenant L. D. Britain, a man with a chin like the rock of Gibraltar, and as tough as the toy soldiers which had carried his name all over the world. With Flight Lieutenant David Keith, a Charterhouse schoolmaster, to help him, Britain took the trade another step forward towards becoming a science.

While I had been plugging away at this training programme John had been busy with the training of the pilots and the final crews. Although he had no liking for the job, he got on with it. And he was determined that the maximum sentence of six months that had been passed on us should apply to himself no less than to any OTU instructor. As the time passed he began putting out feelers, dropping hints in sympathetic ears, and taking a discreet tug or two at any likely strings.

I was more hardened to office life than John, but I was also becoming very restless. Every night the Mosquitos of No. 264 Squadron – one of the first night squadrons to be equipped with this new aircraft – came climbing over the hills from Colerne, and the crisp song of their Merlins, crackling through the frosty, autumn starlight, aroused in both of us an acute longing to get back to squadron life.

As Christmas approached and there was still no definite news of a posting, John began to grow even more restless, and more dispirited and short-tempered. And there was an added restlessness in the air. The Allied landings in North Africa had broken the stalemate, and the tide of war was beginning to flow again; and all we were doing was stagnating in our quiet backwater. January 1943, was drawing to a close when finally John came to me with the good news that at long last we were to go back to flying. There was a sparkle of new life in his eyes as he explained that he had been given command of No. 85 Squadron, and that I was to go with him as his Navigator Leader.

No. 85 was a famous fighter squadron, and its badge – the mysterious hexagon, the origin of which no one could trace – had distinguished its aircraft in the First World War. It had borne the brunt of much of the early fighting in France, and later it had won honours in the Battle of Britain. Converted to a night fighter squadron, it was now stationed at Hunsdon, in the same North Weald sector from which we had guarded the eastern approaches to London in the autumn of 1939.

The squadron was equipped with Mosquitos, and their AI was the pilot-indicator Mark V which I distrusted so much. Now I was going to be able to find out for myself whether it could be made to work. In fact, I knew that, somehow or other, I was going to have to make it work. But that could wait. The important thing was that we were on the move again, and that we were going to an operational squadron in a highly promising sector.

At the end of the month they gave us a farewell party, and we were on our way at dawn the next day.

CHAPTER SEVENTEEN

Second Innings

IT was inevitable that with the change of command of our new squadron there should be a certain amount of uneasiness. John knew well enough that the squadron he was taking over would have its own traditions and customs, that there would be a clinging loyalty to the departing CO, and that there might possibly be a fear that the new broom would sweep too clean. On the other hand, he had his own ideas about how he wanted things done. He knew that he was going to have to step cautiously, and that he would have to be careful not to upset things by making too sudden and too ruthless a change, while at the same time being careful not to court popularity by appearing to be too easy. We both knew that the first impressions were going to be very important ones.

The Officers' Mess for the aerodrome at Hunsdon was in an old country house named "Bonningtons", which sat squat and comfortable among its iron-railed meadows. John brought his big Lagonda to a halt outside the entrance, and we got out. The great moment had arrived. Feeling rather like a new boy on his first day at school, I squared my shoulders and followed John into the Mess.

A group of officers, obviously dolled up and looking very self-conscious in their best blue, drew themselves up as we walked in. It was all, I reflected, very much in the tradition, and I could not help feeling an inward amusement. A young pilot, smiling cherubically beneath a mop of ginger hair well plastered down, came forward.

"Good evening, sir," he said. "My name's Farrell. Will you have a drink, sir?"

I sensed that it was not so much an invitation as an appeal. There was something almost beseeching in the way the question had been asked; and the whole gathering seemed to have frozen into a tense silence as they waited for John's answer.

"Thank you," he said. "A half of bitter, please."

The tension relaxed with an audible sigh, and there was a concerted rush towards the bar. What we had not known was that the departing CO, Wing Commander G. L. Raphael – a vigorous young Canadian who had joined the RAF in 1936, and of whom we really knew very little – strongly disapproved of drinking. This most unusual trait had been weighing heavily upon the more light-hearted members of the squadron. With John's acceptance of the offer of a drink we had, literally, crossed the first bar.

In addition to Wing Commander Raphael there were several other Canadians in the squadron. It was an association which dated back to the

First World War, when the famous Billy Bishop, VC, a Canadian, and the highest scoring of the Allied pilots, had first formed the squadron and taken it out to the Western Front.

Now, we discovered, this happy arrangement was, at the demands of the politicians, being broken up in accordance with a policy known as "Dominionization", a deed as horrid as the word. The move was equally unpopular with Canadians and Englishmen alike, but there was no way of stopping it. Henceforth, it had been ruled, as many Dominion personnel as possible were to be withdrawn into units to be made up exclusively of men from their particular part of the world. The fine, leavening effect of mixing men from all over the Commonwealth so that they learnt mutual respect, toleration, and understanding friendship was lost. Within a few months, all the old stupid jealousies, misunderstandings, and even hatreds reared their ugly heads until, in the worst cases, it was scarcely possible to put Home and Dominion squadrons on the same stations without getting outbreaks of petty violence.

Our first concern after our introduction to the Mess was to get to know all those in the squadron. Of these, the first was the Adjutant, Flight Lieutenant T. J. Molony, known as Tim, a massive and dignified man, urbane and very conscious of the niceties of decorum. In civilian life he was a director of Ladbroke's, the turf accountants; and he had been with the squadron since the early days in France. He also laid claim to being the last man to bowl underarm at first-class cricket, playing for Surrey. Because of this distinction, Tim described himself, using a happy phrase, as "the last of the lobsters".

The Engineer Officer, Flight Lieutenant J. Hoile, was a good-natured, hard-working old sweat of a Regular who knew his job thoroughly and in every detail from spinner to tail wheel. We soon discovered that the aircrew knew well enough that if an engine let them down it could not be blamed on "Castor", as he was affectionately known to everybody.

Hunsdon was strictly a wartime station, and first things had very wisely been put first. There were comfortable, brick crew-rooms, well dispersed parking pens for the aircraft and small blister hangars, and concrete perimeter track and runways.

The airfield was not far from North Weald, our sector station, and the entire sector – which guarded London from anything coming from the east coast across the Essex marshes or up the Thames Estuary – was well known to us from before the war and the time we had spent there during the first four months after hostilities had broken out.

The first morning back on the aerodrome was sheer delight. There was a promise of spring in the air, and we were free again. Everything looked clean and bright, and I could hear the cry of the plover and the snarl of engines being warmed tip. My heart lifted as I pedalled around the perimeter track on a dilapidated bicycle.

I made my way to the flight offices, scattered among the dispersal pens where the engines of the Mosquitos roared and crackled as they were run up, vapour trails spraying from the whirling propeller tips. It was not difficult to locate the home of the Special Signals Officer, Flying Officer E. A. Kingscote, by the forest of radar aerials jutting from one of the huts.

After my first meeting with Kingscote I had the feeling that he was possibly just a little suspicious of me, and that it was probably due to the fact that he might have been getting a raw deal from the navigators. I knew from past experience that they were always all too ready to blame their own shortcomings on to the AI sets the Special Signals people tended with such zeal. I felt now that I would have to be very careful not to express too freely my own opinions of the AI.

From the Special Signals Section I went to the Intelligence hut nearby, and in it there was a bunch of navigators sprawled all over the place in a haze of cigarette smoke. In the middle sat the squadron Intelligence Officer, Flying Officer E. A. Robertson, a wizened, dry old Scot, trying all at the same time to retrieve his scattered papers from the floor, answer the 'phone, and put up most amiably with a merciless ragging from the others. Robbie, I learnt later, was in the fishery business, and lived in Hull. When he answered the 'phone it was with an accent so thick that his caller had on one occasion mistaken him for a Pole.

"Dee-ay-oo he-rr-e!" he shouted. He covered the 'phone and turned to the others. "Wull you fellows no be quiet a minute?" he beseeched, and then he turned back to the 'phone. "No...Dee-ay-oo!"

He was trying to make it clear that he was the Duty Intelligence Officer, known, for short, as the DIO. Turning away from the 'phone in disgust, he held it out with the plea: "He-rr-e...have a go, wull ye! The damned man canna' onderstand his own language!"

When I left Robbie was still warding off in his own agreeable fashion the good-natured attacks of the others. I made my way to Flying Control. The days of a casual blink from the Duty Pilot's Aldis Lamp were over, and by this time there was a most efficient organization, armed with radio and direction finders, teleprinters and landlines, well trained to watch our comings and goings. The square, camouflage-painted Control Tower, I had been told, was called Castle Keepfit, the name being taken from its radio call-sign.

The senior Flying Control Officer, Squadron Leader M. H. Bradshaw-Jones, was out on the balcony. He was a tallish, gaunt, piratical figure of a man, and he was, for some reason unknown to me, wearing a revolver and thigh-length waders. Somehow it all gave him a vaguely nautical air. Later I came to know Brad very well, but somehow I always seemed to be half-expecting him to whip out a cutlass when things got tough and action was demanded. I remembered now that I had met him in the Mess the night before. At that time he had been quietly riding a solo motor-cycle around the billiard table with four passengers on board.

From what I had already heard, the squadron had come to look on Brad as one of themselves. As he showed me around the tower, explaining every detail in a brisk and forceful way, I realized just why the crews held him in such high esteem. Airborne on a dirty night, they could be sure that a watchful eye was being kept on the weather, that they would be recalled in time if it got too bad, and that they would be given accurate homings with everything properly laid on and waiting for them. The voice would remain friendly and calm and confident no matter how hectic things might become. Perhaps the highest tribute they could pay him was the reassuring expression I was to hear later as they buckled on their harness and glanced at the thickening mist.

"It's all right, chaps," they would say. "Brad's on tonight."

One of the first difficulties with which I was faced in my job as Navigator Leader was to find some means of assessing fairly the value of the navigators in relation to the positions they held in each aircrew. There was not much chance of being able to check their work in the air because it was almost impossible for more than a pilot and a navigator to work in the confined space of the cockpit of a Mosquito.

There was in existence, however, an AI ground trainer for the particular brand of radar we were using. It was housed in one of the huts, and consisted of what looked like a pair of school desks. At these the pilot and the navigator sat side by side, the AI set and a set of pilot's controls in front of them. With these they could go through the motions of making an interception. It was useful enough for elementary demonstrations, and for checking patter and procedure, but, like all ground trainers, it had very definite limitations. Nevertheless, it did at least give me some idea as to how the crews had adapted themselves to the pilot-indicator AI, and their methods of working with it. I was in for a bit of a shock.

Some of the navigators had developed a patter that I could only describe as most extraordinary. It seemed to consist of a non-stop and bewildering stream of words somewhat like the chanting of a Dutch auctioneer trying to finish off the sale before closing time. Into the ears of the pilot would pour the torrent:

"Left – left – left – still left – 3,000 – steady – steady – dive – dive – dive – 2,500 – right – right – right – level – out – steady – steady – steady – 2,000."

And so it would go, on and on, while I sat dumb with amazement. It was not until I heard the retiring Navigator Leader in action that I discovered where it had all come from. He was a lively, vivacious man named C. P. Reed, a Flight Lieutenant. He was sharp featured and quick witted, and a remarkably fast thinker. The words streamed out of him in a torrent, and I wondered how any pilot could ever take it all in. But the amazing thing was that it worked, and worked well. And what sort of argument could prevail against the unanswerable fact of success?

All the same, I began with the newer navigators to use a more orthodox style, if only to simplify the interchangeability of crews. I had a pretty shrewd idea that Phil Reed owed his success more to his quick thinking than to his style.

There were among the aircrews some well-matched teams. Many of them merged their own pronounced individualities in achieving this. Flight Lieutenant W. H. Maguire was a jovial, prosperous looking man, an ex-instructor and a fine pilot. He had as his navigator a Welsh schoolmaster, Flying Officer W. D. Jones, a short, stocky man who was a great lover of music. Flying Officer George Irving came from Carlisle. His head of flaming hair naturally brought down upon him the nickname "Red". He was navigator for Flight Lieutenant Geoffrey Howitt, a solid and imperturbable individual. Squadron Leader W. P. Green, A Flight Commander, had as his navigator a typical NCO of the best type, Flight Sergeant A. R. Grimstone. Known to everybody as "Grimmy", he was, although unburdened by any unnecessary ambition, keen, quick-witted and reliable. Peter Green was a slightly built, deceptively mild-mannered man, plagued with a nervous stammer which, as I had noticed happened with other aircrew, was barely noticeable the moment he left the ground. There was certainly no trace of nervousness about his flying.

Sergeant G. G. Gilling-Lax, another of the navigators, had only been with the squadron for a very short time when we arrived. He was an NCO of a very different type, and entirely different to the popular conception of what a Sergeant was supposed to be. Greying hair topped a long, scholarly face, and he stooped slightly in a rather dignified manner. His voice was quiet and carefully and evenly modulated. I was not altogether surprised when I checked through the records to find that he had been a house-master at Stowe. I seemed to have on my books an astonishing number of schoolmasters.

One of the more senior navigators – although young enough in years – was Flying Officer F. S. Skelton. I saw little of him as he was just finishing his first tour of flying and was about to go on a rest; but what I did see of him made a lasting impression. He had been through the complete navigator's course, and at first he had been rather annoyed at having to specialize in AI for night fighters, as that was by no means the job of his choice. Known to everybody as Bill, he was tall and handsome with veiled eyes well set in a leonine head. A rather drawling, under-graduate voice tended to complete an impression that Bill was taking the whole business far too languidly ever to be much good at it. I should have known better, and subsequent events were to prove how wrong first impressions can sometimes be.

In Bill Skelton, I felt, there could be more or less summed up the general standard of operating in the squadron: the basically fine material had been softened by prolonged and enforced inactivity. Most of them had got into the habit of doing only perfunctory night flying tests, and their practice in the air was casual, even slapdash. It was the old and very sad story, all the result of a little too much of the playboy in their attitude towards things. I formed the impression that they were good, but not as good as they thought they were, and by no means as good as they could be; and I became anxious to show up their shortcomings, and my own, before the Luftwaffe did it for us.

Early in February, a few days after our arrival at Hunsdon, John and I went off on our first night practice with one of the East Coast GCIs of our sector. It was our first night flight in a Mosquito.

We had already made a few flights in daylight, and we had worked out a rough system for use with the pilot indicator AI. From my set, which displayed to me the whole story of what was being seen by radar, there was relayed to a single, small cathode ray tube set to the left side of the instrument panels in front of John what was supposed to be a composite picture. It showed roughly whether the other aircraft was up, or down, right or left, and when approaching minimum range, the blip on the pilot's tube began to sprout wings, indicating that the two aircraft were getting close to each other. But even then the pilot was almost entirely dependent on the navigator to read off the ranges as they closed in, particularly when they got to the point where they were so close that the pilot would have to keep looking out for a visual on his target rather than concentrating on what was being shown on his tube.

Between us, John and I had decided that I should control the interception during the early stages, using our old and well-tried methods. When we got in close enough for any evasive action the target might take to become effective, John would take over while I merely called out the ranges. And when we were close enough to hope for a sight on the other aircraft, I would chip in when necessary with additional instructions and information so as to free John from the necessity of watching his tube.

At last we were back on the job, and this time in the trim, sleek Mosquito. It was with heartening contentment that I came to the point of getting into the aircraft. There was the small, telescoping ladder that led up to a door, less than 3ft square, on the starboard side of the front of the aircraft. Close on John's heels I climbed the ladder, dumped my parachute pack on the floor, and squeezed through the door into the tiny cockpit.

John was easing himself into the pilot's seat on the port side as I struggled to turn around. A dozen hidden bandersnatches caught at my harness and clothing. The navigator's seat was nothing more than a shelf on the main spar of the wing on the starboard side of the cockpit and set back slightly so that once in position he could relax his left shoulder to normal width just behind the pilot's seat. It made me think of those old Continental racing cars, in which the mechanic crouched half behind the driver's right elbow. I did not have to concern myself now with reloading the guns as we were literally sitting on top of the four cannon and their boxes of ammunition, separated from them only by the floor of the cockpit. Their muzzles were set in the underside of the nose of the aircraft.

John was wrestling with his harness, and I held the shoulder straps up for him with one hand while I turned on the petrol cocks with the other. In addition to all the radar equipment, the navigator had several other things to keep an eye on, such as the oxygen supply, the petrol taps and the lighting switches, since all these were more readily accessible to him than to the pilot. The control of these had to be the subject of a most rigid cockpit drill very clearly understood by both pilot and navigator if trouble was to be avoided.

The rigger who was helping us to get started had collapsed the ladder as soon as we were on board, and he handed it up to me. I slammed the door, checked the catch, and strapped the ladder into its place. Now we were on our own, groping around the still unfamiliar layout for the various switches and cocks. I had already spent some hours just sitting in the cockpit memorizing the positions and functions of all the knobs and taps until I could drop my hand on them blindfolded; but it was only with practice that the routine would become automatic.

There was a whirr of starter motors, and the engines burst into life. In front of me there was a box of controls for the AI set hinged at the bottom so that it could be pulled forward to a position in front of the knees, with the visor covering the cathode ray tubes in a fixed position above it. I wriggled my shoulders forward and pulled out the box, leaning over it to look into the visor. Already I was puffing and sweating and I realized why the old hands had warned me not to put on full flying kit. If anyone as small as I was found it a tight squeeze then how on earth did the broad-shouldered bigger types manage. Unable to believe that I should ever be warm enough in any aircraft at night, I was obstinately wearing everything, including my leather and furlined goon skins.

John signalled the ground crew away and we taxied off around the perimeter track, rolling smoothly on the concrete. Our way was dimly lit by coloured electric lights sunk in the ground on either side, an aid we had not known on our first tour of flying. It felt strange to me, after riding backwards for so long, to be up in the front, facing forward, and be able to watch the pointers of the forest of dials of the instrument panels. The figures stood out sharp and clear as the old smudgy and rather dazzling luminous paint had been replaced by ultra-violet lighting.

"All set?" John asked.

"Yes…all set," I replied. "Gravity tanks on."

The popping from the stub exhausts of the engines close beside the side windows rose to a fiendish snarl. The tail lifted and swayed, and the avenue of lights along the runway came rushing back at us. Then the rumbling stopped and John's right hand came across, reaching for the undercarriage lever. The wheels thumped up into place, and the dim, clustered lights of the Sergeants' Mess streaked away below the nose. We were away, and it was with a glorious feeling of relief that we were really back on the job.

We climbed to the eastward, heading for the North Sea. As we gained height, the temperature in the cockpit became noticeably warmer. The Merlin engines were liquid cooled, and the radiators were set into the centre section of the leading edges of the wings, with only the thin wooden shell of the fuselage separating them from the cabin. I sat and sweated in the Turkish bath of my goon skins. I was regretting my obstinacy in getting all dressed up, but I was thankful at the prospect of our second tour being in a really warm aircraft.

On the other hand, I was not too happy about the change from air-cooled to liquid-cooled engines. And the ear-splitting racket from the stub exhausts of the Merlins was very tiring after the soothing snore of the Hercules. Those radiators offered quite a big area, and it would take only one bullet, or even a piece of flying wreckage to put an engine very quickly out of action.

Soon after we were airborne Sector Control handed us over to the GCI with which we were to work. Both John and I had gained a pretty firm impression that night interception practices had become little more than just cursory routine flights, much the same as with the night flying tests. For one thing, I learnt, much to my astonishment, that it was the accepted practice for the target aircraft to fly always at a height of ten thousand feet, with no variations.

It was our turn first to act as target. The GCI Controller gave us a course to steer, but no height. John said nothing, and climbed to 12,000ft. We heard our playmate being vectored after us, and again there was no height given. Nor did the fighter ask for one.

Over the intercom John said to me: "I think we'll have to shake these people up a bit."

He pushed the throttles forward and pulled up the nose, and the altimeter needles wound their way around the dial until they stood at 20,000ft. Then we levelled out. But there was still no mention of any heights from the Controller. In a little while the echo from the other aircraft trying to get at us appeared on our own set, showing behind and far below. In fact, so far below us was he that it seemed that he did not have any contact on us at all, and very soon he was vertically below us.

"You must have contact now!" the Controller was telling him, the tone of his voice becoming somewhat peremptory. "You're right with him!"

"Sorry," the other aircraft reported. "Definitely no joy."

"Then your weapon must be bent!" the Controller almost snorted.

John chuckled to himself, and then reached out and switched the radio set over to transmit. Quietly he said: "Two Four calling. What do you make my angels?"

There was a brief silence. I imagined that the Controller was probably too stunned to be able to make an immediate reply.

When he did, it was with an obviously restrained indignation at this unseemly interruption.

"Why…10!" he declared, as if outraged at the thought that it might be anything else.

"Are you quite sure of that?" John asked.

There was another pause, and then the Controller replied: "Well…perhaps it's 12."

"You may be interested to know," John said, an icy edge to his voice, "that I am at 20."

There was not much doubt left in our minds that we were going to have to do a lot of sorting out if the Germans were not to catch us napping.

CHAPTER EIGHTEEN

Swing High – Swing Low

MY fear that the Luftwaffe might beat us to it was unfortunately confirmed much sooner than I expected. On the night of the 3rd March, 1943, the sirens were howling and the guns in the Estuary were already shaking the air as we raced for our aircraft and joined in the scramble to get off the ground. After the long spell at Middle Wallop, I had almost forgotten how short the warning could be of the approach of enemy aircraft across the narrow Strait of Dover.

Mosquitos were streaking off down the runway, hard on each other's heels. We elbowed our way into the stream and leapt into the air. We were too late to get to one of the GCIs, but the searchlights were busy as John wheeled out of the circuit and pulled up the nose into a gruelling climb.

The searchlights had been reorganized, and they were now in a regular, box-like pattern grouped around a series of evenly spaced markers. The object was to pack into a small area as many fighters as could he usefully handled. Each fighter as it was airborne was given one of these boxes to work in, and the pilot made his way to his allotted marker beacon and orbited there until the lights in the surrounding box either illuminated a target or formed a cone that was decisive enough for him to follow the indications and so pick up an AI contact.

"Orbit I for ink," we were told by the Controller.

In a very short time we were circling around above the flashing marker beacon. The sky seemed to be full of clustering beams, glaring back from a mass of billowing, broken cloud. Already the ground was alive with the flash of the London guns, and quite close, on the southern edge of our orbit, the air began to twinkle with shell bursts. And all the time I was aware at the back of my mind of a feeling of joyful anticipation. I realized then that the enforced rest of the past six months had done me a lot of good.

John swung around towards a well-knit cone that came sweeping across our box. I turned my attention to the AI set and looked down into the visor, withdrawing from the outside world and probing into that other electronic sphere. We made contact, and the blip started to slide down the tube.

We closed in quickly, and I was soon feeding John with a complete picture, in the same way in which we had worked in the past. We slowed up as we approached minimum range, but John could not see a thing.

"Range about 500ft," I said. "I daren't get in any closer."

"We're still in cloud," John replied. "Hang on a minute."

Remembering the chase we had had with the cloud-skimming Heinkel, we climbed a little, even going as far as to let the picture of the

AI show that we were well above the target. But there was no clearance in the cloud, and reluctantly we dropped down again. There was no bump from any slipstream through which we might have passed, and the cloud continued to flow densely about us.

"Either he's flying in cloud or that thing's lying," John said.

There was a sceptical note in his voice, and all my old doubts returned. "Shall we try firing blind?" I suggested.

But John wisely decided against that. The chances of a hit were too small, and if we did hit it and it blew up, we should almost certainly fly into the wreckage.

This was not a very auspicious start, I thought, and I began to feel depressed. But we were completely blind in that cloud, and finally we had to give up. We went back towards our marker beacon. But the raid was still going on, and with luck we might be able to find another customer who would not be as coy as the last one.

And we did. I got a contact and we followed it as it weaved its way outward bound between the swinging beams of the searchlights. When John looked up and saw a Dornier 217 twisting and turning just ahead of us my faith in the AI was quickly restored.

We closed in for the attack. The twin fins of the enemy bomber stood out clearly, with the long, pencil fuselage foreshortened under the high wing. From where I now sat I was going to watch the battle from a ringside seat. There would be no more peering through the tunnel of the fuselage as I had done in the Beaufighter. Now I had a perfect view of things, with only the clear, wide panel of bullet-resisting glass of the wind-shield between us and the target and any hot tomatoes they might want to throw back at us.

But they did not see us, and John drew up into position and got his sight steadied on to his target. He pressed the gunbutton, but nothing happened. I had braced myself for the thunder of the cannon under our feet, but all I heard was John's exclamation of annoyance. He tried again, but still there was no response from the guns. And then somebody in the Dornier must have given the alarm. The long, slim bomber rolled right over to the left and plunged vertically downwards.

John rammed our nose over, and I was lifted from my seat as the aircraft fell away; but I forced my face into the visor of the AI set and just held on.

The Dornier went plummeting down for several hundred feet, but we were still in contact. Then it levelled out, and started to climb steeply. But we were right behind it, and a few minutes later John again had it in his gun-sight. I was beginning to feel quite affectionate towards the AI set, much as I had maligned it.

"Well, now," John said, "we'll try again."

The Dornier was hanging in front of us, tantalizingly close. And again John stabbed in vain at the gun-button. There was not the slightest flicker of life in our cannon, and a moment later the German peeled off again, apparently thoroughly alarmed, and swooped earthwards. He made no speedy pull out and climb this time: he went straight on down in a long, high-speed dive that kept us well behind, and finally the ground echoes swallowed him up and I could see nothing more of him on the AI. He must have learnt a pretty sharp lesson, and probably went all the rest of the way back to his base at nought feet.

John and I were fuming with rage, too angry even to be able to speak to each other. We landed back at Hunsdon, and a quick examination revealed that a severed lead had put the gun-firing circuit out of action.

One by one our other aircraft came creeping home. Three-quarters of the squadron had been up. There had been eighteen sorties, and of the lot we were the only ones who had even seen a raider. There was an unhappy silence in the crew-room, and I wondered to myself if the others really believed our story. But at least I knew that the AI would work. It might not be as good as our old stuff, and it was certainly no good at all low down, but it would work, after a fashion. And these crews were going to have to make it work.

There was quite a post-mortem over the general failure of the night's operations. Staff Officers arrived from Group and Headquarters, Fighter Command, to hear what we had to say and to ask a lot of questions. There seemed to be some relief when they heard that we had actually got on to the tail of our Dornier, and that we had also followed it down through a peel-off. But I took care not to let my honesty run away with me. I did not want to be saddled with this Mark V AI for ever. I had heard rumours that there was a new improved version of the low-looking set which we had had at Middle Wallop, and I felt that if anyone was going to get it then it might just as well be 85 Squadron.

We could well do with an efficient low-looking set in our sector as we had to cover the coast-wise shipping lanes and the approaches to Harwich and the Thames, all of which were a rich field for the enemy minelayers. There were also the early morning, low-flying enemy reconnaissance aircraft. These appeared with such regularity and such immunity that they took on quite a personality, rather like Von Plonk at Middle Wallop. They became known throughout the Service as The Milk Train.

By now John was feeling well enough established in his new command to start reshaping things in the squadron more in accordance with his own ideas. There was not a great deal to do, but what there was of it needed careful attention. There was plenty of good material, but we had one or two thoroughly bad types, a few well-meaning incompetents, and several willing but tired-out old stagers. John started by wiping the slate clean. The wretched Dominionization scheme set us back a bit. We were as sorry to lose our Canadian crews as they were to go, but there was nothing we could do about it. What with that, with crews going on rest, and with John's purge, we stood in some need of reinforcement. But that was by no means a problem.

The night fighter world was a small one with an intimate and personal quality about it that made us all known to each other. Every good Commanding Officer made it his business to keep track of a good crew that had been sent on a rest. In turn, crews came to have a strong personal feeling for the Commanding Officers under whom they had served. Many of those who had been with John in 604 felt, when the time came for them to return to operations, that their loyalty to John was even greater than that which they had felt towards the squadron. Moreover – and this was a telling point – we in 85 were now in a live sector, whereas 604 were languishing in the wilds of Cornwall.

As a result of a lot of long-distance telephone calls and flying visits made by John to OTUs and Headquarters, Fighter Command, some familiar faces began to appear as guests in the Mess. And shortly after that a trickle of our old and well-tried crews began to swell our ranks. It was not long before the trickle became a stream, and somebody was heard to refer to 604 as "85's OTU."

There were some, no doubt, who thought that it all rather smacked of "jobs for the boys", but I could not see that that mattered so long as the right boys got the right jobs.

One of the first in the procession was Edward Crew, who came to take over command of B Flight. He had as his navigator Freddie French, now a Flying Officer. Freddie had never quite recovered from the terrible crash he was in while he was with us at Middle Wallop, but he was determined to go on with his job.

Another of the crews from our time at Middle Wallop that soon joined us was Flight Lieutenant Bernard Thwaites, and his navigator, W. P. Clemo, who was another of my schoolmasters, a little older than the average, a thoughtful man who took his pleasure in solitary nature study rambles. He sported an enormous pipe with a deeply curved stem, and when he spoke, which was rarely, the words emerged reluctantly between puffs and in a gruff undertone. Our old friends Johan Räd and Leif Lövestad also came to us after their rest. They were the forerunners of a formidable Norwegian contingent that was to join us in the months to come.

And there was another arrival which proved that I need not have worried for a moment about being saddled forever with our pilot-indicator AI. Within a week of that disastrous night of failure a travelling circus landed at Hunsdon. It was equipped with Beaufighters and a mobile ground trainer, and its object was to coach us in the use of the latest version of low-looking AI, known as Mark VIII.

The Beaufighters were doubly useful as they gave me an opportunity of flying with all the operators and of gaining some idea of how they were all performing. It was the first real chance I had of weighing them up as the ground trainer had only given me a rough idea of how they were doing. Although the new gear was strange to them, and the technique was slightly different, the basic principles of operation were the same; and I found that I could tell quite easily from the way they worked what a difference there was between the bodger, the slowcoach, and the quick, clear thinker. It was gratifying to find that after John's purge the surviving operators appeared to belong in varying degrees to the clear thinking category, which promised well for the future of the squadron. I appreciated the fact that it would also make me look to my own laurels.

Towards the end of March, we received the first of the new Mosquitos equipped with the low-looking AI. John immediately got to work on it – No. DZ 302/G – grooming to his satisfaction his third R for Robert, the letter he always used for his own aircraft. The graceful nose of the Mosquito had been altered in order to make room for the AI scanner. It had also been extended with the addition of a somewhat bulbous snout, which gave the aircraft a bibulous air, somewhat after the fashion of a music-hall comedian.

But no sooner were we settling into our stride with our new equipment than there developed a new threat from the enemy. It was really a case of going from one extreme to the other. Our new AI enabled us to see low down and go after the mine-layers and the Milk Train; but now the Germans went in for extremely high flying aircraft, right at the opposite end of the scale.

More than three months before, while we were still at Avening, we had seen one day a steady, white vapour trail, infinitely high, and writing a clear line of warning across the azure sky. A tiny speck of silver at its head, too high for the sound of its engines to reach us on the ground, had tracked across the sky from the south. It had turned in a wide arc over Gloucester, and had then leisurely made its way out again. All the time the anti-aircraft guns had put up a ridiculous show by plastering the sky a good 2 miles below their target.

This was the first sight we had of the German Junkers 86P, an unarmed reconnaissance machine fitted with a pressurized cabin which enabled it to fly not far short of 50,000ft. It came again, and during its third visit a specially fitted Spitfire had managed to stagger up close enough to frighten it off. But the threat remained. If a reconnaissance aircraft could get up as high as that then it would only be a matter of time before it was followed by lightly loaded bombers. If daylight made it all too risky for them, they would turn to coming over at night. And that would bring us into the picture.

Plans were very quickly laid to meet this new threat. The Westland Aircraft Company were given the job of producing a high altitude night fighter, to be called the Welkin. In the meantime the de Havilland Company got to work and converted a few of their photographic reconnaissance Mosquitos to high flying night fighters. It said a lot for that company that their superb team of designers, having only just met our demands for a machine that could be fast and manoeuvrable close to the ground, could now, in a few short months, adapt the same basic design and produce an aircraft capable of operating efficiently 9 miles up in the sky.

At the end of March a third flight was formed within the squadron with the object of conducting operational trials of these high flying Mosquito XVs. To give them extra lift in the rarefied upper air, the wings of the aircraft had been given long, tapering extensions which drooped visibly when at rest. The cabin was pressurized, and entrance to it was through a small, double hatch under the nose. The armament was restricted to two small machine-guns, bolted on under the belly of the aircraft rather in the manner of the old Blenheims we had had at the beginning of the war. They would not produce a very formidable weight of fire, but it would be enough to puncture the pressure cabin of the 86P and either cause the pilot to turn blue or rush down to a lower altitude. Wide, paddle-bladed propellers had been fitted to the engines to give a better grip on the thin air, and a host of other ingenious but less obvious details had been built into the machine. By some miracle of supercharged plumbing the engineers had persuaded the engines themselves to function efficiently at all heights. And to top it all off, the whole aircraft was painted a glaring shade of sky blue.

We enjoyed the usual crop of awful stories about "the bends" and boiling blood, and what happened when the glass cracked. But our daring young men stepped unscathed – and the right colour – from their first trips to a height of 8 miles. There were one or two instances of flights being curtailed when the navigators started to turn blue through a defect in their oxygen equipment, but this did more good than harm because it started an unprecedented rush in the checking and overhauling of helmets and oxygen masks, something that all my nagging had failed to accomplish.

John was just as eager as anybody to see for himself how these high flying aircraft performed. About three weeks after they had come to us – and after the development crews had done their job – we carefully checked our helmets and masks one afternoon, crawled up through the narrow double hatches, and sealed ourselves into one of the aircraft. John ran up the engines, and we watched the gauge as the air pressure in the cockpit was built up by the pump which was to keep conditions in the cabin at 10,000ft below our actual height above the ground.

I watched the waving wing-tips flexing upward as we started to gather speed for the take-off; and after an incredibly short run we were soaring into the air. The altimeter needle was almost spinning around the dial as the earth shrank swiftly away below us. In two minutes we had passed the 10,000ft mark, and in ten minutes we were nearing 30,000ft. It would have taken us the best part of forty minutes to climb to that height in our orthodox, heavily-armed Mosquitos, even by flogging the engines hard.

The earth below us began to look remote, a world apart, a faraway pattern of tiny fields and toy lakes and little smudgy scars that puny man called towns. A layer of broken cloud formed the base of our new world, and even that was far below us. We were free in the empty sky, and we could look up into the vast, indigo depths of frozen space. The small, fierce sun threw harsh shadows on the wing, and as we climbed the sky became darker and darker, and the windows began to frost over until only part of the windscreen and a few patches at the side remained clear. This was all quite different from what I had known of even our fairly regular flights to the higher altitudes of about 25,000ft. The cabin pressure was at an artificial 32,000ft, but the altimeter needle, slowing down now, had just passed the mark for 43,000ft.

I became vaguely aware of a slight pounding in my ears, and there was a strange, blinkered feeling around my eyes. Pins and needles tingled in my left knee, and my lungs were pulling heavily, sucking in oxygen. But these things were only incidental, and I was there to do a job. There was another of the Mosquitos about somewhere, and we were to do a radar interception on it.

Up at that height the spinning scanner of the AI set never even glanced at that far off earth, and the responses on the cathode ray tube were as clean and as clear as a May morning. Only the firm, sharp arc of the blip from our target showed up, circling the tube and shrinking towards the centre as we drew nearer. If only all our interceptions could be as clean as that one!

John was satisfied, and at his word I looked up from the AI set, up and out into the hard, bright glare around us. A dense stream of white vapour was pouring back over our heads, and for a few seconds it seemed to me to be coming from nowhere. Then, right in front of us, I saw the other aircraft. So perfectly blended were paint and sky that the wings and the fuselage of the Mosquito were only barely visible. The blue paint that on the ground had looked so blatant was now blending perfectly with the deep indigo of the background, and only the dark oil streak beneath each engine cowling showed up clearly. But behind, of course, the dazzling white vapour trails streamed out for miles.

John turned back on the homeward run and we changed places with the other Mosquito so that they could check their AI. I looked around, and through the half-frosted windows I could see the sweeping curve of the horizon. It was the first time that I had seen for myself that it really did curve, and that the earth was round. It was a breath-taking view. From Portland, in the west, the distant coast skirted the Isle of Wight along to Dungeness, and then out to the North Foreland. A silver finger pointing inland marked the Thames Estuary. Eastward and northward the curving line ran on hazily to the deep encroachment of the Wash. From my side as I looked down we appeared to be over Chelmsford. But when John banked over to the left and peered down through the frosted window on his side he reported that we were over Hertford. We were both right, but although the two towns looked from our height of over 40,000ft as if they were very close together, I found when I checked my maps that they were 24 miles apart.

With the arrival of May the weather began to improve. The Germans were still sending over short, sharp reprisal raids – using their Dornier 217s and Junkers 88s – on London and the Home Counties; and although twice John caught sight of the elusive enemy bombers I could not hold them long enough for him to get in a shot.

Peter Green and Grimmy opened the scoring with the new A.I. We saw their victim fall in flames as we were hopefully chasing the sky trying to find the enemy. Geoff Howitt and George Irving also scored a victory that night, shooting down a Dornier 217. A strange thing about that episode was that the pilot crashed with his aircraft and lived whereas the rest of his crew, who had baled out, were all killed.

Edward Crew and Freddie French celebrated their return to us by having a battle soon after they arrived, and they chalked up a Dornier 217 as probably destroyed. Gilling-Lax and his pilot, Flying Officer J. P. M. Lintoff, were also busy, and they spread a Junkers 88 all over Bromley.

In my own case, I simply could not break the evil spell which seemed to have settled over my operating, and I was becoming jumpy and depressed again, with a growing sense of frustration. I could not bring John into a position for a combat. If he felt any misgivings he did not show them, and he uttered no word of reproach. In fact, early in May he took me down to Ford to try out a new Anglo-American AI set which FIU were in process of putting through its trials. This set struck me as being bewilderingly complicated as it was entirely different from the sets we had become used to; but it was full of possibilities for the quick-witted operator.

For some time past a rumour had been in circulation that the squadron was going to be moved. A week after John and I returned from Ford the rumour was confirmed. But our destination was kept a secret, to be revealed at a ceremonial presentation by the AOC of the newly designed squadron badge. Then we learned that we were headed for West Malling, the plum of the whole of Fighter Command. It was the night fighter station for the famous Biggin Hill sector, lying athwart "Bomb Alley", the short, and direct, south-eastern approach to London from the Channel ports. Biggin Hill had featured prominently in the Battle of Britain: it was still the liveliest and most vital sector to defend. We were in luck.

CHAPTER NINETEEN

Fast But Not Furious

T HE squadron made the move from Hunsdon to West Malling on the 13th of May. John and I were not there as we had gone to the Westland aircraft works at Yeovil, in Somerset, where John was seeing how the Welkin was coming along. Long afterwards we heard that the absence of John's restraining influence led to a departure of the aircraft of the squadron that was something to haunt the dreams of any flying control officer for the rest of his days. For ten minutes the exuberant pilots beat hell out of the airfield. By a miracle no one hit the Control Tower, although later Brad did find that the tips of the propellers of one of the Mosquitos had clipped a swath out of the turf.

While this devilment was going on John and I were motoring quietly across the peaceful countryside of Hampshire and Somerset, lush and green and radiant with blossom in the bright spring sunshine. We passed a very pleasant day at the Westland works, climbing all over the almost completed Welkin. It was a rather ungainly monster, and what we saw was the prototype. It never reached the production stage as the Germans soon gave up their attempts to fly over the top of us.

On the way back from Yeovil we had arranged that John should leave me at Ford. I was to go through the Navigator Leaders' course at the school there before I started work at West Malling. We had lunch at the Spread Eagle in Midhurst and then we lingered for a while by the lake in Cowdray Park. We both felt that there was a great deal ahead of us, but just for that one day we could relax. We took off our jackets and sat back in the open Lagonda and enjoyed the warmth of the sun, and it was all very peaceful.

I always found it pleasant going back to Ford, and now that they had the Navigator Leaders' course going it was of additional interest, and I listened with the closest attention to talks by L. D. Britain and David Keith and by some of the visiting lecturers. We saw demonstrations of equipment in the FIU workshops, and I learnt all I could about the new AI – Mark X as it was called by us – as I foresaw that we might be using it ourselves before long.

There were six of us attending the course, and we were very comfortably boarded out at the Bridge Hotel in Arundel. Each morning a brake collected us and took us to the airfield for the day. In the evenings, after dinner, we would stroll along the quietly flowing Arun, beneath the old grey walls of Arundel Castle, for a quiet drink at the Black Rabbit. And then back through the warm dusk, tossing pebbles into the air to fool the bats in the way Johan Räd had taught me at Middle Wallop.

I realized from the outset that if I was to do any good on the course

I should have to keep my wits about me. But even then I made a sorry mess of my test interception. The AI set I was to work with gave trouble right from the time of take-off, and I was still fiddling with it trying to get it to work properly when the target crossed our path and caught me napping. But my instructor gave me the benefit of any doubt that might have existed – which was more generous of him than I should have been had I been in his place – and I was duly passed.

In order to try and make up for what I considered to be my poor showing in the test I muscled in twice on the night flying programme during my stay at Ford. On my first trip there was some activity going on, but even though we went as far as pushing our noses right into the flak over London my luck was out and I did not get the slightest sign of any contact. In fact, I had a shrewd idea that we were the aircraft at which the guns were firing with such gusto.

On my second attempt we were put on to an outgoing raid, and we went after it in a steep dive. We picked up a lot of speed and went into an even steeper dive, but we could not catch it. I began to wonder whether it was the Mark V AI playing up or if we were possibly after a new kind of opponent. I already knew that something different was happening in the night battle, because the Luftwaffe had just started sending over fighter-bombers at night, and it was going to take all the guile and speed we had if we were going to catch them.

We had found, a month before, while still at Hunsdon, that the raiders coming over had become extremely agile. On one patrol I had had two contacts which had led up to John getting fleeting visuals. But the enemy had been taking violent evasion with constant changes in speed, and we had lost them.

On the very next night four German aircraft – Focke-Wulf 190 fighter-bombers – landed in this country, two of them on the aerodrome at West Malling, and two of them in the fields nearby. What had caused them to do that we did not know. It might have been that they had run out of fuel, or possibly their navigation had gone astray. In any case, we knew after that just what we were going to be up against.

The aerodrome at West Malling, a few miles to the west of Maidstone, was deep in the midst of the orchards and hop fields of Kent. When I arrived from Ford, the Garden of England was at its best, the whole countryside alive and aglow with fruit blossom and spring flowers.

The airfield itself was a grass one with a strip of Somerfeld track – wire mesh pinned down over the turf – to form the main runway for take-off and landing, with a concrete perimeter track surrounding it. Brick crew-rooms and offices for the squadrons were dispersed around the fringe, hidden among the plum trees of a half cleared orchard. The overall effect was more that of a garden city than an RAF aerodrome.

The surrounding countryside, whichever way one looked, was thick with woods and orchards, and to the north the long, clean line of the Downs swept across the skyline, until it broke where the valley of the Medway wound through the hills. Of the grim battles which had been fought in the skies over this part of England in the difficult days of 1940 there remained little sign. Here and there one occasionally found a few grass covered craters where a bomb load had been jettisoned or a scar on a hillside which marked the grave of some stricken aircraft.

Over dinner the night of my arrival at West Malling I heard exciting news about the fighter-bombers the Germans had started using. During the time I had been away there had occurred what could only be described as a red letter night in the history of the squadron: they had destroyed their first FW 190.

We had all known from the beginning that we were going to be up against something that would be pretty hard to catch. The FW 190 was one of the Luftwaffe's latest single-seater fighters. Once it had got rid of its wing drop tanks and the 2,000lb bomb that it carried externally under its belly it was quite a fair match even for a Spitfire. It could easily run away from us if it chose to do so, or make rings around us if we caught it.

The picture was a gloomy one, but there was another side to it with certain vital factors which might alter things completely. First of all the German single-seater pilots would be less experienced than our own at night flying. That would lead them to pay a great deal of attention to their navigation and even to the fundamental matter of keeping airborne. Then they would not be able to fly at full speed all the time for fear of running out of fuel. And finally they had no radar, and they were completely blind below the tail. With skill and a little luck, we felt, we might be able to accomplish what we had always aimed at in night interception: not a battle, but a quiet case of murder. If we did our job well it would all be over before the German pilots even suspected our presence. If we did not do our job well, then woe betide us!

During my absence the squadron had thought a lot about all that they were now faced with, and their reaction had been to make up a kitty to be awarded to the first crew to destroy a FW 190. The prizes included bottles of gin, whisky and champagne, and £5 in cash. Tim Molony, our adjutant, held the stakes.

The squadron had been at West Malling only three days when, on the night of the 16th of May, the sirens began to wail as the German fighter-bombers came streaking in across the narrow Strait of Dover. B Flight were on duty. The 'phone started jangling, and as Peter Green snatched it up they all jumped for their kit. To their astonishment and disgust they were told that they had been ordered to stay on the ground; and no matter how much they argued there was no reversing the decision made by someone higher up that No. 3 Squadron – which had a flight at Manston – should take care of the raid with its Typhoons.

For nearly an hour they sat on the ground and fumed while the Typhoons, not having AI, raced blindly and uselessly around the night sky. Fortunately, the Sector Controller was a man with some courage. Seeing that the Typhoons were getting nowhere he took the matter into his own hands and ordered them back to base. In their place he ordered off 85. That put an end to their fuming and with whoops of joy they raced for their aircraft. After five minutes of hectic jockeying around the perimeter track the pack was off.

Through all this excitement, Tim Molony had been peacefully sleeping in his own bed in the Mess. But two hours later he was awakened by a thunderous hammering on his door. He sat tip, blinking, as a swarm of jubilant aircrew surged into his room. Tim was accustomed to the high spirits of his flock, but before he could make any protest the shouts of the intruders clearly explained what had happened.

"Come on, Tim…disgorge!"

"Peter's won the jackpot!"

"Give, Tim…give!"

"Peter's got a 190!"

Tim rose to the occasion and the kitty was cracked as Peter and his men pieced together the story. He and Grimmy had been the first to get off the ground. They got contact 3 miles behind a homeward bound raider, and they got within range for an attack – it was a FW 190 – as they reached the sea. Peter shot it down near Dover.

While that was going on Geoff Howitt and George Irving, following a searchlight cluster, picked up a contact near Hastings. Their customer was a little more wily, and was diving for home at high speed, taking evasive action as he did so. But they chased on out across the Channel after him. Before he could reach the safety of the French coast they shot him down. He crashed into the sea, and they pulled out only just clear of the waves. That was the second FW 190 destroyed.

Bernard Thwaites and Will Clemo were also after one, chasing it right to the French coast. But there they were recalled. On the way back Clemo snapped up a freelance contact crossing their bows. Thwaites made sure of that one and blew it up from only 50 yards astern, collecting some of the wreckage in the air intake of one of his engines. But that did not prevent him from having a crack at another of the raiders. He fired three times, and each time he saw hits. A large object fell off the raider, which disappeared, but he was able to claim it only as probably destroyed. That made the score three destroyed and one probably destroyed.

To complete things yet another crew, Flying Officer J. D. Shaw and Pilot Officer A. C. Lowton, after a difficult time with searchlights which

XIX

insisted on illuminating them and not their quarry, caught a raider near Gravesend and opened fire. They flew through the wreckage as the enemy aircraft disintegrated, and they came back with their windscreen coated with soot.

That night's sharp encounter with the new menace resulted in four FW 190s being destroyed and one probably destroyed, and the congratulations poured in. There was a signal from the Sector Commander, Group Captain A. G. Malan – known to the world as "Sailor" and for his prowess in the Battle of Britain – and another from the Group Commander, "Dingbat" Saunders.

The bogey of the FW 190 had been debunked, although everybody knew well enough that they would continue to be a difficult problem. In moonlight we should have to make our approach with special care; on dark nights the small wing span and bulk of the German aircraft would mean getting uncomfortably close on AI before they could be seen, with even closer shooting to ensure results that would be lethal. Even the improved performance of the searchlights might prove to be an embarrassment to us as their efforts to illuminate these new raiders might drive them to even more violent evasion. It was by no means easy for even the best of the searchlight crews to keep their beams from wandering on the pursuing Mosquito: the bare quarter of a mile separating the two high-speed aircraft weaving around at a height of 4 or 5 miles allowed little or no margin for error.

The 190s continued to come over, however, and our crews went on knocking them down. John, of course, had been very keen to get one, and during my absence at Ford he had taken with him as his navigator Flying Officer O. C. Townsin, an able and experienced operator known to all of us as Bert whom I had seen instructing at Usworth and who was now on his second tour of flying. But the jinx that had dogged John's return to operations had not come on my course with me. It had stayed with John as their AI had packed up when they were almost within visual range of one of the raiders.

Shortly after the squadron's arrival at West Malling a "Wings for Victory" dance had been held in the Mess. At the height of the party news came by telephone that Lintoff and Gilling-Lax had just destroyed another FW 190. Tim Molony had an inspiration and he immediately put it up for auction, describing it as:

"One Focke-Wulf 190…owner having no further use for same…needs attention."

Since the burnt out remains of that aircraft were at the time lying at the bottom of the River Medway it would have needed a great deal of attention. But the bidding was brisk and went to £105, which made a good addition to War Savings.

155

West Malling was just off the main London to Maidstone road, a fortunate state of affairs because it had enabled the village to retain its old world charm and local character rather than becoming nothing more than an untidy prolongation of the dreary south London suburbs.

At the western end of the village there was an attractive old church, and just beyond that stood the Manor House, which became our squadron Mess. It was a mellow, creeper covered, Georgian house, with a beautifully kept walled garden at the back. The garden in front of the house was terraced, with a drive leading to a sunken road, across the other side of which there was a long, reed-banked lake, the home of ducks, swans and moorhens.

The swans quickly became the object of great interest to the aircrews. Every afternoon the great birds went through their night flying tests. The lake was very narrow, and they could only become airborne along its length, and in a cross wind or calm air that called for some strenuous flying. The wild beating of their wings became more and more agitated as they proceeded on their take-off down the lake. One could almost see the look of anxiety coming on their faces as they began to run out of lake and had to make up their minds whether to put on full boost or throttle back for another run.

The Manor House had formerly been used, we were told, as some sort of convalescent home for elderly ladies. We found a list of rules for the patients, one of which stated that ladies could not be accepted unless they were capable of walking upstairs without assistance. This was naturally preserved, with that particular rule heavily underlined, and was smartly produced at parties whenever anyone started showing signs of falling by the wayside.

Our job at West Malling was the defence of London, standing guard from the Foreland to Beachy Head against anything that might come across the narrow seas. Many of the raiders went through our area and on north across the Estuary, to the east of London, and these we had to take care of as well. Because of the shortness of the run they had to make and the closeness of the enemy coast, a lively vigilance and lightning scrambles were essential if we were to do our job properly. These factors, added to the high speed of the fighter-bombers, called for big changes in the tactics we had been using in the past.

It was most important that the Controller should have his fighters ready and in position, preferably with some height advantage over the enemy, at the very first sign of activity. The vectors he gave to try and cut off the enemy had to be bolder and his judgement of the final turn finer if we were to avoid a hopeless stern chase.

At all times two standing patrols were maintained throughout the night. The only thing that would stop that was if the weather became so bad that it was impossible to fly. We had two GCI stations – "Skyblue" and

"Recess" – with which we worked, each one controlling one of the patrolling aircraft, and we also got help from one of the low looking stations of the coastal radar chain. While they were waiting, the aircraft would make practice interceptions on each other, each GCI taking it in turn to position the attacking fighter. As soon as the indications of the GCI cathode ray tubes showed that the enemy were forming up over France for another swoop, the standing patrols would be sent out across the Strait almost to the coast of France, and made ready to pounce. At the same time the telephone back in the crew-room at the aerodrome would start ringing.

Life at night in the crew-room in Bomb Alley was very different from what it had been at Middle Wallop. No longer did we sleep at readiness, and gone was the almost leisurely take-off. We sat around in various stages of flying kit, depending on our position in the pre-arranged order of patrol, talking or reading or listening to the radio. Always in the background there was the chatter of the inveterate card players which rose and fell with the fortunes of the game.

A scramble late at night usually produced something in the nature of a well ordered stampede similar to that of a fire station turning out. At the sudden ring of the telephone down would go all the books and the cards, and the radio set would be quickly silenced. The next crews to take off would be on their feet as the Flight Commander reached for the 'phone, and there would be a tense hush as he listened to the voice rattling in the earpiece. Then he would nod at the waiting crews and they would start for the door. He wasted no words on the telephone, merely answering:

"OK. We'll be off."

Picking up his own helmet he would call to the Flight Sergeant in charge of the ground crews that the next four aircraft were to go off, and at the door he would turn back for a word of explanation to the others.

"Fifteen plus forming up over the Somme. You had better stand by."

Outside in the darkness the Flight Sergeant would be calling to the airmen already on the alert. "Crews for C, M, L and Q."

There would be the sound of running feet, and torches would flash. "Where's Arthur got to?" a voice would shout. Another would call out: "Bring another trolley-acc."

In quick succession the engines would come to life, raising their voices in a deafening pandemonium of crackling exhausts. Navigation lights would whirl and there would be clouds of dust, and the aircraft would he on their way around the perimeter track. For a moment the lights would disappear behind a corner of the orchard. Then, one by one, the green starboard lights would flit along the runway, lift, sway, and then flick out as the aircraft were airborne into the darkness, and the drone of the engines would fade away to the south-east. Already the sirens would be wailing along the Medway, and the thunder of the Dover guns would be shaking the air with the heavy pulsing that could be felt rather than heard.

On the night of the 13th of June, John and I missed all that familiar excitement: we were one of the fortunate crews already in the air when the raid began. We had gone off on patrol just before midnight, and we were beating up and down the Channel off Dungeness at 23,000ft when "Skyblue" warned us that a fast customer was on the way in. The Controller timed our converging courses to a nicety, and the blip came scuttling across my cathode ray tube only a mile and a half ahead and well below us. I had no fears about overshooting, only of being outdistanced. John opened up the engines as I brought him around in a tight diving turn, and we went howling down after the raider.

The range closed only very slowly, and the blip was as steady as a rock. This must be a new boy, I thought, one of those they-will-never-catch-me-at-this-speed characters I had been hoping to meet. The only thing to worry about now was the searchlights. If only they would leave us alone! On the other aircraft went, hell bent for London, and not the slightest sign of a light broke the soft velvet of the summer night. And all the time we were creeping in.

During this, we heard later, the telephone in the crew-room at West Malling rang again. The Sector Controller was on the line.

"You'll be interested to know," he announced, "that there's a 190 approaching the aerodrome, and that your CO's close behind him."

They all rushed out of the crew-room and looked up into the dark sky. From the south there came the heavy, lumpy snarl of the German radial engine. Swiftly it drew nearer until it was right overhead, its noise beating down through 4 miles of warm, still air. The familiar howl of the Merlins of the Mosquito could also be heard, and as the two aircraft drew closer together the noises of the engines blended into one.

At that moment John saw the other aircraft against a patch of cloud. I looked up from the AI set, and there was no doubt about what we were after: it was an FW 190 all right. The single exhaust flickered below the fuselage; the short, straight wings still had the drop tanks hanging from the tips; the big, smooth bomb was still clutched fiercely to its belly.

John very briefly touched the trigger, and the guns gave one short bark. The enemy aircraft reared straight up on its nose, flicking over and plunging vertically downwards. It all happened with an incredible speed. Standing up and pressing my face to the window, I watched the blue exhaust flame dwindle as the aircraft hurtled earthwards.

Those watching from the aerodrome were apparently entranced with what was going on. They heard the one short bellow of the cannon and the echo from the surrounding hills. The note from the 190 changed its song and grew louder and louder and higher and higher until it was a tortured scream, which ended abruptly in a great red flash that silhouetted the trees to the west, followed by a crump that shook the ground and rattled the windows.

We had broken the spell, and had made the first kill of our second innings. At first light I drove over to Borough Green to have a look at the place where the raider had gone in. There was not much to be seen. In the middle of a field of waving corn a group of farm workers stood around a hole large enough, in their words, "to put two charrybangs in". The 190 had gone in with its bomb, and all we could find of the aircraft was one wheel, tyre still inflated, the twisted propeller blades, a cylinder or two from what remained of the engine, and the cannon with a shell still in the breech.

The pilot had had an astonishing escape. When the aircraft had flicked over into its dive he had been catapulted through the roof, breaking his arm. Suddenly recovering from the shock of finding himself marching against England without his aeroplane he had managed to open his parachute. He was picked up by a searchlight crew, and, apart from his broken arm, he was not much the worse for wear. I told the farmhands about this, and their air of grim satisfaction over the crashed aircraft vanished. One old man reached for the nearest weapon, a villainous hay fork.

"Where did they take 'un?" he demanded.

CHAPTER TWENTY

Midsummer Fires

I T was not to be expected that the Luftwaffe would continue to tolerate the casualties we were inflicting upon them without trying out some changes in their plans. Their raids were not on what would be called a big scale, as rarely more than twenty or thirty aircraft a night ranged over the Home Counties, reaching as far as London, or up the East Coast as far as Harwich.

Although the material damage caused by a score of 1,000lb bombs scattered over so wide an area was relatively small, these raids were nevertheless having, from the German point of view, the desired effect. The nightly wail of the air-raid sirens and the tremendous uproar of the greatly strengthened anti-aircraft defences were quite enough to remind the long-suffering civilians that they were still under attack.

But this small, if effective, force of raiders had been losing up to a fifth of its strength on some nights; and in that sort of contest it was the proportion more than the total number lost that decided whether or not the operation was a success. A loss of 20 per cent was enough to hurt, and the enemy brought all his tricks into play to try and ease the smart.

They began by intensifying their efforts to outclimb and outrun our Mosquitos, and even before the end of May they were giving our crews some hard chases. Lintoff and Gilling-Lax in one interception had to climb up by steps, gaining speed in one step and height in the next, and so on until they caught up with a Junkers 88 flying at a height of 29,000ft. And we soon realized that with the fighter-bombers that we were up against there would be very little chance of catching them without an initial height advantage. The Germans knew this as well as we did, and the more wily pilots of the Luftwaffe were climbing up to 30,000ft over their own bases before starting off for England.

From that height they would come in, sometimes gathering speed in a shallow dive, drop their bombs while still at 20,000ft, and then dive out again, "like scalded cats", as the newspapers put it, hurtling back across the Channel until they were able to level out over the safety of the French coast, at not more than 1,000ft.

To help their pilots find their way back the Germans projected two searchlight beams vertically on the coast near Dunkirk. They stood like goalposts to mark the limit of play. As yet we were strictly forbidden to cross into enemy territory with the precious secret of our AI on board. At the other end of the field, when the raiders headed towards London, our home goal was clearly marked once the show had started by a highly impressive display of shell bursts, tracer and rocket showers which we referred to somewhat disparagingly as "Pile's Fireworks", named after the Commander-in-Chief of Anti-Aircraft Command.

With the arrival of July there came a short, uneasy lull in the activity. We sharpened our weapons and wondered what new tricks the Luftwaffe had in store for us. The old, old battle with the unserviceability of our equipment was always with us. With such new devices it could hardly be otherwise; and the very magnitude of the power compressed within so small a box brought its own troubles. The Genie would burst his bonds, and the intense keenness of his magical vision burnt out his eyes faster than they could be replaced.

Some of the complexity of manufacturing the AI sets was explained to us when we were taken to visit the Osram factory at Hammersmith. They were making some of the special valves or our sets, and the factory boffins proudly presented us with an extra-special, hand made job whose vital parts had been gold-plated in order to give a longer working life for our own private Genie. Sad to relate, this back-room enthusiasm did not mean much: we burnt the thing out on our very next sortie.

At this time we lost Edward Crew when he was promoted to the rank of Wing Commander, and given command of No. 96 Squadron. We toasted his promotion and our loss in champagne, which flowed in a regal fashion from a great silver Victory Cup which had been presented to the squadron by one of the local residents, Lt-Col. Sir Albert Stern. Edward's place as B Flight Commander was taken by Geoff Howitt.

A little later in the month the weather broke, and throughout one afternoon an all-weather section stood by at readiness while the draggling clouds blotted out Wrotham Hill, and the rest of the crews kicked their heels behind the rain-blurred windows of the Manor House.

We were just sitting down to tea when we heard the roar of Mosquitos taking off. Howitt and Irving and Lintoff and Gilling-Lax, the two standby crews, had been scrambled to meet a wave of sneak raiders coming in under cover of the bad weather. We looked out of the windows, and then at each other. The cloud seemed to be almost down to the ground, and none of us envied those crews their job.

Twenty minutes later we heard the sound of aircraft approaching, but now the notes of the engines varied, as if the pilots were jockeying for position. There was an outburst of firing from the Medway guns, followed by a rattle of machine-gun fire, and the unmistakable and throaty roar of cannon. By then we were all out on the drive in front of the house. But we could not see anything through the blinding rain. The note of the engines changed, and the drone rose to a howl, rising in pitch to a scream, and then it cut off abruptly with an ominous thump.

We were silent as we waited for news. When it did come through on the 'phone it was in confusing and contradictory fragments. A Dornier 217 had crashed near Detling, just across the Medway valley, and the anti-aircraft guns, as usual, were claiming it. But the GCI Controller had put Lintoff in contact with the raider. He had seen the two blips on his cathode ray tube merge and stay together for seven minutes. Then they had faded, and he had seen and heard nothing more.

It was not long before the 'phone rang again. Geoff Howitt and Irving had landed safely at Bradwell Bay – across the other side of the Thames Estuary – creeping in from the sea under the weather. And shortly afterwards there came news that Lintoff and Gilling-Lax had been found. They were both dead in the wreckage of their aircraft at a place only 2 miles from where the Dornier had crashed. When it was found that the Dornier had been hit by cannon shells from the Mosquito the anti-aircraft claim was withdrawn.

It was the fourth victory for Lintoff, but in his eagerness to get at the enemy he had over-reached himself and had gone in. Both he and Gilling-Lax – who had only recently been given his commission – had just been awarded DFCs. They were a bitter loss to the squadron.

We were not kept waiting long to find out what the next move would be from the Luftwaffe. In fact, it was made within a week. Intelligence had warned us that we could expect the Germans to start using a new, fast, manoeuvrable, two-seater fighter-bomber. This was the Messerschmitt 210, or, in its later form, the 410. It carried a pilot and a gunner-navigator seated in tandem, with the latter operating by remote control two rearward firing heavy machine-guns mounted in blisters on either side of the slim fuselage. This was to be the Germans' answer to the Mosquito, and by all reports it was going to be a formidable one. We all sat for a long time in the Intelligence Room studying photographs and models, carefully noting every detail, memorizing the outlines of the new aircraft from every conceivable angle.

Nigel Bunting, a Flight Lieutenant, and one of the old guard in the squadron, was the first to make closer acquaintance with the 410. Freddie French was flying as his navigator, and they were at 20,000ft over the Strait of Dover when the GCI put them on to a raider heading up the East Coast. Within a few minutes, Freddie suddenly got two contacts on the AI, both at a range of 3 miles, one well below and the other above. Looking down, Nigel saw a red light, but he was too experienced a hand to be drawn. That red light looked altogether too much like bait, and he decided to have a go at the higher, unlighted contact.

Climbing at full power, Nigel began to close in, and when they were still 7,000ft behind he spotted two bright exhaust flames ahead. They had been at it for fifteen minutes and had climbed to 25,000ft before they were close enough for Nigel to get a really good look at the outline, now clearly silhouetted against the bright glow of the northern sky. There was no mistake about it: there were the two engines trailing bright yellow exhaust flames, with the narrow fuselage and the twin barbettes bulging on either side.

Nigel closed in until he was 200 yards astern, and he worked his gun on to the target. Then he hit the slipstream and was put completely off his aim. He dived to recover, and began to ease up into position again. The Messerschmitt flew on as evenly and as steadily as an air liner, and the German gunner had missed his last chance. Nigel's second aim was true; and with flames streaming from the fuselage the enemy raider rolled over on to its back and dived vertically into the sea 5 miles east of Felixstowe.

That summer of 1943 was a splendid one, and in our spare time we wandered through the orchards and the hop fields or swam in the lake at Mereworth. Not that I had a great deal of time to spare: I was always busy with the training programme and checking on the work of the crews, quite apart from our own turn on the routine flying that had to be done. In addition to that, John had his finger in every interesting or worthwhile pie, and was all the time off on visits to FIU, Defford and TRE, Sector Operations, Group and Fighter Command, and quite often I went with him.

Such had been the speed of its development that radar in aircraft was being used by this time for all sorts of different purposes. In our own case – AI equipped night fighters – the developments were still going on. But we had passed from the early experimental stages, and we were now using equipment of more advanced design that was far more reliable and efficient. And so it was that the earlier types of AI were now released for use over enemy territory. Although that use, we knew, would be severely hampered by interference and height limitations, it would nevertheless give our stalwart intruders far more chance of chasing the enemy around his own country as well as providing some warning from a threatened attack from behind.

Some of the more agile and adventurous radar equipped intruder crews soon developed a system of tactics whereby they even allowed themselves to be intercepted, waiting for the attacker to move in, more or less dangling him on their invisible radar string. And then, with a very nice timing and a vigorous use of their aircraft, they would whip right around on to the tail of the other aircraft and quickly complete an interception of their own.

Bob Brabham, who had been running John's score very close, was now in command of No. 141 Squadron at Wittering. One afternoon in July he landed at West Malling with several other aircraft of his squadron before taking their AI equipped Beaufighters on intruder operations over Germany that night. Their navigators looked rather enviously at our low-looking AI sets, but when I pointed out that we were quite blind behind they had second thoughts about it.

There was also a most secret unit operating from Drem, in Scotland,

and Derek Jackson had been doing some interesting experiments there. One of these was the development of a method of homing on the AI transmitters of the German night fighters. The Luftwaffe now had AI of a sort, although technically it was a long way behind ours and scarcely up to the standard of even our Mark IV, which, with us, was now obsolete.

For so long our night fighters had been operating in a purely defensive role. Now, with the increased activities of the intruders, and with additional gadgets such as that being developed by the people at Drem, it was quite obvious that the offensive night fighter was on the way.

Another of Derek's jobs had to do with the effect of "Window" – the strips of metallized paper or tinfoil dropped from bombers to confuse the radar picture – upon our own AI. It had long been known that the use of "Window" would disorganize the German radar reporting system and so greatly reduce our own bomber losses. But since the Germans would inevitably employ it, in turn, against our own defences, we had to make sure that our night fighters could operate through it. Derek had found that that was just possible with the old type of AI, given a first-rate operator, but that it was fairly easy with our more up-to-date equipment.

It was to this unit at Drem that Peter Green was now posted, his tour of operational flying having come to an end. To lose two Flight Commanders within five weeks was a severe blow to the squadron. But the general standard of our crews was so high that John was able without hesitation to fill both gaps from within our ranks. A Flight was taken over by Bill Maguire who was promoted to Squadron Leader, an event which enabled his navigator to congratulate his pilot in his own Welsh fashion.

"Good. Now you'll have to pull finger properly, man," he said. "And don't think I shall call you sir, either."

Another of the old-timers who came back to us was Phil Reed, who sportingly gave up his chance of a Navigator Leader's post with another squadron in order to come to us and re-crew with his former pilot. I soon found that he had not altered at all his extraordinary style of operating; but when John and I took him up in a borrowed Beaufighter for a routine check, he soon put me to shame by giving John a much slicker interception than I had managed during my demonstration of the accepted method of doing things. To crown it, he and Nigel Bunting celebrated their reunion a few nights later by knocking pieces off a 190. After that I stopped worrying about style. I told all newcomers that it did not matter how they gave their patter just so long as they got results.

While on their rest, Bill Skelton and another ex-85 pilot, Branse Burbridge, had crewed up together. They returned to us, and after one check flight it was obvious to me that the rest, the period as an instructor, the change of pilot, or some happy combination of all these factors had set Bill on the way to becoming a master craftsman.

Branse and Bill were deeply religious both in upbringing and in outlook. During the first six months of the war Branse had been a conscientious objector on religious grounds; but later he came to feel that as a Christian his place was in a more active role. It was not without much heart-searching that he had brought himself to the belief that his active participation in the war was necessary. But having once accepted the task both he and Bill applied themselves to it with all the fervour of a crusade.

Of particular pleasure to me at this time was the arrival of another old 604 stalwart. Partly as a result of John's general efforts to get the rest from operational flying limited to six months, Pat Patston had at last managed to escape from his OTU, and he now came to us to carry on with his second tour.

At the same time Bert Townsin left us to become Navigator Leader of 29 Squadron. I saw him only once again, and he was looking puzzled and rather worried. They were operating from Ford, and they had been having trouble with the Milk Train. I knew only too well all about the difficulties in chasing things low down, and I tried to commiserate with him.

"They must be using a radar altimeter," I said. "We'll never get below them without submerging."

"That's not the only trouble," Bert warned me. "Our chaps reckon that Jerry's operating in pairs. The first one acts as bait, and the second tags along behind and jumps our fighter while he's busy with the interception. We've lost two crews already."

I had heard the report that the Germans were believed to be operating in pairs; but somehow I felt that in this case it was Isaac and not the Germans who was to blame. Our fighters carried no radar altimeters at this time, and even a very small error in the setting of those we had could, when flying very low, cause a fatal accident.

"More likely they dipped a wing," I suggested. "It's awfully easy to lose 50ft in a turn."

But Bert was not satisfied with that idea. What he did learn I never found out, as a few weeks later he and his CO went out after the Milk Train and did not return.

Throughout July the temperature steadily mounted, and in the orchards all around us the luscious fruit hung heavy, and the dusty lanes were pungent with the tangy smell of the ripening hops. When we were on duty we would sit outside the crew-room waiting for our turn to fly. We would talk and watch the glow as it crept around the northern sky and until the first chill in the air drove us inside to pass the hours until dawn. Then we would drive back between the dew-spangled hedgerows to the Manor House, and go to bed and sleep until midday.

After a bath, a drink and lunch there would be another night flying test, and then another night on duty. And then the two nights that followed were free: the first for carousal, if one felt like it; the second for an early night in bed and deep, refreshing sleep. It was a wonderfully carefree life for now we felt that the war was going our way, and we had only our personal problems, whatever they were, to worry us.

Following one of our trips to Defford, John took a night off and we went on to Predannack, in Cornwall, to visit 604 Squadron. They were now on the job of ranging on daylight patrols far out into the Bay of Biscay. It was good to see again so many familiar faces, but there was one I sadly missed. Fred Larcey had been flying with the CO of the squadron who had taken over from John. They had gone out one night from Ford against a wave of 190s, and nothing more had been heard of them.

I was due to fly back to West Malling with Lieutenant Tarald Weisteen, the latest recruit to our Norwegian contingent. But the weather report the next morning told us of cloud sitting tight over Dartmoor, so we gave ourselves up without regret to a few pleasant hours of sunbathing down in Mullion Cove nearby, watching the gulls doing circuits and bumps around the great crag of rock just off-shore.

Tarald Weisteen was very different in physical structure from most of his compatriots. He was small, dark and slight of build. But his mind, like his features, was keen and taut. He had joined the Royal Norwegian Air Force before the war, and was a regular officer. He had gone through their War Academy, and was an established fighter pilot when hostilities broke out in Norway. It was said of him that he had had quite a time flying against the Luftwaffe in Gloster Gladiators until the resistance was overwhelmed. And then he managed to escape to England.

On our way back to West Malling – we were flying in the squadron Oxford – Tarald astonished me by asking my advice about whether he should remain below cloud or climb above it. I hesitated about giving an opinion, and several seconds passed before I realized that I was really basking in a reflection of John's reputation, and that Tarald was willing, for that reason, to place my opinion above his own sound judgment. He was one of those eager, willing people who did not hesitate to ask for and to profit by advice. I soon found that he handled the aircraft with an easy grace. Later I arranged for Freddie French to go into partnership with him, as his navigator, and they soon became a happy and effective team.

We were by no means left in peace during this time. The Luftwaffe kept up their attacks, making the most they could of their limited numbers by sending in mixed raids of FW 190s, Me 410s, and J 88s. This mixture of fast and comparatively slow types, and the presence all the time of so many of our own bombers returning from raids, made the job of identification by ground control extremely difficult. Visual recognition by the night fighters became even more essential than before; and it helped a great deal when we were issued with Ross night binoculars. Though they had no great magnification, these glasses had an amazing power of collecting light. We tried them out after dark, standing at the door of the crew-room. A vague blur to the naked eye 200 yards away took on with the help of the binoculars the clear outline of a Mosquito, with the squadron letters plainly readable on the fuselage.

Halfway through August the Germans put on a sharp raid on Portsmouth, and although most of the raiders passed through the sector next to ours – which was under the control of the GCI we had known as "Boffin" – our own GCI managed to thrust us into the fringe of things.

Three times during the course of the raid they gave us contact, and each time I sweated after our target – they were all coming in fairly fast – and brought John in to visual range.

The first one was flying as straight as an arrow. We were closing in quickly, and I brought my new binoculars to bear. It turned out to be a Beaufighter. The second waited until we were within 3,000ft, but before John could see it the pilot started a tight turn to port. That was a little puzzling, for he could hardly have seen us, unless the Germans were now equipped with radar tail warning. But that pilot had chosen the wrong man for a winding match, and after a couple of turns John was well inside and rapidly closing in. Our target then steadied up and we saw that it was another Beaufighter.

Our third customer was moving a great deal faster, and although he flew straight on it took us some time to catch him. At John's word I looked up from the AI set. The strap of the glasses caught in my harness, but even without them I could see that this one was no Beaufighter. The fuselage was much too slim and delicate for that: it was far more likely to be a Me 410. I fumbled impatiently with the strap and finally got the glasses to bear. Our target leapt into clear profile. This time it was a Mosquito!

Just over a week later we were patrolling up and down the Channel at 17,000ft while those not on duty enjoyed a cocktail party at the Manor House. About midnight the GCI Controller warned us that there was a bandit crossing us from starboard to port on a north-westerly course. That heading, we realized, would take him not to London but across the Thames Estuary in the direction of Harwich.

Then suddenly the blip flashed up on the AI, and we went turning into our curve of pursuit, climbing as hard as we could go, the whole aircraft quivering with the effort. Our target was still 2,000ft ahead of us when it crossed the East Coast, and the searchlights came jabbing up in a ragged bunch. The German pilot did not wait to be illuminated: he immediately started a violent, corkscrew evasion. John had not managed to catch sight of him and it was all I could do to hold on to the blip.

But the German had apparently seen as much of England as he wanted. Still without being seen by us, he whipped around and dived back across the Channel, going like the wind. At my urgent shout John wheeled around on a wing-tip, and down we went after the other aircraft. The Mosquito quickly gathered speed and we were just managing to hold our own, bouncing about like a power boat in a rough sea.

Our engines were howling and the whole airframe was shaking. I braced myself as best I could, pressing my face against the rubber visor. Slowly the blip began to creep in…1,000ft…800…and then John caught a glimpse of an exhaust. The howl of the engines became wilder, and we were bucketing down at something like 400mph. And there the range remained stuck.

Three times John caught a fleeting glimpse of the exhaust, and now he knew what we were after. It was not a 410 this time, but one of our old customers, a 190. Down and down we dropped, swallowing hard to ease our cracking eardrums, and still we could not work off that last few hundred feet that separated us.

Then I felt the aircraft steadying up, and the note of torment from the engines relaxed. On the AI set the blip came sliding in. John now had the other aircraft firmly in sight. My tensed muscles relaxed as I straightened up. We were down to 2,500ft, and almost across the Channel. Close ahead of us the welcoming searchlights of the German goal posts raised their reassuring arms to light the raider safely back home. I disentangled the Ross glasses from all the rest of the harness with which I was encumbered and brought them to bear, and suddenly the blurred silhouette ahead of us looked so clear and close that I very nearly dodged back in my seat. Even the blue flame of the exhaust seemed to be fluttering only a few yards in front of me. To be gazing at a hostile fighter at such close range seemed almost indecent.

"It's a 190 all right," I told John quickly, hoping that he would get the business over as soon as possible. "I can even see the black crosses on it."

The French coast was by this time almost under our nose. John pulled up and fired. There was a flash from the fuselage of the 190, but it went on flying. John fired again, scoring hits, and the target seemed to wilt and stagger. We swooped over the top of it, dodging bits and pieces of wreckage, and John wheeled around to keep us clear of the enemy coast. As we turned away the 190 hit the beach in a splash of red flame not far from Dunkirk.

I watched the fire for a while as we flew quietly back across the Channel, and I wondered for a moment if the pilot had managed to bale out. I was a little shocked when I realised that I no longer cared very much. It had been our turn do a bit of fire lighting, and my only emotion was a feeling of satisfaction at having completed the job.

CHAPTER TWENTY-ONE

The Enemy Within

L ATE summer began to turn to another autumn, a golden autumn, and the unpicked fruit of the orchards weighed down the trees. I had only to lean out of the window of my office at our dispersal point to help myself to luscious great plums, dripping with juice. Just beyond the end of the aerodrome the camp fires of the hop pickers sent their sweet wood smoke curling into the sky as the city dwellers settled in for their traditional annual working holiday.

Life at the Manor House had taken on something of the orderliness and settled comfort that we had known at the Pheasant when we were with 604 Squadron. But in contrast to those days we now had enough contact with the war to be free of the pricks of conscience that we had known before, and we could feel that we were honestly earning our ease and comfort.

The WAAF ran the place, for us, and except for lunch and night flying suppers when we were on duty we rarely visited the Station Mess. The Assistant Catering Officer at West Malling was Helen Tyson, a Warrant Officer in the WAAF, and after she had finished her day's work on the station she would come down to the Manor House, roll up her sleeves, and supervise the cooking of our dinner. Helen had a son in the Army, and she took a most considerate and motherly interest in all of us. The feats she performed with the issue rations were scarcely short of miracles.

Another of the WAAF who watched over us was a woman of uncertain age named Nina. She maintained a mature and generally unruffled dignity, but there was a sultry touch of fire in her appearance that suggested something of the gipsy in her origin. Nina served behind the tiny bar, and she kept the unruly types in their places with a polite but ruthless efficiency. Sometimes, when the drinks had flowed on late into the night, she would allow herself to be argued into reading palms. At first it was nothing more than an amusing game. But twice within a few months Nina had looked at a man with troubled eyes, and had abruptly closed his hand, leaving it unread and refusing all explanation. And in each case the man had been killed flying a few nights later. That it should happen twice was too often for the good of the game, and after that it was generally agreed that Nina would not read any more palms.

As a protection against possible damage, the walls of the living rooms at the Manor House had all been covered temporarily with sheets of plaster board. David Langdon, the cartoonist, who had at one time been the squadron's Intelligence Officer, came to stay with us for a couple of days, and one night he went to work on the panels in the anteroom. Starting with a life-like portrait of Bill Maguire staring with astonishment at a small bird that had just fluttered from a nest in his luxuriant moustache, the drawings progressed in licence and ribaldry as Langdon worked his way around the walls of the room. The next day, Arthur Woods, a Flight Lieutenant, and one of the latest pilots to join us, and who was also a film director and a talented artist, painted ornate frames around the drawings, setting them off to such advantage that when the time came at the end of the war to hand the Manor House back to its owners the panels were carefully cut out and hung in the Station Mess on the aerodrome.

In addition to the newcomers, we were still receiving quite a number of old friends among our replacement crews. The massive Per Bugge and his navigator, Claus Björn, came to us after a tour of flying in the Mediterranean. These doughty Norwegians, like many of our own crews, did not believe in going on a rest, and they usually arranged that they merely had a change of scene. Although they belonged to the Royal Norwegian Air Force, they were serving in British squadrons, which gave them the chance to make skilful use of the subtleties of international relations to arrange for nothing more than a change of squadron as they approached the end of a tour of flying.

Towards the end of his first tour with 604, Per had pestered various people about arranging a posting for him to the Mediterranean. At last he got his own way, but no sooner had he and Claus left England than some bright mind at Air Ministry woke up to the fact that Norway was not formally at war with Italy. Instructions were immediately sent out recalling them to the United Kingdom.

But Per knew all about taking evasive action, and three months passed before these instructions caught up with them. And in that time they had, amongst other exploits, shot down an Italian Cant Z 1007 B – Per was a stickler for detail in his aircraft recognition – thereby setting the staff an awkward poser. They did not have the heart to annul Per's claim, but on the other hand, they could not officially condone something that might be regarded from the point of view of international law as an act of piracy. So, much to Per's indignation, they awarded him "one unidentified aircraft destroyed", and he and Claus were sent back to England.

This question of going on a rest after a certain amount of operational flying continued to be a vexed one right up until the end. It was an extraordinary revelation to me to find how greatly men varied in their apparent ability to stand up to nervous strain, and in their reaction to it. In our comparatively safe job of home defence the strain of operational flying was so very much less than it was on offensive operations that for a long time it was ignored. There was, in fact, some justification for the view that with so many intruders flying around the Operational Training Units – not to mention all the other hazards connected with training – there was far more strain and risk involved in being an instructor on a so-called rest.

But however slight the strain, and no matter how long it took to build up, it was there as a very natural revolt of the human system against repeated exposure to risk, whether present and real or merely potential and imagined. It was there inside each one of us, a secret enemy within. I felt that it was as if each of us started with a certain capital, a sum of something—was it fortitude?—which we spent, sometimes over a short period, sometimes over a much longer stretch of time. But when it was gone life became a torment with the spirit flogging on a bankrupt body. That was what we called the twitch.

It was the size of this mysterious capital sum which, it seemed to me, varied so enormously. With some it seemed to be almost inexhaustible; with others it seemed that they started off with a very meagre allowance. I could never make up my mind what it was that determined a man's wealth or poverty. It was certainly not courage because some of the poorest I knew in that particular quality were amongst the bravest. Perhaps it was more self-confidence, and a sane and well-balanced approach towards life. Of one thing I was sure: no man could control his wealth. Nor could he be blamed for his poverty. He could only enjoy the one and try and hide the other. Nor could I be sure what it was that drained away that precious capital. One man would pay heavily after being badly shaken by an incident that another would take easily in his stride at little or no cost. A lot of wastage, I began to feel, was through influences quite unconnected with the risks that were taken in flying, but which became aggravated by circumstance. There might be some domestic worry, or some unresolved inner conflict, or an inability to be able to cope with the job to one's own personal satisfaction.

Most of us had come to recognize this state of affairs without a great deal being said about it. We just went about our lives happily enough, maintaining a guarded neutrality with the secret enemy, slapping him down with a joke about the twitch whenever his voice was raised too insistently. I had heard that voice myself towards the end of my first tour of flying, in the last days at Middle Wallop, and I had come to accept it as a natural outcome of the job we were on.

There were a few supermen who seemed to be able to carry on indefinitely, quite unaffected by anything that might happen. Unfortunately, and too often, this inspired many others less resilient and resourceful to flog themselves unmercifully in their efforts to do the same. To many of these the twitch was an unspeakably shameful thing whose presence within themselves they would never admit. They usually went on until, if they were pilots, they killed themselves and their crews, their overtaxed minds and bodies blundering eventually into some fatal error of judgment. If they were navigators, they gradually lost their ability to concentrate on their work, and so became hopelessly inefficient and unreliable.

In some cases the outraged system took its own way out, developing stomach ulcers or obscure nervous complaints. It was not a question of malingering because the complaints were genuine enough. Many of the afflicted would go to the most extreme lengths to conceal their troubles, carrying on until they were literally carried out, still protesting loudly against the suggestion that they were due for a rest.

There were not many who flew continuously on operations, paying little or no attention to the matter of going on a rest. One of those who did was Ginger Farrell, who made a name for himself as an outstanding personality of 85 Squadron. Ginger had joined the RAF at the age of eighteen, soon after the war started. He was on the sick list for a short time in May 1945, and after that he was sent to a headquarters staff job on a convalescent rest. But that lasted only a month. He then went back to 85, and eventually, at the age of 23, became Commanding Officer of the squadron. And he had also, by that time, married.

Immediately after leaving the RAF – of the six years he was in the Service practically the entire time had been on intensive and operational night flying – Ginger went straight to work studying to become a doctor. He passed all his examinations, and started up in practice. And then came the settling of the account, with an almost complete breakdown in his health. It will always be to his credit that this misfortune did not impair in any way Ginger's never-failing cheerfulness.

Shortly after Per Bugge and Claus Björn joined us at West Malling I became involved one day, much against my inclination, in a rather heated discussion about this matter of operational strains and stresses. It was all largely because of Björn's fondness, for an argument. As I entered the room he was asserting with some vehemence – and a Norwegian accent – that aircrew who "turned jellow" should be shown no mercy.

I did not know what had started it all, but I could see that tempers were becoming a little frayed. In the interests of peace I intervened, trying to explain to Claus that it was not a question of a man turning yellow. It was the duty of a Commanding Officer – and of a Navigator Leader also for that matter – to watch over his crews, I told him, and to see that they were sent on a rest while they still had a chance to replenish their reserves of strength, and before they broke their aircraft and killed other people. Also, it was a matter of making sure that the few crews that could be employed at a time within any sector should be at the peak of their efficiency. The motive behind the system of sending people on a rest, I tried to explain, was not soft pity. It was not even common humaneness. It was just very sound economics.

When I left Claus was still arguing. I was beginning to feel a little unhappy about him. He was introspective and intensely proud, and if he had had any misgivings about himself he would never for a moment have admitted it.

Another thing that was giving me cause for thought was the way in which aircrews kept watch at night. We had seen for ourselves how casual some of them were and, given the right conditions, how easy it was to surprise even the most alert. There were times when we were told the strangest tales by those shot down by our own squadron. There was even one report by a captured German pilot who claimed that he had been attacked simultaneously by three night fighters. There were others who claimed that they had been victims of a direct hit by flak. That was quite a common delusion, and we took it as a tribute to our tactics and the destructive power of our four cannon.

During the "Bullseye" exercises, when training aircraft from the bomber OTUs were engaged by the sector searchlights and subjected to dummy attacks by the night fighters, no lights were shown by either side. The fighter signalled that it had made an attack and had fired by flashing its navigation lights on and off. The bomber indicated that it had fired at a night fighter by flashing a torch from the gunner's turret.

Time and time again on these exercises we found that we could make our usual stalk and pull up and hold the bomber in the gunsight and sit there for several minutes before there was any response. Sometimes we would even finish the attack and pull up alongside the bomber, flashing our lights. The rear turret in the bomber would then suddenly swing around and the gunner would happily report another fighter shot down.

The odds, of course, were all in our favour, with radar to limit the pilot's field of search to the small and most important sector of the sky, and the ability to make an approach carefully chosen to give us full advantage of the prevailing light. But I had a feeling that many of the less experienced bomber crews paid far too little heed to the unseen but very real danger from night fighters, compared with the very healthy respect they had for the all too visible flak.

Not that the flak was not dangerous. From our vantage point of safety high above the Channel we could sometimes see, on a clear night, the inferno of shell fire going up from the Ruhr. There were times when we saw the fireball of a stricken bomber, and that was a sight to appal the stoutest heart. Whenever a damaged Lancaster came limping in to West Malling – it happened quite often – the minds of the crew of the bomber were nearly always occupied with the flak.

"Night fighters?" they would comment, with a grin. "We shoot 'em down!"

And there was a ring of very real conviction in the way they said that. At the same time, how could we, who had not been out there, going through what they had faced, presume to tell them anything? How could we explain that the ones they shot down were the bunglers and the inexperienced, and that they would never even see the one that would probably get them in the end? It was all well and good for them to be nonchalant about the German night fighters, but we had already heard that mounting losses were beginning to worry Headquarters, Bomber Command.

With experience, of course, the bomber crews became far more wily customers to tackle. As we found out, a fully operational Lancaster taking full cork-screw evasion called for a great deal of chasing, and that was without the tail and mid-upper gunners pumping lead at us. In fact, one of the most successful of the German night fighters admitted after the war that he often broke away from our bombers once they had seen him and had started shooting, and left them alone and went off in search of another less on the alert. With the density of the main bomber stream, he did not have far to look for another target.

We knew that before long the ban would be lifted, and that we would be allowed to take our radar equipped night fighters over enemy territory to meet our opposite numbers in the Luftwaffe. But for the present we could do no more than listen. There were many times when the main stream went out over our part of the country, a great procession of heavy bombers, unseen, but shaking the air with the thunder of their engines. We could only stand and look up into the darkness with feelings of awe and pity, knowing how heavily the odds were stacked against them.

And by day the bombers of the United States Army Air Force were beginning in ever increasing numbers to join in the battle. There was something inspiring and very comforting in the sight and the sound of those mighty hosts climbing up in their hundreds through the morning haze, solid evidence that the tide had turned, and that now the big battalions were on our side.

All day long those American bombers would be out over enemy territory, battling with wave after wave of German fighters, all too vulnerable in the broad light. Late in the afternoon their formations would come streaming back with ominous gaps in the tight boxes, and the stragglers striving to maintain height with smashed engines and feathered airscrews and tattered wings, lobbing down where they could to unload their wounded or find out just where they were.

I spoke one day to the tail-gunner of one of these strays which had landed at West Malling. He was a tough little man after the fashion of the characters portrayed by James Cagney. He crawled stiffly out of the cramped position he had been in since dawn, and in the most unruffled way he started to dismantle his guns, rubbing the barrels lovingly with a piece of oily rag. He chewed steadily as we talked.

"Have much trouble with the Kraut fighters?" I asked.

"Sure. They keep comin' on in," he said. "But we got plenty o' dis stuff, see." He waved a gun barrel over his shoulder towards the ammunition trays. "We don't get paid nothin' for takin' it back, so I just keeps givin' it away. De old one-two, see."

I asked him where they had been to, but he was very cautious about that. When I pressed him he told me that they kept a navigator to worry about it. I suggested Munich, or Augsburg, but he shook his head.

"We bin around," he said. "We bin a ways." He chewed pensively for a moment, struggling with his geography. Then his face lit up, and he asked: "Say, what's dat lil country…next to France?"

Our successes against the fighter-bombers led inevitably with every raid to faster and higher and more elusive chases. The Luftwaffe were quick to appreciate the damage we were inflicting, and they seemed to be constantly on the alert. But the squadron had reached a pretty high state of proficiency even with the equipment we had; and we now heard that we were going to be the first squadron to receive the new Mark X AI, the new gear which John had taken me to try out at FIU.

On the night of the day Italy surrendered – the 8th of September – the scale of the Luftwaffe's fighter-bomber raid was only seven aircraft, of which three were destroyed, all by 85 Squadron. John and I were working with one of the GCIs when the little wave of bombers came rushing across the Strait. We were turned to the north, and we quickly picked up a contact east of the North Foreland.

We were just settling down to the chase, flying north-west at 22,000ft, when the raider turned north. That, again, indicated to us that his target was not London, but even if he were aiming for the Harwich area the course he was on would take him to the east of it. The thought crossed my mind that he might be trying to give the forts in the Estuary a wide berth.

It was a dark night, and our quarry was hard to see. I kept pressing John in closer and closer, becoming more and more uneasy as the blip on the cathode ray tube approached minimum, range. We were in to 1,000ft, and then 800.

"I believe I can see his exhaust," John said; "'but hang on."

We were still closing in, and down to 700 and then 600ft, and the blip was scarcely more than a flicker beating at the very fringe of minimum range.

"It'll be out of control any moment," I said; and despite my effort to conceal my anxiety I knew that my voice sounded almost panic-stricken.

"It's OK," John replied. "Take a look."

With infinite relief I looked up from the AI set and sat back. The other aircraft was barely visible against the overcast sky, nothing but a dark blob and a wafer thin wing around the little blue exhaust flame. But when I brought the Ross glasses up the whole thing leapt into startling clarity. It was a 190 all right, with the wing-tanks still in position and the single big bomb suspended under its belly.

I kept watch through the glasses while John fired. The flash of the bits was dazzling, and immediately the two wing-tanks dropped off. Looking horribly, big and close, they came tumbling back and flicked past right and left just under our wings.

But the 190 flew on, weaving gently from side to side. John immediately dropped down into the blind spot under its tail. From there, scarcely 30ft below the other aircraft, and too tense to be able to speak, we waited and watched uneasily for the German pilot to make up his mind about what he was going to do next. I imagined what he must have been thinking as he craned his neck around to see what had hit his aircraft. There were no guns firing, there were no searchlights, and there was no sign of any tracer from anything behind him. Would he play safe and make a break for home? Would he come looking in earnest for us? Or would he carry on to his target?

For several long minutes the game of cat and mouse dragged on; but which of us was the cat I was not at all sure. Then the German straightened up and continued evenly on course. John gave him a few more seconds to settle down. Then he dropped back and steadily pulled up for another shot.

Again there were flashes from the hits, squarely in the fuselage, and this time the other aircraft slowed right up, swinging in its tracks in an uncertain way. Again John dropped down into the safety of the blind spot; but now it was not so easy to stay there. With the throttles cut right back and the engines popping and stuttering, the Mosquito slithered along right below the 190, swinging wildly as John struggled to avoid over-shooting. For a horrible moment I thought we were going to charge right ahead and into the German's line of fire; but John had things under control. He gradually side-slipped off our extra speed until we were sitting snugly again as close as a shadow beneath the other aircraft.

I watched the 190 through the Perspex roof, as it hung like a hawk just above our heads. Almost idly I brought the glasses up for a closer look. What I saw made me suddenly shrink back in my seat. It looked so close that it seemed that I would only have to reach out to stroke the black crosses on the wings. But it was not the crosses that had given me such a bad jolt.

"He's still got that dirty great bomb on," I said, trying hard to keep my voice steady.

That 190 must have been badly hit from the two attacks John had made. And badly damaged bombers usually try to jettison their load. I pictured the pilot, perhaps desperately wounded, groping in his fume-filled cockpit for the release switch, and the butterflies ran riot in my stomach. I simply could not take my eyes off that monstrous bomb, grotesquely magnified through the glasses, hanging just above our heads. Would it come straight through the cockpit of our aircraft, I wondered, or would it just take off one of the wings? As if it would make any difference!

But John knew that we were in the safest position, bomb or no bomb, until he could get into place for another attack.

"Wait a bit," he said. "We'll see what he's going to do."

While we waited, and I watched with fascinated horror, the sweat trickled down my sides and my back. Such a very long time passed, it seemed, before the 190 began to draw ahead again.

"Ah, well," John said at last. "'Third time lucky."

He pulled up close behind the other aircraft, not more than 75 yards away. Again there were the strikes as John's firing hit home, but this time they were followed by a brighter flash. The whole cockpit cover broke away and the pieces came flashing back past us.

Then suddenly our cabin was filled with a thick, white vapour that swirled out from behind John's seat and blotted out the view. I turned and saw it squirting from the cabin heater. Although I could not smell anything, my first thought was that it must be petrol. I quickly jabbed my finger in the stuff and then, ripping aside my mask, stuck it in my mouth. It was a relief to taste a sickly sweetness.

"It's all right," I exclaimed, "it's Glycol."

John, who had guessed as much, was already feathering the port aircrew, and trimming the aircraft to fly on one engine. Some of the flying wreckage of the 190 must have pierced the port radiator in the section that supplied the cabin heater with hot air. I gathered my wits together, turned off the hot air, and started to get a fix as John turned slowly westward towards the coast. The 190 had disappeared beneath us. We could only hope that it had been well and truly fixed by that last burst, as we were in no shape for a winding match.

Before long we were crossing the coast and turning on to a course for base, and John was calling for an emergency homing. He was paying a lot of attention to the instrument panel, and muttering in a puzzled way something about the height. I was looking out of the window, trying to locate our position. We seemed to be well up the coast of East Anglia. I could just make out the black fingers of the waterways indenting the coast, and far ahead I could see the broader streak of the Thames Estuary flanked with searchlights.

"You'd better put your 'chute on," John said, "just in case we have to step out. We seem to have lost a devil of a lot of height."

Although he did not sound worried there was a puzzled note in his voice, and it was the first time I had ever heard it.

"I could have sworn we were at 15,000," he added. "Now we're down to 5,000."

The needle of the altimeter was steady enough as we watched it. I thought that perhaps what was rankling in his mind was the fact that the thing should have escaped his notice, almost as though in defiance of the absolute sense of mastery which characterized his flying, even though he had had a battle and the cockpit was full of Glycol fumes and he was on one engine with an emergency radio transmission to cope with.

I switched off the AI so as to conserve our failing batteries, as we edged a little further to the west, aiming to cross the Estuary at a narrower part just clear of the balloons and the gun zone.

The voice of the Sector Controller sounded thin and weak in the headphones as he tried to fix our position. He sounded more worried than we were for he could not guess what we now knew: that we were over land, on course for base, maintaining height, and with the one good engine running quite sweetly.

The searchlights were still coming and sweeping seawards as the last of the raiders went racing back to France. Far off to our left a red pin point of fire burst in the sky. It swelled and became a ball and hung there for a moment, and then plunged into the sea. Someone was still on the job.

We crossed the Estuary, and suddenly the carpet of the darkened land ahead was broken by a fairy ring of tiny lights. From within the ring a cone of the canopy searchlights sprang up and stood there like a luminous teepee; and outside the circle the red neon beacon of West Malling was winking its greeting. They had heard at the aerodrome that we were in trouble and, air raid or no air raid, they had switched on everything they had to guide us home.

We were quickly back over the airfield, and John went into a right hand circuit, following it with a touch-down that was as light as a feather. There was good news waiting for us. A gun site and a Coastguard station had both reported seeing our 190 crash into the sea off Aldeburgh. It was the destruction of this enemy aircraft that was John's nineteenth confirmed victory.

Although it was a satisfactory ending to a most eventful night, it nevertheless left me feeling vaguely uneasy. I had not liked that long, long wait sitting under that bomb; and for the first time in the four years that we had been at war I had felt an inner rebellion. I forced myself to brush it aside, and I sat down with zest to our night flying supper, and after that I slept soundly.

But I was not sorry when John announced a little later that he was going to take a few days' leave. Only the mountains could provide the sort of peace I needed, and I took the night train north to Windermere, and made my way up to Ambleside. It was good to be away from the sound of aeroplanes for a while, and to be able to breathe in the peace and quiet on the cloud-flecked fells of Cumberland. It all seemed to be very far away from the war, with the clouds trailing silently across the rocks and pouring down into the gullies.

At Grasmere I came upon a party of young Hostellers, and I joined forces with them. They were gay and light-hearted. No doubt they had their secret troubles too; but for a few days nothing would matter to any of us but the weight of a pack or the rub of a blistered heel.

One day we were just below the broad crest of Helvellyn, and we sat there eating our sandwiches in the warm sunshine, sheltered from the wind by the crags behind. Before us stretched the vast amphitheatre of rocks that towers above Red Tarn, sweeping around in a great curve by Swirral Edge and Catstye Cam to the misty cleft of distant Patterdale. Lying back against the rocks I listened to the soothing, whispered chorus of tiny sounds that we call silence. The wind rustled with a sigh over the rock slabs, and there was a far-off bleating of sheep, and the waters of the becks rushed with an unending and muffled roar down to the sea; and closer at hand there was a clatter of stones and the ring of clinker and triple hob nails striking the good hard rock as a party of walkers came scrambling tip across Striding Edge.

And then, adding almost imperceptibly to all the tiny sounds, there came out of the east a familiar and discordant note. Reluctantly I opened my eyes and sat up, and I listened to the throb of the engines of those faithful old Ansons. And there they were, two AI training Ansons from Ouston, the target stooging on towards us, the interceptor just behind it, weaving wildly from side to side. I could imagine only too well what was being said on the intercom.

"Hard right...steady...hard left...no...right again...no...Oh...it's gone!"

They were hard at it, learning their trade, and even up there in the mountains, safely tucked away in a niche in the rocks, I did not seem to be able to get away from it.

CHAPTER TWENTY-TWO

Tough Customers

B Y the time I got back to the squadron after my few days' break I was feeling refreshed and eager to get on with the job of mastering the new Mark X AI.

We now knew that we could rely on the Germans to step up their efforts as the nights began to lengthen, which was another reason why the sooner we mastered our new weapons the better. The Luftwaffe had already been mixing Junkers 88s in with the fighter-bombers, and Intelligence had given us a warning that we could expect to meet Junkers 188s, a faster and more powerful version of the 88 with pointed extensions to the wings to give a better rate of climb.

On the 1st of October a Wellington fitted up as a flying classroom arrived to train us in the use of Mark X. The navigator's compartment of the converted bomber had been darkened with blackout curtains so that even in daylight the cathode ray tubes of the new set could be watched by three or four pupils sitting in a row with an instructor on what we called "the mourners' bench".

While we were learning about this new equipment we had to go on operating with the aircraft equipped with Mark VIII AI, testing in the afternoon and flying on operations at night. What with that – which kept us pretty busy – and changes in the crews, the routine life of the squadron never lacked variety. Geoff Howitt had been posted to an OTU, having completed his second tour of flying, and in his place there arrived another old friend of our time with 604, F. S. Gonsalves, who took over B Flight. Geoff's navigator, "Red" Irving, became an instructor on the new Mark X AI.

The Luftwaffe did not keep us waiting long for an increase in trade. At the end of the first week in October they gave us one of the busiest nights we had had for a long time. They came over in three waves of mixed types: fifteen in the first, thirty in the next, and twelve in the last. It was a pathetically poor show in numbers compared with the sort of effort that our own Bomber Command was sending over Germany; but the Luftwaffe were clever about the way in which they employed the limited number of aircraft they had, and that night's operations must have given the civilians the impression of large scale raiding.

There were some interesting – not to say disturbing – features about the night's activities which gave us some indication of the difficulties in store for us. Per Bugge and Claus Björn had a most infuriating time intercepting and identifying no less than five friendly aircraft before they came to grips with the enemy and damaged a Me 410.

Tarald Weisteen and Freddie French had a different kind of exasperation to contend with. As they were chasing a 410 they were persistently illuminated by the searchlights. In spite of that, they shot it down in flames. But when the blazing wreck was a bare 500ft from the ground the anti-aircraft guns got off a few rounds at it and claimed it as their victim. They were awarded half of it. Tarald, who was usually very correct and proper, for once exploded, reverting to his native Norwegian.

"Fahn!" he exclaimed. "Those bloody guns! Which half did they shoot down, I'd like to know?"

Some trouble with searchlights and guns was also experienced by Bernard Thwaites and Will Clemo, and that might have accounted for the fact that they were spotted by the enemy aircraft they were chasing while they were still some distance behind. On the other hand, it was bright moonlight, which might have given them away. Whatever it was, the 410 started taking violent evasive action and sent back a stream of tracer. But Bernard doggedly closed in to 300 yards and fired several long bursts which stopped the enemy tracer and brought back a shower of oil instead, presumably from one of the engines. This unfortunately completely obscured his windscreen, and that was the end of the combat.

But it was Bill Maguire who had the most interesting experience that night. Jones was away on the Navigator Leaders' Course, and Leif Lövestad was flying with Bill. The GCI Controller had just warned them that there were two hostile aircraft flying in line astern and a mile apart when they caught sight of some airborne lights below their starboard quarter.

Bill was not the type to be deterred by the possibility of a trap, and he quickly turned and dived to investigate. He began to close in on this blatant customer, who was carrying a red light on the port wingtip, a yellow one on the starboard, and a very bright white light on the tail. But while he was still a good 2,000ft behind it, the mysterious stranger went into a tight turn, trying to get on Bill's tail.

Bill was a master at that sort of game, and there was nothing he enjoyed more than a winding match. For several minutes the two aircraft turned in the moonlight. But all the time the Mosquito was turning just a little bit tighter, creeping around on to the tail of the 410, which Bill had by that time been able to identify. With a final effort he swung the spot of his gunsight along the line of the fuselage of the enemy aircraft and out in front of the nose, shrewdly judging the amount of deflection he would have to allow. He fired, and the strikes flashed along the fuselage and the wing.

That was apparently just too much for the German pilot. He must have realized that he could not out-turn the Mosquito because he pushed his nose down and dived at full speed for the cover of the cloud below them. Bill went right after him, and managed to get in another burst from 300 yards just as the enemy disappeared into the cloud. It so happened that another of our aircraft was patrolling below the cloud, and the crew saw a burning mass come hurtling down through it and crash into the sea. That meant another confirmed destroyed for Bill.

But in spite of these successes there were three things worrying us. In the first place there was interference from the searchlights. But that could hardly be avoided: we knew the difficulties with which they were faced, and we tried to be patient about it. The second thing was that although we were getting used to being fired at by our own anti-aircraft guns we could bear that with less fortitude because it could be dangerous as well as frustrating. It was true that we had no business to be operating over a gun-zone unless the guns had been informed; but that was not always easy to arrange in the heat and confusion of a concentrated raid. Nor was it fair to expect a very busy aircrew, fully occupied with the business of an AI interception, to keep track of their exact position relative to the guns. However clearly we could see the other man's point of view, it was not easy to keep one's temper from becoming frayed when our own guns started doing their best to blast us out of the sky.

The third disturbing factor with which we were now faced was something entirely different. It was fairly obvious that Bill Maguire's 410 had sensed his presence at a range of 2,000ft. Although there was bright moonlight, conditions were such that we did not feel that the German gunner could have spotted the Mosquito at that range. Could it be that there was some sort of liaison with the second German aircraft flying nearby? Or could it be that the German aircraft were now fitted with some form of radar tail warning? It was possible that our hard won advantage was threatened, yet again, in the endless battle of counter-measures.

On that particular night John and I were airborne along with the rest of them; but our AI gave trouble right from the start, and we finally had to give up. We were on our way back to base when a faint echo drifted in at one side of the cathode ray tube. I quickly realized that it was very close to us.

"There's something coming in from the left," I exclaimed. "It's just going to cross close in front of -"

"Yes...I can see it," John cut in.

The other aircraft had crossed our path, almost at our own level. John turned in barely 200 yards behind and dropped down below it. I brought the glasses up to have a closer look.

"It's a Jerry all right," I said. "88 type...but it's got long pointed wings."

"Let's have a look," John said.

He pulled up a little closer to the other aircraft. Perhaps I had sounded rather dubious about my identification, and he did not want to take any chances. I began to wish that the moonlight might have been a little less bright.

"It must be one of the new 188s," I suggested. The shape of the other aircraft was being magnified by the glasses into clearer detail. "Anyway only the Junkers have those long engine nacelles," I added. I felt that we were hanging about too long. "I can see his external bombs now," I said, trying to clinch the matter.

"OK, then," John said. "In we go."

He pulled up the nose, and the Junkers began to sink down into our line of fire. But before John could open up there was a flash from its under gun position and the hot tomatoes came streaking straight back in our faces. The windscreen shivered instantly into a mass of hair-line cracks. Instinctively I ducked. Then I heard our cannon pounding in a prolonged, angry burst, and I sat up again.

Our windscreen was completely opaque, and John was firing blind, waving the nose of the Mosquito around in the hope that he might get in a lucky hit. It seemed to have discouraged the wide-awake German gunner because there was no answering fire. And there was no sight of the Junkers through the side windows as we swung away towards land.

We looked around and took stock of things in the cockpit. There were three bullet holes near the top left-hand side of the windscreen, close to John's head, and the whole of that corner was sagging in an ominous way. John throttled back so as to reduce the wind pressure.

"Emergency homing for base, please," he called on the radio.

It was becoming altogether too much of a habit, and I felt the old gnawing in the stomach beginning again now that there was nothing I could do but wait. I had my parachute on, but I knew that if that windscreen caved in things would happen far too suddenly and too violently to give us much of a chance.

I forced myself to think of other and more useful things: both engines were apparently all right and there were no signs of any fuel leakages; the controls were in order; the radio appeared to be working. John had not said much, and suddenly I was struck with an awful thought.

"You didn't collect any bits, did you?" I asked.

"No," he replied. But there was a shade of doubt in his voice. "I got a face full of glass, but I think they are all little bits. How are you?"

"I'm all right," I assured him. "I ducked." I could feel the powdered Perspex working its way down the back of my neck. "You'd better have my goggles," I added after another look at the bulging windscreen. "If that screen caves in it's going to be a bit draughty in here."

"All right. Stick them over my helmet. I think there's a piece near my eye, but I don't want to disturb it."

We had crossed the coast while we had been talking. I started thinking about what I should have done had John been blinded. I could have handled the aircraft back as far as base all right, but landing it would have been an entirely different matter. We had, in fact, already talked about our course of action in the event of John being knocked out. With that knowing smile of his he had advised against my trying to put a Mosquito down. In my own mind I had planned that I should try and bale him out over base, after which I should take the aircraft to some deserted spot and jump out myself.

John brought us in on a gentle, sweeping dive over the aerodrome. The windscreen was still holding, and John was watching his approach through the wide window as we came curving in. At exactly the right moment he checked and straightened out, and then we were rumbling across the grass as smoothly as ever. Again there was quite a reception committee to meet us. Their torches formed a ring around us as I opened the door of the aircraft and I pushed out the ladder. A barrage of questions came up at us.

"What happened?"

"Are you all right?"

"Did you get him?"

John came down the ladder after me. He smiled ruefully at the anxious faces.

"I was the victim of an unprovoked assault," he stated.

Our squadron Medical Officer – Flight Lieutenant E. Mortimer, known to us for obvious reasons as "Rigor" Mortimer – promptly carted us both off to Sick Quarters. I sat and watched while he went over John's face with a pair of tweezers, gently pulling out the tiny fragments of glass. One piece was embedded within a fraction of an inch of his left eye. John had been very conscious of it all the way back, but he had resolutely refrained from rubbing or touching it.

At last Rigor was satisfied that he had fished out all the pieces, and that there was no serious damage. Then he turned his attention to me. I busied myself with shaking out the last of the pieces of glass from my clothing, hoping that he would not notice the unsteadiness of my hands. The stuff had even got down into my socks. I tried to make some foolish little jokes about it because I was only too well aware of the way in which Rigor was giving me one of his searching looks. I did not want any of his nonsense, no matter how right he might be or how well meant he intended it.

By the time I got away from Sick Quarters the last wave of the raiders was on its way out. The northern sky was still ablaze with the fury of the London barrage. The air shook with the thunder of the guns, and the whine and crump of the shells gave back that peculiarly hollow answer from the sky that AA fire made, almost like an echo. The long arms of the searchlights, barely visible in the moonlight, swept out the last of the homeward speeding raiders over the battle-scarred Weald of Kent; and the desperate howling of the German BMW engines and the deeper snarl of the pursuing Merlins of our Mosquitos spoke of the fun we were missing.

Gradually the tumult died away with a last parting rumble as the Dover guns warmed the heels of friend and foe alike. And with it the tumult within me – the disappointment at being baulked in our chase, the anger at being so easily shaken. The fierce exultation at being alive and well – slowly quietened as I stood there in that peaceful, moon-flecked lane. Roundly damning the moonlight, I set off to walk to the Mess in search of the precious egg.

But John and I were not the only ones having difficulties. Shortly after our escapade another of our crews – Flying Officer E. R. Hedgecoe and Sergeant J. R. Whitham – were chasing a Junkers 88 in the bright moonlight when they ran into trouble. The 88 spotted them as they closed in and started taking very violent evasive action. But Hedgecoe hit it, and it went into a steep dive. Intent on finishing it off, he went down after it at full throttle. He fired again, and there was suddenly an ominous roar of air through the aircraft as something broke loose. The plastic nose must have shattered. The Mosquito went into a spin, and Hedgecoe and Whitham blacked out. But Hedgecoe quickly came around, and he managed to recover from the spin, only to discover that the aircraft was quite unmanageable. They both had to bale out, landing, fortunately, just inshore.

Only a short time before that, Hedgecoe – who had started as an Accountant Officer, and had then remustered to aircrew – had had the plastic nose of his aircraft break up as he was diving during firing practice at the sea targets on the range at Leysdown. He managed to land at Eastchurch on one engine with pieces from the broken nose stuck in the starboard radiator.

But these mishaps we could take in our stride as they were nothing more than the normal hazards of operational flying. Our trouble with the ground defence was another matter altogether, and it was at this time that it reached a climax.

One of our crews was almost continuously engaged by the searchlights and the guns while they were chasing a Junkers 88. Not until it had dropped its bomb and turned for home were they able to close in without interference and shoot it down. They were luckier than another crew made up of our latest Norwegian pilot, Lieutenant P. Thoren, and one of my promising ex-schoolmasters, Pilot Officer S. P. Benge, who had been with the squadron for some months, and who had been commissioned at the same time as Gilling-Lax.

Thoren and Benge were hot on the heels of an outward-bound raider, and as they got to the coast near Dover the anti-aircraft guns opened up. The GCI Controller who had given them the contact was busy with another customer, and no one ever found out for certain just what happened. There was another friendly fighter close at hand, but it did not fire its guns. At all events an aircraft which the gunners claimed they had shot down was seen to fall into the sea. The raider continued on out across the Strait – it was seen to do so by the GCI – but nothing more was heard from Thoren. It was not until the following day that pieces of an aircraft were found floating in the water, and were identified as part of his Mosquito.

To make matters even worse, Thoren had only just married a Norwegian girl, and tempers in the squadron were running pretty high. We all felt that it was high time that the liaison between the guns and the fighters was properly tied up. It was possibly the upset over this affair that accounted, in part, for the exceptional craziness of the party which developed, quite spontaneously, a few nights later. We found that these parties usually blew up that way.

A whole bunch of decorations had been showered upon us that day, including a DFC for Will Clemo and a DSO for me. In my own thoughts it struck me as rather ironical that I should be the first radar navigator to receive this high honour just at a time when I was beginning to feel that I was failing rather miserably at my job. That I was not doing as well as I should have was a very disturbing thought, but I pushed it aside, and, along with the rest of them, I occupied myself with the gaiety of the moment.

But the squadron continued with the good scoring, although soon afterwards we did lose another crew after a battle near the French coast. That was more than evened up, however, by two of our crews shooting down two raiders each. And on the 15th of October thirteen enemy aircraft started towards England. Only eight of them crossed the coast, and of these four were destroyed. Bill Maguire and Jones distinguished themselves by shooting down a Junkers 188 and a Me 410 within the space of twelve minutes.

Our targets were nearly all fast, highly elusive customers, and the pressure was beginning to tell on our hard driven engines. They had been persistently flogged over a period of months, and they were beginning to crack up in the middle of chases. Halfway through the month Branse Burbridge and Bill Skelton had a starboard engine pack up when they were 1,500ft behind a hostile raider. And a few days later Johan Räd and Leif Lövestad had an engine failure when they were only 1,200ft behind a Me 410. There was nothing the infuriated crews could do but switch off the burnt out engines and limp home.

It was probably for some purely political reason – intended, perhaps, as a timely counter to the growing suspicion that London's defences had more sound than fury – that the decision was made to operate a couple of night fighters over what was known as the Inner Artillery Zone. The guns were to limit their fire to a height of 18,000ft, and the fighters were to patrol at 20,000ft or above. I felt that the idea was merely for propaganda purposes with the hope that there might be a spectacular battle with plenty of cannon fire overhead possibly finishing up with an impressive flamer.

Having watched the London barrage from afar, I hoped that there would be no errors in the height at which they set their fuses; and remembering our battle over Southampton over two years before, I viewed with mixed feelings the prospect of sending down a flamer into the centre of London.

Two crews were chosen for the job. One was made up of Rory Chisholm and George Cooke, a Flight Lieutenant on Rory's staff at FIU at Ford and John and I were to be the other, from West Malling. The plan was put into operation on the 23rd of October. From our lofty seat over the great metropolis the blacked-out city looked lifeless and deserted as we waited for the enemy to arrive. The only signs of life were out on the suburban fringes where the Underground trains emerged from their tunnels with an eerie green flashing.

That night we did not even get a contact. But two evenings later we were scrambled rather too late, because we scarcely had time to reach the height at which we were supposed to operate before we were turned to the south to meet the first raider. I got a contact almost immediately, but it was well above us and we had to turn after it, still climbing as hard as we could. In doing that we inevitably lost range, and a few minutes later we found ourselves at the edge of the gun zone still in contact but some 3 miles behind.

And then the guns opened up and the fun started. I glanced outside to see what it looked like. The anti-aircraft display was fantastic as it tore the night apart just below the place where our target should have been. Our customer must have been equally impressed because I found when I turned back to the AI set that he was throwing himself about all over the place.

There followed a few moments of hectic manoeuvring, and it took all my breath and all John's skill to keep up with it. Then the raider dropped his bomb, turned and dived for home, going like the wind. We went down after him, our ears cracking, out across Kent. We were slowly closing the range, and we crossed the coast less than a mile behind our target. If the quivering airframe and the screaming engines of our aircraft held together, I thought, we had a good chance of getting him. But we had dived in a very short time from the Arctic cold of 25,000ft, and the moisture from the warmer air below began to cake in solid ice on our windscreen. In a few moments it was opaque, and although by the time we had pulled out of our dive the range had closed to 2,000ft we could see nothing through that sheet of ice. But the blip was still there, and from the way it was behaving the raider showed no signs of slowing up. We continued after it until we were 30 miles out across the Channel with the windscreen still iced up and our target still just out of reach. We had done our best, but that best was just not good enough, and reluctantly we turned back. When we landed we learnt that Rory and George had had no better luck.

The elusiveness of the raiders now coming over was becoming far too common an experience with all of us; and I began to be haunted by the fear that the only ones we would be likely to catch in the future would be the unwary or the overconfident. If, as we suspected, the Germans now had some form of radar tail warning, then they would only be unwary if and when the stuff was not working properly; and it would have to be a very over-confident crew that would ignore a positive radar warning. Our own bombers flying over Germany were operating in a solid stream of aircraft so dense that any aircraft seen astern was more likely to be a friend than an enemy. But the raiders over England were few and far between, and the Luftwaffe pilots could pretty well be sure that anything showing up behind them would be one of our night fighters.

On the last night of October I had cause to think that perhaps our fears about the tail warners were justified. John and I were on patrol under the control of one of the GCI stations; Bill Maguire and Jones were in a position under the direction of the other. The raiders started coming in. There were layers of broken cloud from 10,000 to 24,000ft. That might have proved to be a handicap; but in spite of it the show started promisingly enough.

Our customer was flying fast but straight, and my hopes began to rise as the range closed from 4 miles to 2,000ft. It was too dark to expect a sighting outside 1,000ft. But suddenly the blip soared upward and came racing back. It was as if our target had stopped more or less dead in its tracks.

I dared not tell John to climb for fear of ramming it, and we went slithering on almost into minimum range. John had cut back the throttles and lowered the wheel at my first warning cry to slow up. The aircraft designers had not yet got around to answering our pleas for air-brakes.

The blip on the set hovered at the top of our AI coverage. Then it slid over quickly to the left and dropped away.

"Hard left and dive!" I exclaimed. "It's a peel-off."

John whipped up the wheels, opened up the throttles and nearly cartwheeled the Mosquito to the left almost before I had finished speaking. But our target was dropping like a stone, and the range had opened to 6,000ft. We lost a couple of thousand feet in height on our new heading, and then I saw the blip coming back and mounting the tube again as the other aircraft levelled off. I breathed a bit easier and started the final stalk all over again. This was the real stuff: the type of evasion which we had decided from our own practices would be the most effective and at the same time the most difficult to follow. But could we slow up quickly enough if we had to? I wondered if the other aircraft had air-brakes, or if it had merely been my own carelessness in closing in too fast.

Although we were at full speed again we were only slowly closing the range. It was down to 3,000ft, then 2,500. I was determined not to be caught napping again. Two thousand feet...

"Brakes!" I yelled as the blip shot up and back, just as it had before.

The urgency of my cry brought an immediate response from John, and again we went through the same exhausting experience: the turn and dive, with the loss of the hard-won range.

"I caught a glimpse of him that time," John said in the midst of his juggling. "A 410…right overhead."

We started the chase all over again, and again we all but caught up with him. But this time, as we closed in, he changed his tactics. Instead of climbing he stuck his nose down and went into a weave that was so violent that he very nearly escaped from the side of the narrow beam of our AI.

I was too late off the mark to get inside his turn, and very quickly I was weaving behind our target as wildly as any first-week pupil. John had no sooner wound the Mosquito into a rate four turn as hard as he could go to the left than I was demanding of him the same thing to the right. And he kept on seeing the 410 flashing past his nose on the other tack.

It went on and on, and before long a sort of dull, hopeless despair began to numb my brain, and my voice began to crack. But I still went on with what I hoped was an incisive patter, pouring it out like an automaton. All the time we were diving fast down through the various cloud layers. And every time our weave crossed that of the target my heart was in my mouth as the blip on the AI set went shooting wildly at our level from one side of the cathode ray to the other, and coming right into minimum range as it crossed dead ahead of us.

I tried everything I knew to reduce the weave and stop our swinging backwards and forwards in time to turn inside the target, but that German pilot never let up for a moment. At last even John realized that we were getting nowhere, and the interception more or less died of exhaustion. In the painful silence that followed I looked at my watch. We had been at it with that contact for thirty-five minutes. I had done what I could truly call my damnedest, but it had not been good enough.

The raids were all over when we called the GCI, and they sent us home. On the way back I felt so despondent that I could have jumped out. Was that the best I could do after all those years of experience and practice with a pilot who could turn on a sixpence and who was quite prepared to risk my leading with his chin right into minimum range? It was a sickening thought.

I walked into the crew-room and threw my gear down on the table. The other navigators, after one look at my face, carefully refrained from asking how we had got on. Croaking hoarsely for tea, I sat down gloomily to write out the interception report.

The door opened and Bill Maguire and Jones came in, blinking in the light. There was written on their faces only too clearly a look of exhaustion and despondency. They told us that they had been in contact with a 410 for 39 minutes. They had been through the same experience that John and I had faced, and with no better result. What we had to face now was the bitter fact that although those two 410s could not have done any useful bombing they had nevertheless kept both our standing patrols very busy while the rest of the raiders slipped past and got on with their job.

A few days later Intelligence brought us the results of the interrogation of the crew of a Junkers 188 which had recently been shot down by the squadron. The prisoners had made the definite statement that their aircraft were now fitted with a rearward beamed radar, known as Neptun Gerät. So our suspicions were confirmed, which only served to make the outlook even gloomier. Although we should be able to cope with 188s whether they had radar or not – we had the advantage in speed and manoeuvrability – the 410 was a different matter as it was just about on level terms with the Mosquito. With the radar tail warner they would have a definite advantage over us when it came to trying to intercept them.

All this bore a close relationship to the way in which the moon had affected our work, and the important part it played in our changing fortunes. In the earliest days of AI we had welcomed moonlight as it had helped us out when poor sets and poor operating had lost us so many customers at close range. But as our skill had increased and the enemy had become more wary we had welcomed the dark nights which cloaked us from the vigilance of the German air-gunners. Now our customers were becoming tougher and tougher, and we began to long again for the moonlight which would enable us to catch sight of them at greater range. We did not want to have to rely only on our radar, with its inevitable time-lag, when the target's evasion in the last stages of the interception was most effective. Our night fighting was becoming an ever increasingly complex business.

CHAPTER TWENTY-THREE

The Odds Against Us

W ITH November came the bad weather, and we had to face the fact that we had the long dirty nights of winter ahead of us. We also had a new AI set to master, an enemy forewarned – or, rather, rear-warned – and more than a match for us in speed, and old Isaac waiting to pounce on airframes over-stressed and engines grossly overtaxed for longer than was good for them. The prospect was not exactly a rosy one.

But the morale of the squadron continued to be reassuringly high, which was only to be expected: although the competition was getting tougher and tougher, we were in the forefront, and we did have the pick of the trade. Keeping the pace going, Hedgecoe, with Norman Bamford – now a Pilot Officer – as his navigator, scored the squadron's fiftieth night victory by shooting down a FW 190. Bamford had been with us in 604 at Middle Wallop, and he had just joined us for his second tour.

We were also lucky in having two more old friends from the 604 days join us in Basil Duckett and John Selway, both returning for more operational flying after their rests. Basil crewed up with Gonsalves to form what proved to be a long and fruitful partnership.

John Selway's stay with us, although also fruitful, was cut short in a somewhat dramatic fashion. He had been with the squadron only a few days when he went off with Norman Bamford, his old navigator, on his first operational patrol of his second tour. John Cunningham and I were away that night on a visit to Ford. When we got back to West Malling the next day we were told that Selway was in hospital and on the danger list.

Wasting no time on his first patrol, Selway had started off in cracking style by shooting down a 190. Shortly afterwards Bamford got another contact. They closed in rather quickly, and got a visual on a Ju 188. But when the range was at about 1,000ft, with Selway trying desperately to slow up, the German pilot pulled the old trick of suddenly throttling back. The gunner was vigilant in his look-out, and a bullet from his first burst cracked into the Mosquito at the exact point between the resistant windscreen and the armour just below it, and smashed through the instrument panel.

Selway felt something hit him a severe blow in the belly, and for a moment he lost control of the aircraft, with the altimeter and the airspeed indicator out of action. But he managed to regain control, although he was feeling dreadfully sick, and was afraid he was going to faint. But he held on and flew back to base, made a good landing, and then walked unaided to the crewroom.

For a while he just stood there discussing the affair with the others in his usual lighthearted fashion. He started to drink some tea, but fortunately Rigor Mortimer snatched the cup away from him, thereby possibly saving his life. When he started to undress the onlookers were shocked to see that his clothes were liberally soaked in blood. Rigor whisked him off to hospital, where an emergency operation was performed and the nose of a bullet was removed from his liver. And that put an end to John Selway's second tour of flying.

The following night London was raided again; but our patrols were all foiled by the cunning evasive action taken by the enemy. Everything was quite normal until our fighters had closed in to just beyond visual range. And then things really went mad. The evasion was not a matter of gentle weaving: the raiders now went in for violent corkscrews, climbs almost to the point of stalling, and full-blooded peel-offs.

Some of the faith that a night fighter pilot had to have in his navigator in following this sort of evasion might be explained by suggesting that a car owner should try driving a very fast car, with no lights and no brakes, on a dark night down a winding, unlit road close behind another equally fast car with no lights driven by an unarmed desperado who is swerving violently and making unsignalled crash stops. Let the car driver then shut his eyes and keep them shut, and let him rely entirely on his passenger's instructions to keep him out trouble; and at the same time he must keep closing in on the car he is chasing.

So far as the navigator was concerned, he was in the position of the passenger, breathlessly trying to keep the blinded driver on the road, to hide the fact that at every bend he kept losing sight of the other car, and all the time doing his best not to imagine what would happen if he found their quarry broadside across the road just around the next corner.

We realized only too well that something was going to have to be done about this rearward looking radar the Germans were using. I had heard that it was beamed to some extent into a narrow cone some 20 degrees in width, so I hit on the idea of trying to make an approach from the quarter, or as nearly outside the German beam as the narrow coverage of our own Mark VIII AI would allow.

On the very next night I tried it out, holding contact on the other aircraft at the extreme edge of our coverage. All went well until we were in to about 5,000ft, and then, over-anxious to maintain our closing speed, I allowed the target to get too far on our beam. Suddenly the blip disappeared, and although I turned in quickly towards where the target should have been I could not pick it up again. Feeling as red in the face as any novice, I had to confess to John – who, naturally, was somewhat indignant – what I had tried and failed to do.

"Well...never mind," he said. "Don't burst into tears."

That was just what I felt like doing from sheer frustration. And to add salt to the smart I found when we got back that Bill Maguire and Jones had got a 410 using nothing more than the conventional approach. I knew that I should have to forget my experimenting until we started using our new Mark X AI. That had a wider sweep, which would make more feasible an approach from the quarter.

Early in the month an epidemic of influenza swept through the Station, and we in the squadron were not spared. But, fortunately, activity on the part of the Luftwaffe came to a standstill with the waxing of the moon. The Germans were as quick as we had been in the past to see that their advantage now lay with the darkness; and it was just past the middle of the month before they came over again. When they did come they were as elusive as ever. Throughout the moonless nights that followed our crews doggedly tagged after the raiders without once getting in a shot. This constant and tough practice raised the standard of AI operating to a pitch where most of them could hang on to anything. But if it was one thing to hold on at a manageable distance, it was quite another to close that last half-mile and make an attack.

John and I had our troubles along with the rest of the squadron. We chased one raider all the way to the target and out again, cutting the corners of his weaves, trying every trick we knew to reduce the range. This one did not stop for any fooling about, but just kept diving at full speed for home, weaving as he went. Again I had that horrible touch-and-go feeling that I was leading with John's trusting chin as we worked our way in that last 2,000ft.

We were by then three-quarters of the way across the Strait, and down to within 1,500ft of the water. The German pilot, so nearly home, levelled off and straightened up on course. With an inner glow of relief I saw the blip steady up on the tube and start creeping in towards minimum range. It took on that familiar, miraculously glued-on appearance with no movement at all to either side or up or down that I had come to recognize when John was following something visually.

But his welcome words releasing me from the set were not spoken until he must have sensed the query in my voice.

"It's all right," he said. "I can see him. But the screen's iced up solid."

With the feeling of misgiving now mingled with my relief, I looked up, and there plainly visible through the roof panel was a 410. But when I bent forward to look through the windscreen I could see nothing at all, not even a blurred outline.

"We'll hang on a bit," John said, "in case it clears."

There was disappointment in his voice, and I could tell that he had no more hope than I had that it would clear. It would take time for that thickness of ice to melt, and to attempt to do any shooting before it cleared would be a sheer waste of ammunition.

The precious minutes ticked by and the unsuspecting enemy, so tantalizingly close above us, sped on towards France. Our windscreen showed no sign of clearing and finally the enemy coast showed up through the side windows.

"It's no use," John said. He sounded disgusted. "We'll have to let him go."

So back we went, after all that, with our guns unfired, back empty handed again to the chilly routine of filling in an AI report.

With incidents such as that it was all too easy, wrapped up as we were so completely in our own little job, to lose one's sense of proportion. But what we were going through was a very intense experience, and I began again to feel the haunting fear that I was failing at my job. London was being bombed quite regularly, and I found myself become obsessed with the thought that I was not doing much about putting a stop to it. I had, also, a purely personal interest in the matter in that my mother and my sister and most of my friends were still living in London. But then that was equally true of so many others in the squadron, including John. I became more and more conscious of the thought that every incoming raider that evaded us carried a bomb that might kill a lot of people, even a dozen mothers, and it began to prey on my conscience. We had quite enough to worry about without letting such thoughts upset us too much. But from that I went further, and I began to wonder if the job was not getting beyond me, and if it would be better for John to try another navigator. Perhaps he should have someone younger, someone who could think quicker and who would be up to his standard and that of the squadron.

Later, of course, I was to see that I was being much too introspective about it all, worrying far too much about things that were altogether too intangible, even becoming morbid in my outlook. But the conscientious navigator, like the keen fisherman, found that it was always the ones that got away that haunted his dreams. And I was having far too many that got away.

The influenza worked its way through the squadron and then abated, and we were able to get back to our routine of two nights on flying and two nights off. Nearly everyone had suffered from it, including John, who was so robustly healthy.

While he was on the sick list I flew one interesting and lively patrol with Gonsalves. We got a contact, but almost immediately another friendly fighter turned in behind us. And then the Dover guns opened up and started plastering all three of us. Fortunately they did not hit us, but in evading both the flak and the friendly fighter I lost contact with the one we were chasing.

All this time we were feeling our way with the new Mark X AI. The first of the new Mosquitos with which it was fitted had arrived early in the month but there was a great deal we had to do before either we or the aircraft would be ready for work on operations. Most of us were getting a fair idea of how to use the new gear, and as December came in I began to feel impatient about getting into the air with it as I had worked up some pretty high hopes about its possibilities. The ground crews worked hard to get the new aircraft up to the standard required, and in the meantime we had to keep the night watches going with our cruelly tired Mosquitos and the old type of AI.

How tired our aircraft were we found on a routine patrol at the beginning of the month. John and I took off and I went straight on with my routine cockpit drill, changing the petrol cocks over to the main tanks, switching off the navigation lights, and getting on with the job of tuning in the AI. But from the start I was vaguely conscious that things were not quite normal, and that John was taking a remarkably long time to settle down. Having satisfied myself that the AI was working and in order, I sat up, and I found that John was still fiddling with the trimmers and rocking the stick from side to side. He turned to look at me, and saw that I was watching him.

"There's something very strange about this aircraft," he said.

"How come?" I asked.

"I don't know. She's very slow and sluggish. And just look where the trim is!"

I bent forward, and I could see that the lateral trim – the adjustment that corrected any tendency to fly one wing low – was turned fully one way.

John was obviously puzzled. "She seems to want to roll to the left," he commented.

It did not sound like a very auspicious start to a patrol, but we continued on course, slowly gaining height. If anything drastic was going to happen it would be just as well to have some space underneath. I wriggled around on the seat and tried to look out at the tail and the wings while John moved the controls about.

"Everything looks normal enough," I reported. And then something caught my eye. "Half a jiffy, though…there's something peculiar…"

It looked like the white, improbable face of a Doomie faintly raising itself over the trailing edge of the port wing. Folding myself up, I forced my head into the narrow space behind John's seat in order to try and get a better view. John was craning his neck around to try and see but his harness held him clamped down too firmly.

"We seem to have something hanging on the port wing," I told him, "just behind the centre section."

John was nearly strangling himself in his effort to see what was happening, and I was wondering if I should ever be able to get myself unfolded again. Finally I got my head right across the confined space, and I could see more clearly what was wrong.

"Looks as though we have a flap adrift," I said.

I could see that the flap was sticking up at a grotesque angle, right in the opposite direction to its normal position.

John turned the aircraft slowly around, and went into an easy dive toward base, being careful to keep the speed down. Idly I wondered how much was holding that flap on, and what would happen if it dropped off altogether on the approach. As unobtrusively as possible, I clipped my parachute on to my harness. John looked around at me as I was doing it, but he did not say anything.

Somewhat diffidently I suggested: "How about giving the flaps a try out while we still have plenty of height?"

John was quite unprovoked by the fatuousness of my remark. "I shan't use them," he replied.

There was not a lot of wind to land into without the braking effect of the flaps, and I hoped that the runway was going to be long enough. But I need not have worried. We swept over the boundary with only inches to spare, touched down within a few yards, and squealed to a standstill not far beyond where we usually stopped. Then we taxied in, and I climbed out to find our ground crew gazing with doleful expressions on their faces at the port flap: it was hanging precariously from the remains of one hinge.

As we walked together towards the crew-room John turned to me and gave me a queer sort of look.

"That's the first time I've ever known you put your parachute on without being told to," he remarked.

I was glad of the darkness that hid my acute embarrassment. Was there a reproach implied in his remark? Did he suspect for one moment the dwindling confidence I had in myself and in all aircraft in general? Quickly I covered up with the banal comment that there was nothing like being prepared for the worst.

We said no more about it because neither of us was given to discussing our feelings. There had always been this personal reserve, almost shyness, between us. And yet our mutual understanding was all the deeper, I felt, for being unspoken. At that moment, although I could not bring myself to talk about my troubles, I felt that John understood. There was not much that escaped him.

The job of squadron adjutant was suddenly down-graded to the rank of Flying Officer, and since Tim was a Flight Lieutenant he had to go. It was a sorry leave-taking for all of us; but it was particularly so for Tim because he had been with the squadron since the outbreak of war, and he had come justifiably to regard it as his very own.

To fill Tim Malony's place there came a man of a very different type, Flying Officer F. G H. Custance. He was known to everyone as "Cussy", and before the war he had been an actor. He was no stranger to us as he had been adjutant to No. 3 Squadron at Hunsdon when we were there, and since a change was inevitable he was a popular choice.

The difference between Tim and Cussy was perhaps best typified by what Cussy was pleased to call his operational hat. This tattered and treasured wreck was a soiled, shapeless affair the brim of which hung precariously to a shot-ridden crown. It was said that it had been tossed light-heartedly into the air during a skeet shooting session, and that it had instantly been blown out of the sky by half a dozen shotguns. John viewed That Hat with marked disapproval.

It was only a little over a week after the episode of the loose flap that our tired aircraft let us down again. The weather for the middle of that December of 1943 had turned bitterly cold, and it was a fairly miserable sort of night even on the ground.

We were well on the way towards our patrol beat, snug and secure in our little cockleshell of warm air, before a noticeable roughness in the port engine developed into a vibration that was so severe that John had to feather the aircrew and switch off the engine.

We were becoming used to this sort of thing by now, but we had plenty of height in hand so there was nothing to worry about. The Mosquito, even with our full load on, would maintain level flight quite comfortably on one engine if handled intelligently. It was asking too much of it to climb, so height was a thing to be maintained until one was quite certain of having a safe approach to a clear airfield within gliding distance.

John called up West Malling to tell them that he was returning on one engine.

"How's your weather?" he asked, to be on the safe side.

"OK," the Controller replied. "'I'm putting on the canopy."

Thus reassured, John set the Mosquito into a gentle dive. With the coming searchlights of the canopy to guide him when they came on he would be able to go straight in to land without having to do the usual circle of the aerodrome.

But as we got nearer and nearer to the aerodrome – and lower and lower – the cloud seemed to be getting thicker than ever. I was staring ahead into the murk, but of the canopy, or of anything but cloud for that matter, there was not a sign. We were down to 1,000ft, and we were still pop-eye. John was becoming a little restive, as well he might, as we were soon down to 600ft and the airfield should have been in full view right underneath us.

"I don't think much of their clear weather," John remarked. He switched over the radio to transmit. "I am approaching base. How is it with you now?"

There was a slight pause, and then the voice of the Controller came back, heavy with embarrassment and concern.

"Sorry, Two Four. There's a snowstorm right over us at the moment."

I felt rather sorry for the poor man. How was he to know that a wretched snowstorm would sneak up on him out of the darkness just as we arrived back over base? But there we were, on one engine, and it put us in a bit of a spot.

There was no reply that John could make, but to me over the intercom he said: "Well...I don't know what we do now. But keep a look out for the canopy."

He went into an easy right-hand orbit, turning against the good engine. Staring out of the side window, it seemed to me that the cloud had broken up a little, and I could see the swirl of snowflakes driving past. Then suddenly I saw a white glare beyond the starboard wing-tip, a smudged diffusion of light shining through the swirling mist and snow.

"There's the canopy!" I exclaimed. "Just off the starboard beam."

"Keep your eye on it," John warned.

As if I was going to let it go! We milled around for some minutes, hoping for a clearance, and I kept my eyes glued on that vague smear of light in the surrounding gloom. And as we watched we talked of possible alternative airfields. We were not really left with much choice: we were too low to bale out, and we could not climb; and our nearest alternative was Ford, which was at sea level and offered a safe approach from seawards almost on the deck. But to get there our track would take us uncomfortably close to hills that were too high for us to clear. It would not take a great deal of error in height to run into a stuffed cloud.

I got out my map and began to take furtive glances at it, searching for spot heights and likely routes, and doing some mental juggling with wind speed and direction and magnetic variation. And every time we came around to the north-west of the canopy, where we were nearest to Wrotham Hill, I had to resist the most ridiculous inclination to draw up my feet.

"There's no future in this," John said at last. "We'd better have a try at Ford."

He set course, but just before we left I cast a last wistful look back at that vague pool of light. It was just as well that I did for I found myself looking right down what seemed to be a narrow funnel of clear air. At the far end of it there were the aerodrome lights.

"It's clearing!" I exclaimed. "There's a clear gap right in line with the flarepath."

"Don't lose sight of it," John replied.

He began to turn back to starboard, diving into the funnel. The cloud rolled past, close on either side, and arching over our heads. But out ahead of us we could clearly see the lights of the flarepath. Juggling swiftly with the trim and the wheels and the flaps, John took us in and we were safely down.

At the far end of the runway, when the momentum of the aircraft had carried it as far as it would go, John turned off. At the same time the canopy lights were switched off, and the darkness closed in over us. We could not taxi any farther as the aircraft could not be steered on only one engine. For a long time we waited while the flight van searched in vain for us. Our navigation lights had long since faded to mere glimmers as the accumulators ran down, and we became lost in the sleety darkness.

John's voice grew hoarse over the dying radio; and the apologetic reassurances from the Control Tower dwindled away to a whisper, and then to utter silence. At last, with an angry glance at the mounting temperature gauges, John switched off the engine and sat and fumed. That last half hour had been a trying experience, and even his seemingly inexhaustible patience was giving out.

But I was content enough just to be sitting there in the aircraft on the ground. Finally a snort of disgust from John roused me. The cold was seeping into the cockpit, chilling our sweat-soaked bodies.

"How much longer do they think I'm going to sit here and freeze!" John demanded.

I slipped the Very pistol from its catch, stuffed my pockets with cartridges, and, scorning the ladder, jumped down on to the wet grass. Here was a chance to summon the van and at the same time to celebrate in my own fashion another victory over Isaac. Walking a few yards downwind I began happily firing off a cascade of gaily-coloured stars. That brought them running.

CHAPTER TWENTY-FOUR

New Tools – New Tricks

MY first impression of the new Mark X AI had been that we should have to breed a new race of radar navigators to handle it. They would have to be men with three or more hands to cope with the thing as it fairly bristled with controls.

As I became more familiar with the set, however, it became obvious that most of the controls could be pre-set during the night flying test. Once adjusted to the satisfaction of the operator they could, like the controls of a television set, usually be left for the night's viewing. But even after these had been taken care of, there were still enough left to bewilder even a cinema organist, and they all had to be located quickly by touch. If, as so often happened, the navigator was also called upon in the middle of an interception to operate one of the several IFF switches or to signal to an interfering searchlight on the Morse key, the well-known expression about finger trouble took on a new meaning.

The presentation of the radar information on the new set was radically different from anything we had known in the past. There were two tubes framed in rectangular masks. The blips appeared, at ranges of up to 10 miles, as small, roughly rectangular blobs on the right-hand tube on which range and bearing could be read and relative courses assessed. A selected blip could then be transferred to the left-hand tube, which displayed it as if there were a large clock face standing vertically in front of the fighter. From this we were able to continue with our technique of telling the pilot where to look in terms of a clock reference.

If the tube of our Mark VIII sets, so often infested with whirling spirals of light, might be likened to a slice of Swiss Roll, the new Mark X resembled more a piece of that sinister looking cut cake, amber in hue and sparsely curranted, sold by the Naafi. It was not long before the radar mechanics were referring to the wads of their choice at their morning tea break by Mark numbers.

The scanner of the new equipment rotated about a vertical axis in the nose of the aircraft so that it could see forward through the whole 180 degrees from beam to beam. It also nodded as it whirled around and so could see above and below the fighter's line of flight; and the extent of its nodding could be varied at will by the operator. This flexibility could be put to good use for cutting out the ground echoes when flying low or for following evasion at close range.

The new Mosquitos were also fitted with a separate piece of radar equipment – tucked up under the roof behind the pilot's seat – which enabled us to use the ground radar beacons, enough of which were scattered around the country to render the fighter independent of ground control for fixings and homings.

Although I knew that we would need all our wits about us if we were going to make the most of this new AI, I felt that the day was not far off now when we would be able to operate with a reasonable chance of success without any help at all from the ground. When that day came we should be ready to go with a vengeance on to the offensive, and to tackle the Luftwaffe over their own territory.

But for all these operations, at home or over enemy territory, bold tactics were necessary, and I constantly preached that to the new navigators coming to us.

"Snap up your contacts," I told them. "Don't hesitate…turn in early…and keep the target on the outside of your turn." I stressed the necessity to try and avoid the long stern chase. "Keep pressing on it. Cut the corners and don't slow up too soon. Keep right on into minimum range…"

And so we came to the fifth Christmas of the war. Our hopes were high, and our enthusiasm for our trade was keen and knowledgeable. The ultimate outcome of the struggle could no longer be in doubt; but we could not allow ourselves to feel in any way complacent while bombs were still falling on London. We had a brief respite, however, and for a little while, as with Christmas of the previous years, no raiders came over to spoil the fun.

My wife, now commissioned, had been moved back to London, and was GHQ, Home Forces, at Hounslow, and she came to our Christmas party at the Manor House. She arrived earlier than I had expected, and she looked rather tired, so I suggested that she might like to go over to the WAAF Officers' Mess for a rest before things got going.

At that moment a boisterous crowd of pilots and navigators came bursting in through the front door. At their head was a young Navy pilot – Sub-Lieutenant T. H. Blundell – who had only recently been attached to the squadron. There was a twinkle in his eye, and one of the sleeves of his jacket was missing.

"Where on earth have you been?" I asked.

"Just around to the WAAF Mess," he replied nonchalantly.

As he went off upstairs singing lustily I found Micki looking at me with an amused gleam in her eyes. A fine place I had suggested for a rest!

Our Christmas at the Manor House was the usual gay and happy affair. Arthur Woods added a little personal touch to things by decorating the place with a number of amusing coloured sketches. When we went to bed we found that he had attached to each bedroom door a more personal cartoon taking off some foible of the inmate. On my door there was a shower of grotesque little gremlins being shooed out from a darkly curtained interior.

With the New Year we were still using our Mark VIII AI in the old aircraft, but the boffins had dreamt up a means of coaxing a little more speed out of our sorely tried engines by mixing nitrous oxide – better known as laughing gas – with the petrol. The plumbers went to work installing heavy contraptions of gas cylinders and pipes in the bowels of the aircraft. The use of the gas was restricted to only a few minutes at a time, but it did promise to give us just that extra power when it was most needed.

The GCI Controllers and their teams were co-operating very well with us in the speeded-up tactics we were having to use by turning us in close behind our targets. It was the drill with them for one of the team to switch over their radio from receive to transmit, or vice versa, on the orders of the Controller. So keen were they that they often anticipated his order by several seconds, and we would hear snatches of conversation from the control cabin followed by the Controller's instruction to transmit before he spoke to us. It gave our aircrews a glorious opportunity to rag them with slanderous references to girlish laughter and the rattle of teacups.

The New Year of 1944 was only two days old when the lull came to an end. John and I were on our old beat over the Strait at 25,000ft. There was a possibility of some business, we were told, with a fast one coming in from the south-east. With that news I felt a disquieting tingling, and my heart began to pound in the most annoying way. The prospect of some trade was gladdening enough, but would I be able to cope with it, or would it all end in another heartbreaking failure? We were turning as the Controller deftly wheeled us in to meet our target when the blip flickered up on my tube. All hopes and fears vanished as I concentrated to the exclusion of all emotion on the action that lay ahead.

The Controller had timed our turn to perfection, and we were a bare mile and a half behind our target with a little height in hand. This customer was not only going fast but he was also taking continuous evasion from side to side and up and down. And that was where he made his mistake: as soon as I got an idea of the type of evasive action he was taking I started cutting corners, and we began to close in.

We were in to 3,000ft and John had just caught a glimpse of exhaust flames when the other aircraft seemed to sense our presence and realize that the evasion he was taking, strenuous though it was, had to be varied. He suddenly turned quite violently to the left, and dived away to the west, still weaving. The time had come for us to use all the speed we could muster to keep up with the diving target, and John turned on the nitrous oxide. I felt the Mosquito suddenly lengthen its stride.

We held the range satisfactorily, but the raider must have felt, or seen, that his manoeuvre had not thrown us off because he wheeled sharply to the left again, holding his turn right through 180 degrees until we were heading east. If we had done nothing else, we had at least turned him away from his target. But I had been a little slow on the turn, and now the range was out to 7,000ft.

Somewhere at the back of my mind that traitor that I was learning to recognize as despair began to stir, niggling away in its own poisonous fashion. It was an effort that I should not have had to waste at this particular moment, and I managed to force myself to concentrate on what was happening. And by now the raider seemed to have had enough. He turned back to the south, and continued diving steeply and still weaving.

But he had lost the initial advantage of the speed of his dive. Our aircraft on the other hand, was still gathering speed, and I had now got the timing for cutting off those fatal corners of his. We were streaking out across the Channel, slowly closing the gap between us, but all the time getting closer to France and the forbidden enemy coast. It was going to be a close thing.

We were down to 18,000ft when John turned off the nitrous oxide; but we still managed to keep closing in, and the range was down to 3,000ft. By the time our height was 10,000ft we were nearly across the Channel. And then the enemy pilot, apparently thinking he was safe, began to ease up. The weaves were ironed out, the dive flattened, and the speed dropped off. The blip on my tube came gliding gently back to where I wanted it. Twenty degrees at 12 o'clock, range 1,200…1,000 and then we had him cold.

I was almost overcome with relief when John said in the middle of my patter that he could see it. I sat back and moistened my dry lips, and reached for the night binoculars.

There it was: a 410. The twin barbettes bulged fatly on either side of its slim fuselage. But why, I asked myself, did he now fly on so sedately after all that strenuous and futile evasion? This was his moment of greatest danger. Looking down through the side window I saw the reason why he had steadied up. The French coast was quite close under our noses. He must have fallen for the oldest temptation of all, and had relaxed with the thought that he was nearly home. I imagined his observer stowing his gear and putting his maps away instead of keeping an eye on his tail-warning radar tube. Well…he had had his chance.

With the coast practically beneath us, John pulled up and fired. The other aircraft was instantly spattered with a cluster of dazzling flashes that ended in a great woof of yellow flame. We lifted with a violent surge, and wheeled away. I saw the enemy aircraft hit the ground in a splash of red fire as we hurried out over that forbidden coastline and started to climb back to continue our patrol.

During the entire interception we had, of course, been on intercom, cut off from the GCI which, in any case, had been busy with other fighters. When John called them on the radio to make his report there was a moment or two of a rather comic muddle. They apparently had our blip confused with that of another fighter much further to the north, and the Controller gave us a vector that would have taken us slap back over France. John chuckled and switched over to transmit.

"I think not," he replied drily. "I am at present steering three four zero."

There was a short pause while they sorted things out, and then our IFF must have flashed up on their tube, and they must have spotted us far to the south and apparently inside the enemy coast. We heard the mush of background chatter – but no teacups – as their transmitter was prematurely switched on.

"Is that him, right down there?" the Controller exclaimed in alarm. "Good God…we must get him out of that! Transmit." His voice changed instantly, and with his usual assurance and calmness he said: "We have you now, Two Four. Continue on your present vector."

The aircraft we had shot down crashed between Le Touquet and Berck. The crash was seen, we heard later, by the Royal Observer Corps on the English coast one minute to midnight. John fired only ten rounds per gun.

John and I took our new aircraft with the Mark X AI for its first operational patrol on the 6th January, but we had to be satisfied with the other fighter on patrol for a target to practise on because we were going through a few days of a lull while the moon waned and the Luftwaffe thought up what they were going to do next.

Jones-the-Navigator and Bill Maguire left us about this time to go to FIU, their operational tour having come to an end. And Rigor Mortimer, our devoted medical officer, went away to start writing the medical history of the war. Bernard Thwaites was promoted to Squadron Leader and given command of A Flight in place of Maguire.

It was on the night of the 15th of January that I got my first chance to try out our Mark X AI against the enemy. We were told that a few FW 190s were coming over above the weather, and the GCI took us over in time to bring us across the path of one of them as it sped homeward. A WAAF Controller was on duty at the GCI, and she gave us a perfect crossing contact and a final vector that should have turned us neatly in behind the other aircraft. If I had been using Mark VIII AI all might have been well, but with the wider coverage of the Mark X I got contact while the raider was still well on our beam and before he had crossed our path. I felt sure that the final vector would turn us in front of our target, and I cut in as John was about to turn and told him to wait for a minute.

The two aircraft quickly converged, the blip moving fast down the tube. This was wonderful, I thought; I should be able to turn in almost alongside him. And then, with the range still at 2 miles, the blip slid across our line of flight and I realized with horror that I had boobed. Surprised, after the previous delay, at the sudden urgency in my voice, John wheeled into the turn. But it was too late: we were by then some 2½ miles astern.

We had a little height in hand, and with that we manage to pick up more speed, which gradually brought us in to a range of 2 miles; but by now the 190 was diving for home and his speed was building up. John held us in the dive with the taps wide open, and we began to bounce and quiver and the noise of the straining engines rose to a howl. But the range stood obstinately at 2 miles. The German was taking no evasive action, so there were no corners I could cut. He was pinning his faith entirely on speed, and the blip stood as firmly fixed on the trace as if it had been painted on the glass. Our own speed was mounting alarmingly, and John remarked that the controls were getting devilishly heavy.

"How are we doing?" he asked.

My patter had all but dried up for want of something fresh to tell him. "Still dead ahead at 2 miles," I said for perhaps the tenth time.

"He's going incredibly fast then," John replied.

I thought I detected just a shade of doubt in his voice. He was watching the airspeed indicator with some misgiving as he made a mental calculation of our actual speed. When he spoke, the news he had shook me.

"We must be doing close to 450. Aren't we closing in at all?"

"No...still 2 miles."

I whipped the visor off the tube and sat back; and John was able to lean across and have a look for himself at that stationary blip.

The way in which the Mosquito was vibrating was getting worse, and the thuds were almost throwing me off my seat. And now there was something else, a strangely unpleasant snaking movement of the aircraft.

"I don't like the feel of this," John commented, as if reading my thoughts. "It's almost as if we were coming apart."

We had not gained an inch, and it did not look as if we were ever likely to catch up. Very gently and carefully John began to ease out of the dive. I watched the blip sink and slide away, still dead ahead of us. That proved conclusively enough that it was real: I had almost begun to wonder if it was a mark on the glass.

As our speed dropped off things returned to normal. We flew quietly back to base, saying very little. I was sick at heart and miserable. After all my talk about snapping up contacts and bold cut-offs I had taken it upon myself to take the interception out of the Controller's hands, and I had made a mess of things. How could I go on telling my navigators what they ought to do when they were already doing better than I was? Perhaps the time had come when I should step down and make way for a younger and more capable Leader.

The discovery the riggers made after we landed left me thankful for John's sensitive hands and his sense of discretion. Under the strain of that merciless pounding in the dive, the plywood skin of the fuselage had begun to break away, and we had slowed up none too soon.

The Luftwaffe still made no effort at any big scale raiding, and we spent a lot of our time around the cheerful fire in our crew-room waiting for the telephone to ring. Although I had been barely a year on my second tour of flying, I found myself beginning to start at the sudden ringing of that 'phone. I also found myself displaying that transparent show of over-eagerness to get into the air, at the same time forcing myself to calm and deliberate movement as I gathered up my kit. I was afraid that somebody might notice that my hands had a ridiculous tendency to start trembling. It was absurd and shameful to feel this barely controllable tension. I had the finest pilot in the world, and just about the most envied post in the business.

It was, perhaps, those, two fortunate circumstances that, perversely enough, helped to inflame within my mind the destructive conflict. Every time that telephone bell summoned us to the job I had the haunting fear of another failure. And yet I was too proud – or too stubborn – to admit defeat, and too keen on the job to hand it over willingly to somebody else. And so I went on, trying desperately to keep my fears and worries to myself, uneasily sitting listening to the radio with one ear cocked for the 'phone, bracing myself against the tell-tale start that would come when it did ring.

Sometimes we listened to the German radio broadcasting programmes for their own troops. I pictured in my mind the way their crews were sitting around, just as we were, and I wondered what they were cooking up for us. One of our favourite turns on their radio was a sentimental contralto crooner of the kind so beloved by the Germans. She was apparently some kind of German forces sweetheart. We called her Glucose Gertrude.

But our favourite number of the lot came at the end of the programme. We would leap to our feet and goose-step around the room shouting the Horst Wessel song in execrable German. Had not our fathers taken the Kaiser's hymn of hate for their own and sung it with the same mocking relish in the earlier war?

At such times there would come back to my mind that night on the Rhine – could it really have been eleven years before? – when Micki and I had watched those children marching along to the same tune. I wondered if any of them were sitting in crew-rooms over in France waiting to come over against us. I was quite sure that there would be no weakening of that fanatical spirit with which they were infected: only death or overwhelming defeat would break that down. We still had a long way to go, and that was yet another reason why it was too early to start getting tired.

On the 21st of January things really livened up. That night the Luftwaffe put on the heaviest raid on England since the winter of 1940–41, sending over 200 aircraft in two waves. FW 190s and Me 410s streaked in first dropping "Window" and keeping our standing patrols busy, and they were followed by J 88s and Do 217s. Then, to make matters even more difficult, the raiders got all tangled up with one of our own "Bullseye" exercises and some of our bombers returning home.

Some of our GCI stations were badly affected by the enemy's "Window", but the controllers were ready for such emergencies, and after using a certain code word they continued with their instructions to the night fighters in the normal way. The fighters knew as soon as they heard the coded warning what to expect so they went on acknowledging the orders and ignoring them, making their own way around with the help of the searchlights, whose radar was not so badly affected, and who were able to be of help. In spite of the confusion, and having their standing patrols drawn off by the first of the raiders, B Flight managed to shoot down two and damage a third of the sixteen raiders destroyed that night, and that brought the total number of German aircraft destroyed by the squadron by day and by night during the war up to 200.

But we were not having things entirely our own way. Against the fighter-bombers we were rarely able to make much headway, as our aircraft were possibly feeling the strain even more than the crews, and engine failures leading to single engine returns became commonplace.

On the night of the 28th of January we were told by Control that Blundell and his navigator, Sub-Lieutenant A. T. Parker, were in trouble. They were close behind a fast raider chasing it out across the Channel, but one of their engines was badly overheating. They would have been justified in calling off the chase, but, being the eager types they were, they were pressing on with it. There was a long, anxious wait, and there came another hurried message. The overheated engine was on fire and they were baling out. That was the last we ever heard of them, and the searchers found no trace of their aircraft.

Ten days later we had another loss. When I got down to breakfast I found everybody steeped in gloom, and when I asked what it was all about I was told that Arthur Woods and his navigator had been killed during the night. The death of Arthur Woods was a savage blow to all of us; but I had a particular reason to feel badly about it because I had, I felt, been rather forcing along his navigator, a young Norwegian Sergeant named J. O. R. Bugge. Although of the same name, he was not related to Per Bugge. He was a wildly keen and very confident youngster, and he had been nagging away at me to let him start flying on operations. He was our newest navigator and I had had doubts about whether he was really quite experienced enough. But that night had been a "Bullseye" exercise and I thought that the practice with an experienced pilot would do him good and also give me a chance to get a reliable report from Arthur Woods on his progress.

They had collided with one of the Wellingtons acting as a target on the exercise, and there had been no survivors from either aircraft. Had I rushed Bugge too much? Should I have warned him more forcibly against trying these thrusting tactics too soon? It was not pleasant to recall what I had told him.

"Turn inside the target," I had said. "Don't hang about," I had insisted.

"Close in quickly."

And now they were all dead. Well, it was too late to start reproaching myself. Indeed, later I came to realize that I had no cause to do so, for there was no hope of catching those scurrying, elusive fighter-bombers unless we were prepared to take chances.

By February most of our crews on patrol were using the new AI, although we could still not claim any score for the new weapon. On the 12th of the month I did manage to bring John close enough behind a 410 for him to see its exhausts, and to keep them in view for a tantalizing three minutes without being able to get in a shot at it. No matter how much he tried, he simply could not coax another knot out of the screaming engines and get in close enough for an attack.

A week later we had another chase, and I was able to get John within shooting distance of a Ju 188. At his first burst the startled customer, hard hit but still very much alive, slipped down out of sight. I ducked my head down into the visor to see where he had gone only to find that the vibration from the cannon had put the AI out of action.

On the following night all those not on flying went up to town to see Terence Rattigan's play *While the Sun Shines*. Cussy, through his connections with the world of the theatre, had arranged the show to celebrate the squadron's Two Hundredth. Afterwards we were invited to a party on the stage with the author and the cast.

It was a wonderful evening, but not even in the gaiety of that very pleasant party could I banish the vague shadow of the depression that hovered at the back of my mind. Our losses weighed heavily, and I could not help feeling that perhaps one of them was through an error of judgment on my part. The smallness of our numbers in a night fighter world and of our casualties tended to make the occasional loss all the more personal. And these tragedies had been going on for such a very long time now. I was finding it harder and harder to dull my senses against feeling badly about them and to shrug it all off.

Had I known that night how prophetic the title of that play was I should probably have been even more depressed, because the next morning John received the news that he was to be posted to a staff job at Headquarters, No. 11 Group. He was to become Group Captain Night Operations.

The next night the Luftwaffe came over in some force. Hedgecoe and Bamford beat us to the draw with the first victory ever scored with Mark X AT. And Branse Burbridge and Bill Skelton rounded things off by shooting down one of those elusive 410 menaces in that confident manner which was later to bring them so much success against the German night fighters.

CHAPTER TWENTY-FIVE

Tour Expired

IT was not easy for me to appreciate the fact that my long partnership with John was at last coming to an end. But since he did not have to go to his new job until the end of February there was still time, I hoped, to get him a combat using the Mark X AI, even if only as a parting gift.

There was plenty of activity which might give us the opportunity for a combat as the Luftwaffe seemed to have taken it into their minds to throw in everything they could muster. They by no means achieved what our own Bomber Command would have called a mass raid; but they did their best with what little they had. Once again, Ju 88s and 188s and Do 217s came over with the fighter-bombers, with fast, high-flying window droppers out ahead of them trying to obscure the radar picture. With the fast and the slower raiders mixed along the window-strewn path they were following and with other friendly fighters crowding in, our navigators had their hands full sorting out their targets. But their constant practice paid dividends, and the fighters, freelancing among the searchlights, went on shooting down the enemy, including the fast Me 410s.

I was desperately anxious to get that one last combat, and a couple of nights after our celebration in town it looked as if we might be in luck. There was quite a lively raid on, and we were in position on our patrol line in good time. And then the AI set went completely, incurably dead. John showed no sign of any disappointment as he called Control to tell them that our weapon was bent; but he must have felt that he was getting a pretty raw deal.

On our night flying test during the afternoon we had found that the AI was not behaving at all well. The mechanics had worked on it, and we had taken the trouble to do another air test with it after dark, only to find that the set that time was completely unserviceable. When we were scrambled at twenty minutes to ten we had taken a spare aircraft, and it was the AI of that one that was letting us down now.

The raid was in full swing as we turned back towards base, and for once I was free to get a good view of what was happening outside. So much of my time had been spent gazing at those cathode ray tubes; and what I saw now was an awe-inspiring sight. All along the way from Dungeness to London there was a constantly moving carpet of searchlights. It was almost as if they were bearing the visitors aloft from box to box on the apex of their cones.

The enemy pathfinders had already carpeted the route with a series of great oval splashes of white markers, turning the 70 tormented miles of Bomb Alley into a dazzling Great White Way. At the end of that floodlit highway the inferno of the London barrage twinkled and flickered above a criss-cross pattern of spouting tracer and rocket salvoes that seemed to split the heavens.

And along its length, on a front 10 miles wide and 5 miles deep, the airborne traffic ran the gauntlet. Fifty or sixty aircraft, for the most part unseen, hurtled along as fast as over-speeding engines could carry them, twisting and diving, their crews either staring out at the waving beams of the searchlights or crouching over their radar sets, watching with agonizing intentness those insignificant looking little blips on the cathode ray tubes whose movements meant success or failure, life or death, to the watchers.

In many ways it was primarily a battle of the back room boys. It was the boffins who had fashioned the weapons which gave to the searchlight and gun crews and to the men in those aircraft the power of magic sight or, when necessary, the means to blind that sight. It was not so much a matter of the battle going to the strong as to the most skilful craftsmen equipped with the best weapons.

My old air-gunner's instinct asserted itself and I did not merely sit looking forward at the fantastic display of searchlights and gun and rocket fire: I craned my neck around to try and keep a watch behind and below our tail as we weaved a way among the busy search light cones, waiting for our relief to arrive. Suddenly I saw illuminated some distance beneath us a Ju 188. It was shining with a dazzling silver radiance in the light of half a dozen beams.

In that chaotic free-for-all there was no time to spare to make any formal inquiries over the radio, and that target was far too tempting to be allowed to slip by. John wheeled over and went swooping down to the attack. We heard afterwards that in doing so we cut almost across the bows of one of the fighters from 96 Squadron which was coming up just behind the enemy bomber.

The 188 was doing a gentle weave by no means violent enough to stand a chance of shaking off the lights. For a moment I was puzzled by a luminous trail that streamed out behind it, and then I realized that some optimist inside the aircraft was shovelling out "Window" by the bucket-load, presumably in the forlorn hope of foxing the searchlights.

John went straight in, and his opening burst hit the Junkers hard. But it was apparently not hard enough, because as he pulled clear of the bomber it dived to the right, and the stream of "Window" became a stream of tracer.

But the searchlights hung on to their target, and I was able to keep him in sight as he weaved away more vigorously now down on our starboard bow. I did not realize that John had lost sight of him and I rather wasted some precious seconds in idle chatter.

"I think he's still shooting back," I commented.

It was either that or he was shovelling out more "Window". Or perhaps he was on fire. The glare of the lights was confusing things.

"How about stoking him up a bit?" I suggested.

"Well, where is he, then?" John demanded.

"Down on the right…"

Again we tilted over, with something of an impatient lurch, and John had the bomber in sight. He swooped down and fired. An explosion shook the other aircraft, and there was no doubt about the live sparks that showered back as we pulled up and over it.

I stood up and peered out, waiting for the fire to take hold. But there was no red flame of burning petrol. There was nothing more than that trickle of white sparks which looked like splashes from a guttering candle.

Then suddenly the searchlights went out. For a few seconds more I could see the faint trail of sparks from the other aircraft, and then that was gone also. For a moment I could not believe that we had lost our chance of finishing off the job. The change in our fortunes had been so sudden, and I had not realized how dependent we were on the searchlights now that our own AI was not working. We saw nothing more of that enemy raider, and our relief having announced his arrival over the radio, there was nothing left for us to do but return to base and put in a claim for another enemy aircraft damaged.

The crestfallen but ever patient radar mechanics got to work as soon as we landed, and we were able to take off again for another patrol an hour before dawn. This time the AI worked well, but by then the Luftwaffe crews were sleeping peacefully in their own beds. We kept up our dreary vigil alone in the greying sky. The time traces on the cathode ray tubes were empty, and I sat and watched the creeping daylight slowly dim their radiance.

The next night, at almost exactly the same time, the Luftwaffe came again. John and I joined in the general scramble to get off the ground, climbing as hard as the flailing airscrews could make it. Again the searchlights were doing very well, and as we got into position we saw a well-defined cone sweeping down from the north with a tiny silver bird glittering at its apex. It was approaching us fast, and just above our level. There was no time to spare to gain any height advantage, so John turned in on its quarter, levelled out to pick up speed, and then was after it, less than half a mile behind. I checked quickly to make sure that the blip was showing up well on the AI in case the searchlights should suddenly go out again, and then I sat back to see how the chase was going.

The other aircraft, was a Me 410, and the pilot did not seem to be worrying a jot about the searchlights. They had him firmly held in seven or eight beams, and each cluster handed him on to the next, somewhat after the fashion in which a fainting spectator at a football match is handed over the heads of the crowd. So far as I could see this German was taking no evasion at all: he just maintained his height and kept going at full speed. If he did know that we were behind him he did nothing about it, other than to keep his throttles wound wide open. And that was all he needed to do: no matter what we did we were not getting any closer to him.

We were still only very slightly below his level, but we just could not make up those few feet of difference in height. We could hold him by flying level, and we could gain 100 yards or so by going into a gentle dive; but we soon lost our advantage with the range opening up again when John tried to pull up.

By this time we had traversed almost the whole length of Bomb Alley, and the coast was not far ahead. We were nearly beyond the aid of the lights, so John decided to try a long range shot. Even if he did not hit the German, he might induce him to start weaving or doing something else foolish enough to give us a chance to close in. The range was probably still about 700 yards when John fired, and we watched hopefully but in vain for the flash of hits. He tried again, aiming a little higher in case the shells were dropping too far at that distance, but with no better result.

I racked my brains trying to remember the aiming pattern of our cannon. Since the gun-sight was mounted several feet above the guns, it was adjusted so that the line of sight crossed the trajectory of the shells at the most commonly used range. Beyond that range the shells would soar above the line of sight for a certain distance before they dropped again. On my reckoning the shells would still be high at 700 yards. We were still not reducing the range at all, and the searchlights were all behind us by now, their beams beginning to stretch out.

"Try one more, aiming low," I begged. "He must be well beyond the harmonizing point."

John considered the point for a moment. He had to think of conserving his ammunition.

"All right...one more, then," he agreed.

He did not sound too hopeful. He fired, but again there were no results. The target did not even swerve.

One by one the searchlight beams snapped off. Our silver bird began to tarnish, the glitter fading to a dull white. For a few seconds it lingered on in sight, a faint grey phantom. And then it vanished. All that was left was the blip clearly beating on the cathode ray tube.

Now that he was no longer illuminated we expected that he would possibly relax a little and begin to drop off some height or speed or both. That would give us a chance to close in and make a proper attack. He did ease up a little, and as we closed in the blip began to creep very slowly down the trace.

If the Channel had been 10 miles wider at that point we might have had him. As it was, we were still 2,000ft behind when the enemy coast showed up. The temptation to go on was almost overwhelming, especially since we hoped that Mark X AI was going to be released very shortly for use over enemy territory. But the word to go had not been given, and John's discipline was too good to risk prematurely our new wonder weapon. Reluctantly he turned homeward, and our last operational sortie with a squadron was over.

It had been a good run for John. Since 1940 he had been involved in thirty-one combats, in the course of which he had destroyed twenty enemy aircraft, probably destroyed two more, and damaged another seven. He had been close on the tail of at least as many again. The memory of all the contacts I had lost while flying with him rankled in my mind, and I could not help feeling that I should have done better in my share of the partnership.

Had John been the selfish type, the seeker after personal glory, he might well have greatly increased his own score. But he was not the man to sweep others aside – particularly junior officers and NCOs – at the first sign of activity. When it came to a chance of getting to grips with the enemy everyone was always sure of having a fair chance; and John always took his turn as it came, and waited until it did come. Only if the weather was so vile that it was dangerous would he over-ride the pre-arranged order to take-off in order to go and see for himself if conditions were good enough for the others to fly. Because of all that, the morale, and the standard of his crews never flagged. The squadrons under John's command never degenerated into a small bunch of so-called aces with a useless tail of disgruntled and unsuccessful crews. Experienced, efficient and battle-tested, all the crews played their part in creating evenly balanced squadrons.

It had been a very lucky chance for me when my name had been coupled with that of John Cunningham on that crew list nearly seven years before. At a rather sad little leave-taking party at the Bull, John and I were presented with silver tankards by the squadron to serve as mementoes of the time we were with them.

John was not a smoker, and he drank only in moderation. But it was known that he had an extraordinary ability to be able to cope with drinking whenever it became necessary. He was now awarded a second bar to his DSO, and at a celebration in the Mess everybody appeared to have made up their minds to see him off. A start was made at a midday session in which John readily joined. His glass was kept filled in such a way that eventually it became a half-pint glass tankard just about full of straight gin. But John was not going to be defeated. He kept working away at it, and by 3.30 he had polished it off. He looked a little flushed, but he was otherwise under control; and gathering himself together, and with just a shade too much precision, he said:

"Well…I think perhaps a little sleep is indicated."

He went off to his room and slept soundly until just after six. When he reappeared in the Mess he looked as fresh as ever, and he went on with the celebration without turning a hair.

In addition to his DSO and two bars and his DFC and bar, John later received from the Americans a Silver Star, at the same time that several others – Gonsalves and myself included – received American DFCs. And by this time John's brother, who was a Marine Commando, and had been badly wounded in the landings in Sicily, had also been awarded a DSO.

Having already handed over command of the squadron to his successor, Wing Commander C. M. Miller, there was nothing more left for John to do but say a few quiet words of farewell. And then he was gone.

There had been other changes in the squadron, too, and Per Bugge and Johan Räd, finding themselves at the end of their second tours, had wangled more postings that would keep them on active jobs. Johan found his way to a Mosquito Pathfinder squadron, and amongst the other exploits from which he survived was crash landing one night on his load of 2,000lb of bombs after engine failure on take-off. After it was all over he returned to Norway and went into civil aviation.

His navigator, the redoubtable Leif Lövestad – he flew on operations for four years without a rest – stayed with 85 Squadron until the end of the war, when he returned to his own country with a permanent commission in the Royal Norwegian Air Force.

Per Bugge was posted from 85 Squadron to a new unit in Scotland being operated by the Royal Norwegian Air Force. They were flying Lodestars on a run from Leuchars to Stockholm, over the top of occupied Norway. He made over fifty round trips before the war ended.

When I asked him later how he had managed to stay on operational flying throughout the whole war, his eyes twinkled as he muttered in his usual profound and scarcely audible way:

"It was quite easy, really. I just changed squadrons at the right time."

After the war, Per joined John's staff at de Havillands, working on the testing of the Comet.

Claus Björn, who had been Per Bugge's navigator for a long time, stayed on with Leif Lövestad in 85 Squadron. After the war he returned with the others to Norway. He had become troubled with some stomach disorder. Nobody seemed to pay much attention to it, but it finally led to an operation, from which he died. I wondered how much of that stomach trouble was attributable to the way in which he had possibly repressed the effects of the strain he was under in order not to be thought "jellow".

I had been with John for so long that I suppose I had taken it for granted that when he went I should also be posted away to some non-operational job. I was therefore rather taken aback – and not quite so obviously pleased as I suppose I was expected to be – when I was told that if I wished I could recrew with another pilot and remain with the squadron.

It should not have been a difficult decision for me to make, and most navigators would have jumped at the chance to remain on the job. The squadron was on the crest of the wave, trade was booming, and the new tools were just beginning to take on a fine cutting edge. To leave all that and all the good friends I had made would be a bitter wrench. And yet I hesitated about staying.

I was trying desperately hard to face up to the truth, ugly though it might be. And the truth, as I saw it, was that I was not coping with the job, not even with John. This constant feeling of inadequacy had undermined my own self-confidence, and I felt that I was rapidly becoming a Leader in name only.

I liked to think that I had helped to put the squadron navigators on the right road to making the best use of their new AI; but if I could not lead them in practice as well as in principle then I felt that it would be better for the squadron if I handed over the job to someone who could. There were in the squadron three or four first-rate, experienced navigators who were quite fit and ready to fill my shoes. And the Operational Training Units were crammed with up-and-coming youngsters all thirsting for a tour of operational flying.

On the other hand, the old sweats like Pat Patston and Freddie French were sticking it out and not making excuses to get away from flying. And so it was that I had to face – more often than not in the still watches of the night – a still uglier truth. Somehow or other, and certainly without my conscious knowledge, I had allowed myself to become inflicted with the twitch. I felt additionally bitter about it when I realized that it had happened in spite of the fact that I had been flying with the finest pilot that any man could ask for, and that I had a job that every navigator in the command would have relished. But at the thought of flying with somebody else, and the exciting and disturbing prospect of going over to offensive operations, I was making excuses. It was extremely difficult to judge fairly just what was happening to me, and to apply to my own case the same impartial reasoning with which I had tried to settle the doubts of others.

After long and trying searching in my own mind and heart I decided to stand down, and to recommend that Bill Skelton should take over as Navigator Leader. Better, I felt, to get out of operational flying than to stay on setting nothing more than a poor example. I have always felt that the decision I arrived at then was the right one; and I have never stopped reproaching myself for making it.

It was arranged that I should go to FIU, at Ford, and early in March, while I was waiting for the posting to come through, I went up to town on 48 hours' leave. I met Tommy in one of our old pre-war haunts, The Swiss

Cottage. He was quieter than of old, and as unhappy as I was. But at the sight of each other our flagging spirits revived.

At our last meeting, while I was still at Hunsdon, Tommy had told me a little about the special unit to which he and Sandi and Nobby Kennedy had gone as air-gunners, and how they had trailed their coats across enemy territory probing the German defences and recording the frequencies of the German radar and radio. Sandi had also told me that it was not much fun for them as air-gunners since they had learnt quite a lot about night fighting while they were with us in 604 Squadron and they had been able to see for themselves how easily a night fighter could creep in unseen. Both Tommy and Sandi survived, and had become instructors at gunnery schools.

Halfway through March my posting came through and I packed up and moved to Ford, the centre of the night fighter world, and one of the most beautifully sited of all aerodromes. I had visited Ford so often before both on business and pleasure that it was really more like a homecoming than going into exile. The tranquil Arun meandered past, and the lush coastal plain stretched unobstructed to the sea 2 miles to the south. To the north the lovely Sussex Downs rolled along the horizon, and the grey battlements of Arundel Castle – as medieval and as improbable as a fairy tale – jutted from the wooded spur that guarded the Arun gap.

It was inescapable that for me the place should be haunted by so many ghosts. It was here that we had spent our last Auxiliary summer camp before the war, in July 1939, and of our little group of air-gunners so many were dead. Jack Love, who had come back to fly from there as a pilot; Jack Beale and Ray Sellars, who had also become pilots; the debonair Stan Hawke; Sid, Nobby Kennedy, Ron Taylor, Roberts, Oliver, Warry. The list was a long one.

But there were happy memories too, and even some of the serious moments had a lighter side. The Officers' Mess had been set up in a requisitioned school, Tortington Hall, and there had been some pretty rowdy parties there. As a result of so many previous visits I knew my way around Ford, and, as I had expected, I found there many old friends. The station was commanded by Wing Commander Gerald Maxwell, a distinguished pilot of the First World War and an elder brother of Michael Maxwell, who had been with us in 604.

FIU was no longer commanded by Rory Chisholm. He had gone to Bomber Command – with Promotion to the rank of Air Commodore – to be the Senior Staff Officer of No. 100 Group, a highly secret outfit recently formed to co-ordinate all the efforts to frustrate the German night defences with radio and radar counter-measures, intruders and escort night fighters.

FIU's Navigator Leader was a tall Flight Lieutenant named Don Spurgeon, aesthetic in appearance, and the possessor of a fine legal brain. He was hard at work on the testing of yet another new type of AI, in which he was being assisted by a slightly built, thoughtful young navigator, a

Flying Officer named Denis Lake. I was put on to the job of working with them to give a third opinion.

After finding out what the new equipment was all about and doing a couple of practice flights in daylight, I went up with Bill Maguire to try a night interception under the control of "Boffin", the GCI with which John and I had first worked so long ago.

Bill was just the same comfortable, vital character that he had been at West Malling. His was a personality full of enthusiasm for living and for the work he was doing.

"I'll just get my electric hat," he said, going to his locker for his flying-helmet, "and we'll be off."

There was an infectious quality about his manner, and one could not help sharing the spirit of joyful anticipation that we were about to do something new and exciting. This new form of AI had several novel features, and Bill was a good pilot to work with. I had flown with him on night practices during the time we were at West Malling, and I knew how grimly he could hang on in a close-range winding match. We did some good work together that night with the new equipment and my enthusiasm began to rise. On the other hand, like all the wonderfully ingenious and intricate weapons produced almost off the drawing-board, this one had snags too, serious snags that would call for a great deal of work.

I approached my meeting with Don and Denis the next morning to discuss the report we were to put in with rather mixed feelings. But I need not have worried as I found that all three of us had come to more or less the same opinion. We were quite intrigued with the possibilities of the new set, but we were cautious about reporting too favourably on it because we did not want the squadrons to find themselves facing a critical period of the war hopelessly handicapped by promising but inadequate weapons.

In spite of our own agreement in principle, we still found plenty to argue about; but Don's cold logic and Denis's imaginative realism prevailed over my natural cussedness, and in the end we produced a report which not only expressed a reasonably unanimous opinion but which was also, we hoped, fair to both the designers of the new set and to the navigators who might have to use it.

I had only been at Ford about a fortnight when the gloomy news flashed around the station that the unit was moving north to Wittering. The huge air fleets gathering for the launching of the Second Front would be needing every inch of space available on the aerodromes along the south coast, and we had to make way for them.

On the 3rd of April we moved away from the place where FIU had worked for so long, and we went to that apparently endless strip of grass beside the Great North Road, just south of Stamford, where the two airfields of Wittering and Collyweston had been joined into one.

We were to share this vast aerodrome with several other units. One of them was a US Army fighter squadron, equipped with twin-engined Lightnings. They were helping to provide the long-range escort for the massive daylight raids the American Eighth Air Force were putting on over Germany. The pilots were all still fairly new to the job, and they could not resist "buzzing the field" every time they returned from a mission, practice or otherwise. And as this buzzing was, as often as not, made crosswind at 50ft or less, they were not too popular with the other users of the aerodrome – including a Blind Approach School – who, having survived the odd hazard or two of nearly five years of war, were not very keen about having their lives jeopardized by boyish pranks.

The trouble came to a head after an American test pilot had been on a visit to the aerodrome and had given a snorting display of acrobatics. Rather carried away by national pride, some of the American pilots made a boast in the Mess that night about the relative merits of the Lightning and the Spitfire. It was a foolish thing to do. The Lightning was a fine aircraft and it was doing a first-class job of work, but it could scarcely be expected to out-turn a single-engined interceptor like the Spitfire. But the challenge had been made.

The next morning the entire staff of the station was out watching the two aircraft as they took off and climbed into position. Cautiously they circled for a while; and then they turned in and rushed at each other. As we had expected, within a few seconds the Spitfire was sitting firmly on the tail of the Lightning. The American pilot put up a magnificent show and did everything but turn his aircraft inside out; but nothing he could do could shake off the tenacious Spitfire. Finally the twin-engined Lightning broke off the match and came spiralling in to land. On the approach the American pilot feathered one of his propellers and came in on one engine, as if to say to the pilot of the Spitfire:

"There's something you can't do!"

But the British pilot was not to be outdone. As he continued on his circuit around the aerodrome he rolled over on to his back and flicked his wheels out into the landing position. Still upside down he turned to make his final approach to land. At the last moment he neatly rolled back into the normal position just in time to make a faultless touch-down. Harmony and a blissful silence was restored to the Mess.

And then suddenly I found that I was posted again, this time to Headquarters, No. 11 Group. John had been pulling at those strings again.

CHAPTER TWENTY-SIX

The Great Day

T HE feeling I had when I entered the famous Headquarters of No. 11 Group at Uxbridge was by no means comparable with the sinking depression that had come over me when I had first arrived at Avening. It was true that I was back to an office job, but this time the office was at the centre of things. And great things were afoot.

Group Headquarters – from which since the outbreak of war there had been directed the air defence of south-eastern England, and from which there was stage-managed the Battle of Britain – lay within the perimeter of the very shrine of the great Bull God of the Royal Air Force. For years before the war, Uxbridge had been the first and terrifying home for all the new recruits. But the Group Headquarters were apart from all that. After entering the sacred portals of the main camp one skirted the sacrosanct drill squares and then descended a slope to a narrow, meandering stream spanned by a rough wooden foot bridge. Once across this Rubicon one was no longer on the forbidding ground of the training centre but in Group territory; and the blatant, distorted bugle calls that blared from the Tannoy speakers in the temples of the square bashers could with relief be ignored.

A path led on up the opposite slope to a hutted camp dispersed among the trees crowning a hill and looking out with a pleasant view across a golf links to the sombre barrack blocks of The Other Camp beyond. There was little to indicate that from just outside the main gates there were trolley-buses and tube-trains rattling their dismal way to nearby London.

After booking in I found my way to John's office, one of a row of poky little wooden cells opening off a dingy corridor in one of the huts. John was busy, but one of the first people I met was George Cooke, now a Squadron Leader, with whom, I discovered, I was to share an office as he, also, was now on Headquarters Staff.

We were, I gathered, rather a self-contained little empire. It was a pleasant prospect sharing an office with George as I had known him for some time. He and Bob Wright had been together in the Filter Room at the Headquarters of Fighter Command at the beginning of the war; and he also had quietly cajoled his way out of that job deep underground into flying as a radar operator. His greying hair and an almost grown-up family were the only indications of his age. He had had his full share of flying on operations, had been wounded in the hand, and was now bringing to some of the problems of the Great Venture the value of his outstandingly successful legal brain. Another feat to George's credit was that he also helped to dispel a sinister rumour that had once circulated amongst the radar operators about the possible effects of all the short-wave radiation to which they were subjecting themselves with their AI sets. In the most practical demonstration possible, George and his wife, having already reared one family, proceeded to everybody's delight to embark upon the raising of another.

After seeing John, I was taken to meet the Senior Air Staff Officer, Air Commodore C. A. Bouchier, known throughout the Air Force as "Boy". He was a brisk, peppery little man with a razor-keen brain which made him explosively intolerant of inefficiency in others; but despite the load he was carrying, he retained a good sense of humour. He was engaged on the colossal task of writing the operational order which was to provide the fighter cover for the launching of the Second Front. On his foresight and thoroughness there would depend the efficiency of the whole of that mighty umbrella of Allied fighter aircraft which would have the job of shielding the invasion fleets from the Luftwaffe.

One of the first things I had to learn in my new job was the structure of the command under which I was serving. Fighter Command, a name which had served so well for so long, had reverted to an old pre-war, and unpopular, title of Air Defence of Great Britain, under the command of Air Marshal Sir Roderick Hill. No. 11 Group was still commanded by Air Vice Marshal H. W. L. Saunders – whom we knew so well as "Dingbat" – and was the most important of the Groups in Air Defence of Great Britain.

Now, in those little wooden cells at Group Headquarters, the Air Staff were racking their brains and sweating over the Invasion Plan that had been evolved, known as "Overlord", a magic word that was spoken in whispers. They had to see that the plan was executed, and nothing must be overlooked and nothing must be allowed to go awry.

John was pretty well tied to his desk for some time after my arrival, labouring away at the paper work which he so disliked. But he knew that this was paper work with a difference, and he was putting his heart into it.

George Cooke and I worked directly under John on night operations. It was essential that someone should be on hand in the office, so while George held the fort there I made the most of my time with a high-speed tour of the night fighter stations, getting to know as many of the people as I could, listening to their complaints and suggestions, and comparing their ideas. The squadrons were moving around so fast that it was quite difficult to keep track of them all. This was particularly true of the units selected to go into 85 Group – one of the groups to take part in the invasion – which were organized on a highly mobile basis.

There was a good deal of umbrage being taken about the selection of the night fighter squadron for 85 Group. Those who were not chosen to go on the great adventure felt themselves slighted and were not at all happy in the comparative comfort of permanent quarters and a defensive role on home stations. Like disappointed children unable to understand why they had been left off the list for the Annual Outing, they watched with wistful expressions on their faces while the more fortunate ones pitched their tents and charged around in a Cowboy and Indian fashion, complete with field cookers and mess tins.

But their disappointment was a little premature. The Luftwaffe, unable to risk its bombers or even its reconnaissance aircraft in daylight, sent over a series of night raids against the most likely assembly areas. Portsmouth, Southampton, Weymouth and Plymouth all had visits from the Luftwaffe, followed by scattered raids on places as far west as Dartmouth and Start Point. These night raids cost them at least 22 aircraft and crews shot down by our night defences.

Out on the airfields there was no escaping the feeling of mounting tension. There were 17 night fighter and intruder squadrons available to keep the night watches, and into that small south-east corner of England where the Battle of Britain had once hung so precariously in the balance there were now crowded 171 Allied day fighter and fighter-bomber squadrons. All day long they roared off the ground, from first light until dusk, blotting out the sun with swirling dust clouds, and drowning out even the deeper throbbing of the great armadas of medium and heavy bombers that were passing high overhead on their way to pound the Reich. It was a good setting for Maurice Baring's words:

Squadrons and Wings, Brigades: a mighty host.

I had been at Group only a short time when, one afternoon, Bob Wright walked into our office. Just back from the Mediterranean, he was looking thin and tired after what he described as "a year of sweating it out in Cairo". At the end of his first tour of flying – which had finished in French North Africa – Bob had gone to the Headquarters of Middle East Command, in Egypt. He had spent the year there on the staff, the latter part of it as Personal Assistant to the Air Officer Commanding-in-Chief, Air Marshal Sir Keith Park, who had distinguished himself as the Air Officer Commanding No. 11 Group in the Battle of Britain. Now Bob was back in England for a second tour of flying; and he was hoping to be able to follow in the footsteps of so many of his friends from 604 and find his way to 85 Squadron.

It seemed to me that Bob had spent an enormous amount of effort since the war started trying to get out of jobs for which by training and through experience he was admirably suited and which a great many people would have regarded as most desirable. He had now been Personal Assistant to three different Commanders-in-Chief, and he had had rare experience as a staff officer. And here he was, yet again wangling his way back to flying. And it was not because he liked it: he admitted quite frankly that he detested it. So I asked him just why he felt compelled to get back to operations.

"What the hell else can I do?" he demanded.

It was a fair enough answer. The compulsion to get to an active job was there in so many of us, an almost indefinable force that had to be expressed. But although I could sympathize with the way he felt, I did not go out of my way to encourage Bob's return to operational flying. For one thing, I felt, as did a lot of other people, that he had done enough of that, and that he would be of far more value on the staff. But more important than that was a vague feeling I had, a premonition which I discovered later I shared with several other people, some of whom were at that time unknown to me, that Bob was headed for trouble.

The word went around that The Plan was complete. All that was needed for "Overlord" was the naming of the day. That was something to look forward to. In the meantime, we had other troubles. John showed me some aerial photographs. They were of some clearings in wooded country, pock-marked with bomb craters. There were a few huts about, and some curious tracks shaped rather like the letter J.

I had already read the Intelligence reports on Hitler's secret weapons, of which the VI was given the code name of "Diver". It was known to be some kind of pilotless aircraft, mass produced and expendable. What I was looking at now, John explained, was the modified type of launching site for the VI which was being built in large numbers along the coast of France just across the Channel. It appeared that the sites were being prepared faster than the bombers could smash them, and the threat was that the Germans were thinking in terms of launching 1,000 of the things a day.

I thought of all the massive and solidly packed rows of equipment, and the densely crowded troops waiting for D Day, the launching of "Overlord", of the docks and the shipping, and of what such an onslaught could do, and it was a dreadful prospect. And that was quite apart from the normal targets such as the big cities and the vital centres of control and communications.

John explained that it was hoped that the Tempests would be able to catch the things. It was known that they would be very fast, and he was not at all happy about the chances of the Mosquito against this new target. I was inclined to agree with him. When I pictured to myself what it would be like making a right-angled interception, diving at the same time to pick up speed, I did not feel very optimistic about our chances. John went on to explain that there was some talk of using a special fuel in conjunction with an extraordinary high boost for the engines, to be used with a strict time limit.

I thought rather gloomily of my friends and relations in London with this new threat hanging over their heads. My mother and sister were still there, and my wife was at that Army Headquarters on the outskirts of London. And John's home was right at the receiving end of Bomb Alley.

"We'll just have to keep our fingers crossed," he said. "If you hear the word 'Diver', you'll know that it's started."

But the weeks dragged on, and nothing happened. My thoughts became more occupied with my own particular job, and I managed to get in another hasty trip around the squadrons. The last call I made on that tour was at Hurn, near Bournemouth, where 604 Squadron – now, to their delight, in 85 Group – were tucked away in a corner of the crowded, dusty airfield. They were in high spirits, and looking forward to things to come. Almost the first person I met when I arrived there was Jack ("Doughy") Baker, now a Flight Sergeant, who had been one of the keenest of the Auxiliary engine fitters at Hendon before the war, and who had been with the squadron ever since.

Doughy told me that there were a few more of the old hands still left in the squadron. He also called my attention to the fact that they still had with them the squadron badge. On a pole by the Flight tent there was a metal plaque bearing the badge which I remembered used to be on the gates of the squadron's Town Headquarters on Hampstead Heath. He told me that Mick Wheadon had gone there the morning after that fine old house had been hit and had rescued the plaque from the ruins.

The officers of the squadron had their quarters in an old school not far from the aerodrome. It was devoid of all furniture and fittings, and in keeping with what lay ahead of them they were making do with candle light and camp equipment, which all served only to raise even higher their already high spirits.

The squadron was now commanded by Michael Maxwell, and his operator, John Quinton, was Navigator Leader. I stayed the night with them, and the next morning Maxwell was summoned to Headquarters. When he returned in the afternoon he had a Top Secret envelope in his pocket, and there was a sparkle in his eyes.

"Does that mean that I ought to be getting back?" I asked.

"I should say rather that it was a good reason for stopping here," he replied.

I was sorely tempted to play truant, and to stay there and join in what was going to happen. But my place was in the office, so I dashed off to catch a train.

I met John Quinton again once or twice after the war. He was very unsettled after he was demobilized, and eventually he rejoined the Air Force. Some years later he was involved in an accident in the air, and he sacrificed his life by giving his parachute to a cadet and forcing him out of their wrecked aircraft before it crashed. For that gallant act he was awarded a posthumous George Cross.

On my way back to Group I passed through London, and I rang Micki and we met for a drink. We chatted of trivialities, but my mind was really occupied with the greatness of the hour. I listened, wondering if there might be any careless talk. But all around us in that crowded bar the same sort of idle chatter was going on, with not a sign of anything untoward. Long afterwards Micki told me that in her work at Army Headquarters many of the vital signals had passed through her hands, but not knowing that I was in on the secret too she had naturally said nothing. We had parted quite casually to return to our separate offices.

When I walked into the Mess at Uxbridge late that evening everything was going on just as usual. There was no excitement, there was no rushing about, there were no furtive whisperings. On the home front, at any rate, the great secret was being well kept.

I headed for the centre of things, the Operations Room, known to so many as "The Hole" because of its depth underground. The way down was along a many-flighted stairway, and it lead into an atmosphere that caught at the throat. It was hot and steamy and stale; and yet it was electric. All doubt that I might have had about anything happening was immediately dispelled when I got down there. Every holder of a pass in the Group was in the place, and there could be no doubt that this was the night we had been waiting for.

Elbowing my way across the Intelligence Room, I looked up at the great wall-maps upon which there was displayed the shape of things: the position of the convoys, with the arrows stabbing across the Channel towards the beaches of Normandy. I went on through the doors into the silence of the control gallery, which consisted of a number of little rooms overlooking the great plotting-table on the floor below. Sheets of plate glass, inclined outward to avoid glare, shut off the subdued hubbub of the tellers and the plotters gathered like croupiers around the table.

In the cabin in the centre of the gallery the Air Officer Commanding sat beside the controller. He was a reassuring figure of massive, quiet confidence. His Senior Air Staff Officer – Boy Bouchier – was already at sea on board one of the Fighter Director Tenders. These were nothing more than GCI control stations on board ship. After all the planning, the SASO was going to get a front-line view of the show, and even now he was watching from the bridge as the dim shapes of that great multitude of craft started groping their way across the Channel towards the Norman coast. The rest of the Air Staff were down there in the Hole in their full strength, along with a dense crowd of liaison officers of all Services, inevitably getting in the way of the more actively employed teams from Intelligence, Air-Sea Rescue, Met. and all the others.

Slowly the hours ticked by, and down on the plotting-table the Plan unfolded as the plastic convoys inched across the painted Channel. It was hard to realize that at last the event that we had all waited for and thought about for so long was actually taking place. It was not long, however, before the table was a welter of plaques as the air patrols crossed and recrossed, mingling with the complicated tracks of the seaborne assault.

The controller sat hunched in his chair, watching his patrols, waiting for the enemy's reaction. But of the Luftwaffe there was no sign.

We sat and waited, sweating in that confined, tense silence. The hardened smokers licked their lips and slipped out now and again for a cigarette. Smoking had been banned because of the over-crowding.

The plaques representing the convoys slowly neared their objectives. Further up the Channel the great air spoof that was to fool the enemy as to the exact place chosen for the landings was slowly working its way towards the Pas de Calais. Our standing patrols of night fighters came and went, and still there was no reaction.

The clock on the wall ticked on, and we yawned and stirred. The faint light must now be gleaming on the bow waves of the ships. The men were probably fidgeting with their weapons, waiting for the word to go. Back on the fighter airfields, the pilots of the day fighters would be buckling on their harness; and the silence would be shattered by the crack of the Kaufmann starters as the aircraft engines sprang to life.

Under the glaring strip lighting in the Hole everybody looked frowsty and haggard. The plots of the first day fighter patrols were being pushed across the board, and one by one the last of the night watch came back from the beaches where the liberation of Europe was starting. D Day was born, and the Second Front was launched, and sitting there deep underground I had seen history made.

I came up into the sharp, clean air, blinking in the bright morning light; and as I looked around I saw on the faces of the others who had been down in the Hole with me a vague, faraway look. They were like a matinée audience emerging from a theatre, not quite able to free their minds from the world of make-believe they had just left behind. But what they had seen was not make-believe.

John was itching to go and have a look at things. On the third night after the landings we went down to Ford, and he moved 96 Squadron there from West Malling.

We climbed out across the Channel, and were taken over by one of the Fighter Direction Tenders. It was a dark night, and there was not much we would see other than the gun flashes and a few fires in the neighbourhood of Caen. Our arrival coincided with that of a low-flying raid on the shipping in the anchorage off the beaches. The Controller put us in to it rather hastily, and I did not get a contact until it was crossing close in front of our bows. John whipped around after it, but the blip eluded me in the ground echoes that swirled around the tube on the turn. The Controller gave us more vectors to try and help, but the enemy raider was now milling around fairly low over the sea, and although I had one fleeting contact I could not hold it.

They had another customer for us, and they sent us in over the coast and inland to meet it. Then they turned us quickly, and brought us slap out across the beaches and the shipping. There was no sign of a contact, and the Controller's voice was raised almost to a shout as he tried to make himself heard over the radio above a fiendish din of gunfire that had broken out in the background. Judging by the noise, there were a lot of people shooting at something. I still had no joy, so I took a quick look outside. From what I saw it was quite obvious that the something they were shooting at was us. After the two previous alarms it had only needed the sound of our engines overhead to start the gunners in the ships blazing away.

Opening the throttles, John went down in a diving curve. I looked out of the side window, and I saw the best firework display I had ever come across. Every gun in the anchorage seemed to be hosing up a stream of tracer, and a fortune in steel and lead must have coned up into the empty vortex of sound that trailed us across the sky. But I did not get the slightest sign of a contact, and at the end of the patrol John turned in the direction of England. As we droned back towards the Sussex coast I reflected sadly that perhaps old gentlemen should not try to come out of retirement. It was all right for John, but I had made a mess of two interceptions. They were, admittedly, difficult ones; but it proved yet again how necessary it was for an operator to be in practice if he was to be of any use.

CHAPTER TWENTY-SEVEN

Weapons of Revenge

WITH my wife now at the Army GHQ at Hounslow, it gave us a chance to meet more frequently, and one Sunday morning, shortly after the flying-bomb attack started, we arranged to get away for a few hours in the country.

As we passed through the barrier on to the platform at Victoria there came to my car, faint but distinct above all the hubbub of the station, a familiar throbbing sound.

"Do you hear what I hear?" I asked Micki.

"Yes," she said, "I'm afraid I do."

We quickened our pace a little. The throbbing quickly became louder and more strident and vicious as we continued walking along a platform that had suddenly become deserted. There was no cover we could take, apart from baling out on to the railway lines, so we made for the waiting train. The lofty roof of the station, already denuded of its glass, looked horribly flimsy, and it began to shake with the wild beating in the air. The dubious shelter of the nearest carriage of the train looked a long way away.

"I suppose it isn't done for ATS officers to lie down in public?" I asked, almost hopefully.

"And I suppose it isn't done for Air Force officers to start running!" Micki retorted.

I had not noticed that the pace of our walking would have done credit to a Rifle Regiment. The throbbing in the air had swollen to a fiendish, staccato crackling, and the ground itself seemed to be trembling. It seemed that the wretched thing must be overhead, but still the din went on getting louder and closer. And then the guns joined in, the shells whining up and bursting with angry cracks close overhead.

Just as I opened the carriage door, the crash of another salvo was overwhelmed by the bellowing crescendo of the last dive of the flying-bomb. In my hurry to get to shelter I trod on the heels of my wife's shoes. The roar of the explosion shook the windows of the carriage. We sat down, panting in the uncanny silence. And then, with a clatter and bustle, the station came to life again; and people grinned feebly at one another with the inevitable self-satisfaction of those who had been bombed but who had escaped.

The train pulled out of the station, crossed the river, and wound its way through the warren of the sprawling suburbs towards the peaceful Surrey hills. Back in London, the rescue squads and the ambulances were converging on the shambles of what had once been the Guards Chapel in Wellington Barracks.

No. 85 Squadron had been transferred to Bomber Command only a few weeks before the flying-bomb attack started. Their new job was in 100 Group, helping to provide long-range night fighter escort for the bombers; and everybody in the squadron was dead keen on this new freelance job because it meant going on to the offensive. It also meant that the navigators had to do a lot of hard work in order to bring their navigation up to the exacting standard required for the long night flights. The aircraft were fitted with Gee and other aids, and they were just getting into shape – it was a rushed job and the squadron was under orders to become operational as soon as possible – when the flying-bombs started coming over.

With the transfer to Bomber Command the squadron had moved from West Malling to Swannington, in Norfolk; and then almost straight away they were switched back to a defensive role, flying from Norfolk to do their patrols against the flying-bombs down in the Channel. Then they were brought back to West Malling to go on to the purely defensive work, on patrols in the area inland between the coastal guns and the balloons.

"They're not taking very kindly to the idea," John told me. "We'd better go down to meet them."

We flew to West Malling in the Headquarter's Oxford, and we got there just after the squadron had arrived. We found that they were indeed far from happy. The navigators were particularly annoyed.

"Just as we were getting into our stride on some real navigation," one of them complained, "we have to come here to do nothing but watch our pilots play at bomb busting."

Bob Wright was with the squadron, and I talked to him about the way things were going. Being, like myself, one of the old timers who had never done a full navigation course, he was finding it all intensely interesting, but rather heavy going. But he stressed the extraordinarily high pitch to which the morale of the squadron was tuned. And, along with the others, he was fascinated with the prospect of doing a full job of navigation as well as keeping a radar watch. On the other hand, he also reminded me that quite a few of them had their families in London. His own mother and father were living slap in the middle of Bomb Alley, a fact that I was to remember some months later.

But, in spite of all this, the squadron were quite happy to be back at West Malling, and living in the Manor House again. I gathered that the amenities of life in Bomber Command, particularly on a new station, were not quite up to the standard of Fighter Command; and it made a break for them before starting in earnest on the more strenuous work ahead. They were at West Malling for a month, and then they finally returned to Swannington and their new job.

Bomb busting soon became a popular diversion for quite a number of the livelier types among the staff officers at Headquarters, and a welcome relief from the tedium of office routine. My opposite number at Headquarters, Fighter Command, had already had a good look at a flying-bomb in the air when his pilot managed to take their Mosquito close alongside one in daylight. He 'phoned me about it, and was full of praise for the technical excellence of the wretched thing.

"They go like a bomb, well of course they would," he said. "But you know what I mean. Nicely finished jobs, too. Flush riveting and everything!"

After that I had to try and have a look at the thing myself. I went on a visit to 96 Squadron, which, being at Ford, was in the thick of things. They had already put up quite a formidable score, and they had managed to get things down to a fairly regular matter of routine, although there were still quite enough hazards about the game to take the edge off monotony.

The job 96 had was to fill a section of the line of fighters patrolling out in the Channel, beyond the guns. It was a dreary enough beat between salvoes, and an awkward spot in which to have engine trouble because between them and their base lay the lethal concentration of the gun belt. Anything coming in low, straight and level, and not through the recognized point of entry for the fighters, could count on being blown out of the sky. As any engine trouble that was going usually occurred after attacking a bomb, the unfortunate fighter had little alternative but to try and get to the coast low, straight and level.

But it appeared that the engines were standing up pretty well to the caning they were getting. Most of the trouble was coming from bits and pieces of the exploding flying-bombs when they were hit. Usually the fighters were only 300 yards behind when they opened fire, and as they were doing about 350 miles an hour there was not much they could do other than fly straight on through the explosion.

I was anxious to find out at first hand what it was all like, and they agreed to let me go on one of the patrols. I went off with Peter Green – who was now one of the Flight Commanders – warned that there was not much for the navigator to do, other than read off ranges, but that I would probably get a good view of everything.

We crossed out over the guns, keeping at a respectable height, just as a salvo of flying-bombs was launched from the other side. It was twilight, and the Germans were probably trying the cunning move of firing the things off at about the time the day and night squadrons would be changing over. But they were wrong in their reasoning and their timing. Both lots of fighters were in position, arrangements having been made that the changeover should overlap.

"Here they come," Peter said. "You can see the things 20 miles on a night like this, and it's difficult at first to judge how close you are."

I could see a number of twinkling flames away over the French coast, but they might have been 10 or 2 miles away for all I could tell.

"Those are too far up the coast," Peter said. "'We had a lot of fun when we first started. Every fighter for miles around tried to go for the first arrival. Now we know better."

More little comets were springing up from the French coast. What was left of the light was behind us; and the exhaust flames of the bombs looked deceptively close.

"This one ought to be within reach," Peter said. He opened up the throttles a little. "We dive in from the quarter. Be ready to switch on the nav lights as we go in. Someone else might be after it."

He had already warned me to keep an eye on the radar, and to let him know when we were 300 yards astern of the bomb. The flame which Peter had singled out was rapidly coming closer, and we were flying along the coast, at right angles to the course of the bomb, trying to head it off.

The hum of the Merlins rose to a snarling howl as Peter turned in on a perfectly timed curve, and began to dive on to the bomb. Reluctantly I lowered my head into the visor of the AI set to read off the range. At the same time I remembered the navigation lights, and I groped along the row of switches with my right hand, trying to recall from memory whether it was the third or the fourth switch from the front.

We went down in the dive, and the sea echoes swirled around the tube of the AI set; and then the blip from our target blinked in from the right and centred itself. I began to call off the range.

"2,500ft…2,000…look out, there's another contact coming in from the left, between us and the target…"

"Oh…b-blast the man!" Peter exclaimed.

He was levelling out as I glanced up from the seat. At that moment the interloper switched on his lights. He was almost directly in our line of fire.

"I'm afraid we've had that one," Peter said.

He pulled up out of the way just as another set of lights flicked on to our right. And then another pair came blundering past below us. The air began to turn blue with highly unorthodox exchanges over the radio.

"One Five coming in for this one," a confident voice announced.

"You'd better not," another voice cut in. "I'm just about to press the tit."

The whole gaggle surged in towards the distant line of quivering fire that marked the guns at the coast. And from the murk below an unseen ship pumped up a hopeful stream of tracer. Against the faint light that still lingered in the western sky I could see a section of Tempests, reluctant to leave the fun, diving into the mêlée. Then someone got in a shot before the waiting guns could have a go, and we saw the splash of flame as the bomb exploded on the water.

As they had promised, I got a good view of things. On the following night, flying with Flight Lieutenant J. A. Dobie, I had an even better view.

Dobie was an experienced hand at the game, and he was calm and methodical about the way he went about things. We set off on patrol, but nothing happened for a long time. I pictured to myself the line of fighters strung out all along the south and south-east coasts, beating up and down like yachts waiting for the starting gun. And then the little twinkling flames began to spring up over the French coast. We made a last check around the cockpit, and settled in our seats.

One of the flying-bombs was obviously heading our way, and Dobie began to get into position, carefully weighing up the relative courses. He was nicely placed as we ran in for the final turn, but of course I could not keep my mouth shut.

"Don't you think we ought to cut the corner a bit sharper?" I pleaded, afraid of being pushed out of things again by somebody else.

"I don't think so," Dobie said. He knew what he was doing. "But I will if you like."

He tightened up his turn, and as a result we found ourselves a few seconds later almost vertically above the bomb, swinging from side to side in order to keep it in sight, and waiting for it to draw ahead. Our height was 2,500ft, which gave us an advantage of about 1,000ft over our target. I flattened my face against the side window trying to see the thing.

"Sorry about the turn," I said. "It's beginning to draw ahead now."

Dobie pushed the nose down, and opened up the throttles. I stood up, and I could see the bomb as it came into view under our nose, its sleek, shark-like sides gleaming in the light of the wavering plume of flame that trailed behind it. Although the frightful racket of its exhaust was barely audible above the howling of our over-speeding engines, there was something awesome and full of fiendish purpose in the unswerving flight of the bomb, something outrageous in its brazen indifference to close scrutiny. I felt a strong temptation to warn Dobie not to get too close because it might see us.

We were rocketing down through the wake of hot exhaust gases, and I had a quick glimpse right into the fiery maw of the beastly thing before I remembered that I had a job to do. I quickly turned my attention to the AI set.

"1,000ft…900…" I told Dobie.

"Right," he said. "Here goes."

I looked up as the guns crashed briefly; and I immediately ducked down again. The bomb had burst just 300 yards ahead of us, and we were rushing at over 150 yards a second straight at the heart of the explosion. For a few seconds the jet of air from the ventilator or close to my head blew hot and acrid; but we were still flying. Sitting up and looking back, I saw that the air behind us was full of glowing red fragments still fanning out and floating downwards.

Dobie was coolly checking his instruments, and pulling up so as to gain precious height. I did a little instrument checking for myself: oil temperatures and pressures normal, fuel all right, even the AI working. But when I looked outside I could see something white sticking up from the elevator balance.

"Don't look now," I said, "but we seem to have a foreign body embedded in the tail. I can't see what it is."

"Have we, though?" Dobie replied. He seemed to be quite unperturbed. "It feels all right on the controls, but I suppose we'd better go back and have it looked at."

When we landed we found that it was only a piece of fabric that had been torn loose. I realized that Dobie had taken it all in his stride, just as all these crews had been doing for weeks past. I was happy to find that with success, even one in which I had been little more than a spectator, the old, easy mantle of nonchalance had come back to me. I had enjoyed my night out; but, on the other hand, I was not sorry that I would not be making of it a nightly occurrence.

Chasing these flying-bombs was not the tame target practice that many people had thought it was going to be, and there were quite a few casualties. Edward Crew had the nose of his Mosquito split open in an explosion following an attack; but he managed to gain enough height to get in over the top of the guns. He held the barely manageable aircraft in the air long enough for his navigator – Warrant Officer W. R. Croysdill, who had also been with us in 604 – to be able to bale out over land, and then he also jumped out. They both got down quite safely, landing near Worthing, although Croysdill slightly damaged his ankle.

The other Flight Commander of 96, Squadron Leader Alistair Parker-Rees, and the Navigator Leader, Flight Lieutenant Geoffrey Bennet, also ran into trouble as they were about to make an attack. They had already destroyed two bombs during their patrol, and they were about to open fire on a third when they were hit by fire which came up with tracer past their nose. They could not make it back to land and they had to jump for it, and they spent the next six hours in the water. But eventually the Navy came to the rescue. The imperturbable Geoff was picked up first, and he had things so well worked out that he was able to give his rescuers a course to follow to pick up his pilot.

But not all the crews were as fortunate as Parker-Rees and Bennett. The low height at which they had to operate – some of the bombs came in below 1,000ft – gave little chance for getting out if anything suddenly went wrong. It was essential, in order to be sure of hitting their target, that they should open fire at a range of not more than 300 yards. Most of the crews that disappeared without warning were probably engulfed in the explosion before they had time to know what was happening. Among the navigators that were lost was James Farrar, a promising young writer.

Finally the Germans were driven back beyond the limit of the range from which they could fire the flying-bombs and still reach England. But even then they had one last card to play. Salvoes of bombs began to appear from the east, coming in across East Anglia. It was quickly discovered that these were being launched from specially adapted Heinkels operating from Dutch bases. With the bomb slung underneath, these Heinkels would fly low over the sea so as to avoid detection by our coastal radar chain until they were within range of London. Then they would bob up to 1,000ft or so and stay there just long enough to perform the perilous job of sending the flying-bomb on its way.

Since the Germans dared not risk these launching aircraft during daylight, the main burden of this new attack fell on the night fighter squadrons stationed along the east coast. It could scarcely be expected of Anti-Aircraft Command that they should contemplate extending the gun belt right up the coast. The interception and destruction of the Heinkels was no easy matter because they operated outside our radar control coverage and even when AI contact was made and an interception was completed it was still a sticky business trying to spot and shoot at an aircraft so low down over the sea.

I talked with one of the crews right after they had landed from a long, tiring patrol off the Dutch coast. They had had a frustrating experience, and they were understandably indignant.

"We were close behind him for miles," the navigator wailed, "but he was so close to the water we just couldn't get at him without swimming. I had to watch the radar altimeter as well as the AI while the skipper tried to spot him."

"Didn't he pull up at all to launch the bomb?" I asked.

"I'll say he did!" the pilot broke in bitterly. "I closed in and spotted him. I could even see the thing hanging under the wing. But before I could fire somebody went and lit the blue paper. There was a dirty great flash as the bomb went whooshing off on its way, and for the next five minutes I could see sweet Fanny. I had to pull up in case I hit the deck, and that was that."

But even these difficulties were overcome. A Fighter Director ship was sent out to help; and then a Wellington was fitted up as an airborne radar control station. This outfit patrolled up and down the Dutch coast with a bevy of night fighters trailing behind its radar beacon. It was all right so long as the airborne director could continue on a straight course, but when it had to change course in the middle of an interception, things for the Controller became highly complicated.

But in spite of all these snags, the fighters did well. They attacked 24 of the launching Heinkels, destroying 16, probably destroying 4 more, and damaging another 4.

Driven back from their Dutch bases, the Luftwaffe made a last effort to maintain the attack from bases in Western Germany. It culminated in the launching of some 50 bombs against Manchester on Christmas Eve, 1944. This vicious thrust caused over 100 casualties, but it was almost the last fling.

But even before the flying-bombs were brought to a halt, the second of the weapons of revenge, the V2, started falling. These rockets were altogether beyond the capabilities of any fighters to intercept so the night fighters played no part in the defensive measures taken against them. All that could be done was for the bombers and fighter-bombers to attack in daylight the rockets at the places from which they were fired. But it was not until the Armies on the Continent had forced the Germans right back beyond range that the threat from this weapon, as with that from the flying-bomb, was finally eliminated.

CHAPTER TWENTY-EIGHT

The Foreign Shore

D URING the time that the home squadrons had been coping with the flying-bombs, the night fighters in 85 Group had been pressing on with the invading armies, fighting a mixed battle of attack and defence against a still more mixed assortment of customers. Sometimes they even ran across a marauding German night fighter bristling with cannon and radar aerials, and only too eager for the chance to whip around and bite its pursuer.

They were rarely without the benefit of close ground control to help them in their dealings with the strange assortment of aircraft the Luftwaffe were throwing into the battle. At first they had the Fighter Director ships, and then, as the battle moved inland, they were helped by the mobile control stations which John Brown had had a big hand in organizing. But the Sultan of Starlight had done more than just organize them: he had also imbued the itinerant controllers with the fine spirit of his own initiative. Following hard on the heels of the advance, they deployed their dust-covered caravans almost into the front lines, and within an hour or two of their arrival at a new site their reassuring voices were directing the fighters with the confidence and calm of a practice interception in a quiet sector in England.

The squadrons in France were thus able to enjoy at least some of the same benefits as those at home. Their primary role was still defence, even though their patrol lines were pushed out so far over enemy territory. But the Germans also had their control system. There was, therefore, every chance of things developing into a controllers' battle, with the opposing fighters as the pawns.

Brownie was to the fore in all this. He had left Starlight early in 1942. Later he had been busy in the North African landings, organizing the running of GCI stations all the way along the coast to Tunisia. From that he had continued with the invasion of Sicily, and then on up into Italy. That unbounded enthusiasm of his was driving him all the time with an urgent, pioneering spirit, and now he was in France, bringing up his caravans close behind the advancing troops. The solid magnificence and comforts of the new, static GCI stations at home were not for Brownie: he had to be always in the van, delighting in the hurly-burly of front-line improvisation.

Although at 11 Group Headquarters we were somewhat preoccupied with the flying-bombs, we also held a watching brief over the affairs of the 85 Group squadrons until they ceased to operate from our home stations; and after they had loaded up their convoys and at last moved across the

Channel we kept in touch with their activities by telephone and teleprinter, although they were no longer under our control.

The knowledge I had acquired of so many of those in our small night fighter world added a human warmth to the cold figures of the reports and statistics that came pouring into our office. It was with a feeling of personal understanding and pleasure that one read of their successes, just as one felt all the deeper the personal grief in their losses. The 100th aircraft destroyed by 604 was disposed of over the Normandy beaches by Michael Maxwell and John Quinton. At the same time we heard that Nigel Bunting – who, a few months before, had been such a stalwart in 85 Squadron during our time at West Malling – was missing, believed killed. Phil Reed had been saved from flying with Nigel that night by an attack of influenza.

John worked hard and loyally at his desk although there were also plenty of official visits to stations and squadrons that he had to make. When he was away I often had to stay behind to hold the fort. But we still managed to make occasional trips together, and it was then that I marvelled again at the extraordinary gift he had for finding, rather like a homing pigeon, the right course to follow to get across country.

We never did any flight planning for these trips for the simple reason that there was never any time to spare for more than a hasty word with the Met. people about the weather, and a grab at a few maps before we were on our way.

"What's the course?" John would ask as soon as we were airborne.

I would make some frantic mental calculations, juggling with wind speeds, variation and deviation, and if I had a computer with me I would twiddle furiously at it for a few minutes. And then I would give him an answer.

"I make it two five five."

"Oh…nonsense!" John would protest.

Then, seeing how crestfallen I was, he would tone it down a little.

"Surely it can't be as much as that? Let's have a look at the map." He would give it a cursory glance. "I'll try two four five for a bit and see how it goes."

I had learnt better than to argue about it, no matter what the computer said. He would steer two four five – or whatever other course he might have decided upon – and after a while our destination would show up ahead, dead on track. It made me feel that I might just as well throw my computer away and work things out by holding up a wet finger to the wind.

It was on one of these trips, coming back from Swannington, in Norfolk, after a visit to 85 Squadron, that John suddenly looked at his watch and commented:

"If we cut across a bit further east we ought to be in time to intercept the airborne show."

We had seen and knew all about the plan for seizing by airborne troops the bridges over the Lower Rhine at Arnhem and over the Waal at Nijmegen, and it had made impressive reading. John altered course and opened up the throttles, and soon we sighted the head of the column converging from the right. We dropped just below it, turned to meet it head-on, and flew the whole length of that gallant, ill-fated cavalcade.

It was a noble sight, a seemingly endless process of tugs and gliders rushing at us from out of the far horizon, and flashing past just over our heads.

We did not know then that John Brown, as keen as a lad with a new toy, was there with them, off to Arnhem with his latest creation, a complete GCI for transportation by air. And like so many of them, he paid the price for all his pioneering. His airborne caravan was scattered, and he did not even have a chance to set up his latest shop. He died fighting with the troops within the dwindling perimeter of that tragic landing.

In the late autumn, just before that last winter of the war set in, I managed to get over to the Continent for a short visit, flying over in a Mosquito of 96 Squadron. It was a miserable day when we set out, and we crossed the Channel under a leaden sky. The further we went the lower the ragged clouds forced us to fly. Finally we nosed our way carefully up the estuary of the Somme to Amiens, which looked grey and dreary under the drizzle. We skimmed over its glistening roofs, and splashed down on to the sodden airfield of Glisy.

The village, just outside the perimeter of the airfield, had been largely destroyed, and the houses that still stood were scarred with fire and bomb splinters. A hopeless air of ruin and neglect seemed to hang depressingly over everything. The people I saw had no look of liberation about them, which was understandable enough in view of what had been happening to them. Their faces bore a look of grey, sunken despair.

I walked around the village, and entered the church, wrecked and smashed, crunching over a welter of splintered woodwork and shattered glass. Plaster saints lay smashed amongst the rubble, and little rivulets of rain dribbled down the cracked stonework of the walls. But serene and enduring above the wreckage stood the altar, and scrawled in red crayon across the front of it was the word Resurgam.

In the fading light I made my way back through the puddles towards the Mess. At the crossroads, two Resistance youths were idly standing on guard. But guarding what, I wondered, and against whom? They fingered their rifles in a restless way. Were they chaffing against a bitterness unappeased, and unable to face, as yet, the grim realities of the peace that was coming their way?

Across the road, a middle-aged woman, drab in the uniform black of the peasant, was bending doggedly over a plough as she coaxed her two horses along the sodden furrows. Here was an unquenchable spirit. She was of the people whose homes had been ruined, whose husbands had been killed, whose sons were in some far-off prison camp. But the soil remained, and must be tilled, and the crops sown, and then the spring would come again. I thought of that word across the altar in the church.

A wan gleam of light glistened across the fields as the sun, low on the horizon, broke for a moment through the driving clouds. It struck and flickered back from the shining metal of the plough-share as the woman turned the horses. And then she bent down again to the furrow, plodding on her way, stolid and patient and enduring.

No. 219 Squadron, which had been transferred to 85 Group, and which had come over to France early in October, was now commanded by Peter Green, promoted to the rank of Wing Commander. He had as his navigator, Grimmy having gone on a rest, Flight Lieutenant D. A. Oxby, one of the most successful navigators in the business. Only recently they had shot down during one patrol three Stukas which had been trying to dive-bomb the bridge over the Waal at Nijmegen.

Douggie Oxby was young, slightly built, with a twinkling, almost roguish eye, and a keen wit that seemed always just about to bubble over. I could well imagine that in the air his commentary would come rippling over in an exuberant but unflurried stream.

I asked Douggie if they had had much trouble with the Stukas over speed. He admitted that they had had to put their wheels and flaps down in order to stay behind the slow and old dive bombers, and that even then had nearly shot past them. And they would have shot down a fourth but for the fact that it fired off a cluster of white recognition signals right in their faces, dazzling them, and forcing them to turn away.

In his time, Douggie had flown with quite a variety of pilots. He had been with a night squadron in the Western Desert, and had seen a lot of activity over Tobruk. He had also served in Malta, again on night operations.

"That was a game!" he commented when he told me about it. "'We were re-equipped with Mark VIII AI while we were there, and we were so short of juice that every operator was considered to be operational after one twenty minute practice."

I thought of the long weeks we had spent struggling with the stuff, and I remarked that they could not have been of much use after that much practice.

Douggie laughed. "We did four sorties from Luqa the same night," he said.

More cautiously I asked what luck they had had.

"One destroyed and one probable," he said. "Both Heinkels. The probable was one of those annoying blighters that won't burn. We chased it down from 12,000 to 1,000ft, and used all our ammo on it, too."

It did not seem to strike him as anything of an achievement to get two visuals and combats straight off the reel with completely strange equipment. There was only a vague regret that they had not properly fixed the probable.

Douggie went on, flying now with Peter Green, to pile up what was, I believe, the record score by any night fighter navigator. He produced 36 visuals on enemy aircraft, which resulted in 26 combats. Of these, 22 were definitely destroyed, 2 were probably destroyed, and 2 were damaged. He was given a Permanent Commission in the RAF after the war, and his decorations included a DSO, a DFC and a DFM and bar.

I got back to England and to my office at Uxbridge in time for yet another wartime Christmas, and there was plenty to do. The home-based squadrons in 100 Group were already well on the way in their new offensive roles, and now they were joined by our night fighter squadrons of Fighter Command. But before this could be done we had to fit them with Gee for radar navigation, and with Monica, a radar aid for keeping a look out astern. The cockpit of the Mosquito, in fact, became so congested with radar equipment and cathode ray tubes that there was barely room for the crew. As one burly navigator commented, there was scarcely room to swing a compass, let alone a cat.

All the time the little teleprinter messages dropped into our "In" tray, recording the scores on both sides of the ledger. The war was drawing to its climax; and it seemed almost as if Isaac sensed that there was a time limit being imposed as he made a determined effort to extract the most he could from his evil chances.

Early in the New Year, FIU took on the trials of some new equipment which necessitated rolling the Mosquito in which it was installed. It was a manoeuvre that was generally discouraged with this aircraft, although it was quite safe in the hands of a competent pilot, and if done smoothly enough. The job was handed over to Bill Maguire, and in his skilful hands there was certainly no ground for any concern.

Bill took off with Denis Lake as his navigator. The first roll went smoothly enough; but the watchers on the ground were surprised to see Bill start a second one. Then surprise quickly turned to alarm when they saw the aircraft flick into a third roll, and, at the same time, start rapidly losing height.

Too late, and much too low, the Mosquito straightened out and began to pull up. It disappeared below the limited horizon, and then to the horror of the onlookers that over-familiar pall of black smoke billowed up. It had just failed to clear the ground, had hit a house, and had disintegrated, and both Bill and Dennis had been killed. The double tragedy shook me all the more because Bill had been one of the few pilots, apart from John, in whom I had always had complete confidence.

Less than a month later, as we were talking in my office one afternoon, John was called to the 'phone. From the first words spoken, I could tell by the shocked expression on his face that it was bad news.

At the other side of the table I could only sit and wait to hear the worst. John made a wry grimace in answer to my unspoken question. He covered the mouthpiece.

"Peter Green," he said. "A forced landing on one engine."

The 'phone went rattling on, and John passed on the information in fragments.

"Flight testing a rogue aircraft. Put it down all right, but hit a bump."

"What about Douggie Oxby?" I whispered.

"He's all right…Peter was flying alone."

So Peter was dead, too. But there was more to come. Peter's former Commanding Officer, Wing Commander Raphael – who had handed over 85 Squadron to John a year before was a friend of the family, and he went to break the news to Peter's wife, who was due to have a baby within a matter of days. A few weeks later someone was bearing the news of Raphael's death to his wife. He had been killed in a completely inexplicable collision in broad daylight between the Spitfire he was flying and a Dakota.

Nor was that all of the bad news, for shortly afterwards we heard of the death of Grimmy, Peter Green's navigator. He had gone to 96 Squadron with Peter, but in August, when Peter had taken over command of 219 Squadron, Grimmy had gone on a rest. Later he returned to 85 Squadron, and he was flying with Flight Lieutenant Dobie – who had also joined 85 some time before – on a patrol over the Schweinfurt area when they were fired at and hit by some of our own flak. Dobie was thrown clear and came down by parachute, but Grimmy was killed when the Mosquito crashed.

It was not easy sitting at my desk receiving those brief messages of triumph and tragedy as they poured in by telephone and teleprinter day after day, and I began to feel almost ashamed of the security of that office. But I made no effort to get out of it. And then, on the 23rd of March, John and I had a close shave. If the incident had ended in disaster it would surely have been through the unluckiest of coincidences.

We were on our way from Northolt to Swannington to pay a visit to 85 Squadron. We were flying in the Oxford, and Tarald Weisteen was with us. I had tossed a coin to decide whether to go with them or to a wedding. On the third attempt I had managed to bring down a head; and I was sitting in my usual place in the Oxford, on the main spar, between and just behind the two pilots.

We were flying over Hertfordshire, just north of London, at about 2,000ft. The naked fields rolled peacefully by, and from an almost cloudless sky the comforting sun smiled down on the frost-cracked earth. It was a healing warmth, and I was feeling very moved by the promise of spring, with its prospect of new life stirring; and for a while I forgot the dreary matter of death and rejoiced in the exhilaration of flying again, in the vibrant lift and flow of the air around us.

And then, like a sudden blotch in the blue sky, there appeared a small, reddish cloud about half a mile ahead and high above us. It had not formed slowly, as most clouds do. At one moment there was nothing, and then, in a flash, it was there, complete, ugly and menacing. As we flew on, gazing in astonishment at this phenomenon, smoky tendrils spread outwards and downwards from its billowing heart.

My thoughts had been with pleasanter things, but at the sight of this intrusion my slumbering brain awoke. This was no cloud: it was a V2, a rocket, exploding prematurely in the air. John had already realized what it was, but his curiosity overcame his caution, and he continued to fly on towards the expanding smoke cloud. In a moment it was nearly overhead. Then something big and black smacked down heavily into a ploughed field just ahead of us. The oil spurted up as it went in, and all over the field little puffs of earth began to spring up as smaller fragments of the rocket rained down.

Too late, John had realized our danger. There was no time to turn aside as the air all around us was filled with assorted ironmongery. John and Tarald, with only the thin Perspex roof above them, shielded their heads as best as they could with their arms. I sat watching with fascination as pieces of casing, cylinders, gear wheels, nuts, bolts and straggling lengths of wire went whizzing past. This was indeed a shower. And from a great height.

At last the air cleared. It did not seem that we had suffered any damage, except for a small piece knocked out of the tail plane. I uncrossed my fingers, and started breathing again. John turned and circled over the field. Some farm workers were running out to gather souvenirs, and one of them made for the most tempting prize, the big casing that we had seen crashing to the earth.

"I wonder how hot that thing is?" John commented.

If the man had been a thermometer he could not have given us a better answer. He had taken a good grip on the casing, but then he instantly let go of it and start hopping around sucking his fingers.

We turned back on to the course for Swannington. I did not know what the others were thinking, but I was casting my mind back over the years, wondering about all those who had been killed through stupid little accidents, and the fantastic twists that fate can sometimes contrive, especially when one tempts her by tossing up three times.

CHAPTER TWENTY-NINE

Master Craftsmen

O NE of the memorable evenings in the affairs of 85 Squadron was the occasion upon which, just before they went to Bomber Command, some of the officers were honoured with invitations to a dance at Windsor Castle. It was arranged by Peter Townsend, who by then had become a Group Captain, and an equerry to His Majesty King George VI. John and I were also invited to attend. It was a delightful evening for us, and the natural charm of our Royal hosts soon put at ease even the most self-conscious of the guests.

The only time that there threatened to be any sticky moments was when it came to making suitable conversation with the charming but very young ladies present. Five years of Air Force Mess life, of boisterous and rather animal exuberance, and of almost constant shop talk were not perhaps the best of conditioning for such an occasion, and there were moments when I think we caused Peter Townsend more than a little anxiety.

But the young ladies had been well briefed, and when the conversation flagged they had one stock remark, based on the prevailing difficulties of private transport, which ran:

"Did you have far to come?"

After three successive dancing partners had led off with this remark, some spirit of mischief induced me to spike the guns of my next partner by getting in the question myself. I was deservedly disconcerted when I received the perfectly casual reply:

"Oh...no. Actually, I live here."

The pleasant evening came to an end. The hour for the carriages arrived, and the guests glided away in a succession of stately limousines. The time had come for the Royal Air Force to seek out its transport.

Most of those of the squadron who were there seemed to be travelling in Ginger Farrell's car, a quaint vehicle which went – that was, when it could be induced to start – by the becoming name of "Lilly-Gal". The five or six who were with Ginger moved away from the lighted doorway into the merciful obscurity of the blackout. And to the remaining guests waiting for their cars there came from the darkness a vivid sound picture of what was happening.

"Bet she won't start."

"How's the battery?"

"Flat as your hat. Where's Kent Nowell?"

"I'm in front. Where's the flamin' handle?"

"Shush! We'll have to push."

There came a scrabble of feet on the cobblestones, a tinny clanking, and some hard breathing.

"Now!" someone bellowed.

There was a crack that shook the precincts, followed by muffled shouts of triumph as the engine started up. Then, with a roar somewhat like that of a flying-bomb, and with bodies clinging to the wildly swinging doors, "Lilly-Gal" was launched.

It was with this same spirit that the squadron launched itself, along with the other night fighter squadrons transferred to 100 Group, upon its new job in Bomber Command. It was known that the Germans had long since set up for themselves their own radar ground control stations; and it was also known that they had built up a formidable force of night fighters, the skill of which was being reflected in the rising losses in our own bombers. Now our own night fighters were to go along with the bombers to try and ward off those of the Luftwaffe.

The crews of these long-range escort night fighters found themselves faced with a task that was very different from that of the defensive night fighter. In the first place, they had to work out their own style of navigation. It always remained a mystery to me how the radar navigators managed, watching the AI set most of the time, keeping only the flimsiest of logs scribbled on a knee-pad and juggling with Gee and other navigational aids, to find their way around. It all called for the most meticulous pre-flight planning.

The enemy, of course, had all the advantages of the home team, just as we had known them when we were on the defensive. They had their own ground control, their own navigational and homing aids, and their airfields were close at hand. And, if it came to the point, they had friendly territory to jump into.

All the experience of the intruder squadrons and the knowledge and information gained from the pioneer offensive patrols were put at the disposal of the night fighters, and in a very short time they were ready for their new jobs. The new Commanding Officer of 85, Wing Commander C. M. Miller, with Flying Officer Robert Symon as his Navigator, opened the score by destroying a Me 110 over Melun. Then the Squadron had had to change over to the job of helping with the flying-bombs; but towards the end of August they were back at Swannington and had settled down to the business of long-range bomber support.

From then on the real scoring started in earnest, even though they had a lot of snags to overcome with the later models of the Mosquito, with more powerful engines, with which they were re-equipped. For a while these new engine installations were a nightmare. Power failure on a four-engined aircraft was sufficient cause for anxiety: but when one out of two stopped perhaps hundreds of miles from base and surrounded by hostile fighters, the situation could become serious. At best it meant a long, exhausting haul back home, with an anxious eye on the gauges and an ear cocked for the beat of the one good engine. As one pilot so feelingly put it:

"One runs out of engines so quickly!"

In spite of the efforts of the engineers to get at the root of the trouble, single-engine returns became almost commonplace. Gonsalves, now one of the Flight Commanders, and soon to command the squadron, and Basil Duckett came all the way back from Germany one night on one engine. Branse Burbridge and Bill Skelton even had an engine catch fire over Hamburg. They had a few hectic moments while Branse feathered the aircrew and operated the fire extinguisher. But the fire died down, and they, too, came limping back across the North Sea.

But things did not always go so well. My premonition about Bob Wright turned out to have something to it. After joining 85 Squadron he had crewed up with an old friend of ours from the earlier days at Middle Wallop, Flight Lieutenant Brian Keele, who had followed the popular road from 604 to FIU for a rest, and then to 85 Squadron for second tour of operational flying.

Early in November, Brian and Bob had an engine failure during a night flying test. Coming in to land, they had crashed almost on the perimeter track. Brian was killed, the flames from the wreckage driving back the attempts that were made to rescue the crew. Then Corporal Tom Woodhead, one of the ground crews of 85 Squadron, dashed right into the fire and pulled Bob, unconscious and badly burnt, out through a hole in the blazing fuselage, a most courageous act for which he was later awarded the BEM. They took Bob off to hospital, but he was not expected to live.

When I heard of what had happened I thought of all the trouble Bob had gone to, leaving a life full of interest in the United States, and it seemed hard that he should end like this. But after a while it was found that he was going to live. John and I went to see him in the RAF Hospital in Ely. I was glad, selfishly, I am afraid, that no word of mine had contributed to his efforts to get back to flying because he was a haggard and hollow-eyed sight as he lay propped up in bed in the Burns Centre of the hospital waiting to have skin grafts. His only comment – apart from a few rude remarks about the behaviour of aeroplanes – was to speak words of the highest praise for Tom Woodhead and the RAF Medical Service. He also seemed to be particularly intrigued with the Nursing Sister who was taking care of him; and although that was only running true to form for all patients in hospitals I took it as a sign that he was on the way to recovery.

Even then, Bob was not quite through with the enemy. Months later he left the hospital and went on his first sick leave to his home in Kent. Twenty-four hours after his arrival there a V2 landed 50 yards away. Bob was blown out of the wreckage of the house straight back into hospital, along with his mother and sister. When I heard of it, I remembered what he had said about his family being in Bomb Alley when he was with the squadron at West Malling. It also, at the time, made me additionally conscious of the fact that my wife, who had been transferred for duty at the War Office, was billeted high up in a block of old flats close to Victoria Station.

The risk our offensive night fighters ran in inviting the attentions of the Luftwaffe, though still a bad second to the watch Isaac kept over things was naturally much greater on the enemy side of the sea than it had been when we were on our defensive patrols over England. Apart from the danger from flak, there was the certain knowledge that everything intercepted, regardless of whether it was friendly or hostile, was liable to shoot on sight. And yet, so far as our night fighters were concerned, everything had to be identified before it could be attacked.

But the rising tide of successes mounted steadily through that last autumn and winter of the war, in spite of the usual handicap of the weather. By VE Day the 100 Group squadrons alone had destroyed 236 enemy aircraft in the air, and had claimed 12 probably destroyed and 64 damaged. They had also accounted for 21 destroyed and 62 damaged on the ground.

But what was of far more importance than the score of the enemy destroyed was the way in which the numbers of our own bombers shot down by the German night fighters shrank rapidly and in the most satisfactory way until they became almost negligible. So far as the crews of the night fighters were concerned, they were unanimous in their high-spirited claim that they had the most interesting job of the war. And when I saw them setting off on their long-range, freelance missions my conscience nagged at me again with an ugly whisper that I had, by my premature retirement, missed this culmination of all that we had worked and hoped for.

It was in the nature of these long-range night fighters that they should approach their new job with the keenest anticipation. They had spent long years on the defensive; they were all experts in a highly technical battle of skill, wits and physical endurance; and now that they were at last let off the leash they made the most of their chances. As fighters they had been trained to think aggressively, and when that aggressive spirit was rewarded with ever-increasing success their morale soared even higher than it had been before.

There were, naturally, losses on our side, just as there were crews that met with outstanding success. The doughty Hedgecoe and young Norman Bamford, having finished their period of rest at FIU, went to 151 Squadron at Hunsdon, Hedgecoe, with promotion, to be a Flight Commander. In some inexplicable way they ran foul of Isaac on their first flight with the squadron, and they were both killed when they crashed coming in to land.

Micky Phillips and Derek Smith had the misfortune to be caught between two fires. They were investigating a radar contact; and at the moment they got a visual on it and realized that it was one of our bombers it opened fire and set one of their engines ablaze. The next moment a German night fighter came up behind them and shot them down. They both survived that and spent the last six months of the war as prisoners in Germany; but, after they were released and had returned home, Derek died following an operation.

Of all the crews I knew during the war, the most interesting, to my mind, was made up of Branse Burbridge and Bill Skelton. At the end, Branse was one of the Flight Commanders of 85 Squadron; and Bill Skelton was the Navigator Leader.

Not only were these two the most interesting and capable young men, but they also flew what was probably the most extraordinary of all the long-range escort patrols ever accomplished. Many times I talked over the details of that patrol with other people who belonged to the night fighter world, and we all agreed that it was an outstanding effort. Brian Keele and Bob Wright, who were in Branse's flight, were also on the same show – it was only a few nights before they crashed and Brian was killed – and much later Bob told me of what had happened when they got back, and of the typically modest and almost casual way in which Branse had announced their success when he and Bill landed in the early hours of the morning.

From the moment they crewed up together for their second tour of flying, Branse and Bill hit it off together both on the ground and in the air. They had the perfect and all too rare understanding that characterized the best crews, and which enabled them to work together almost as one man.

It was not only that Branse was an excellent pilot, and that Bill was a first-rate navigator: they had also developed the ability to anticipate each other's moves, to work with a minimum of chatter and without friction and argument, and almost to read one another's thoughts; and the months of the gruelling work flying from West Malling against the fighter-bombers in the raids on London had put the final polish on their individual skill and on their work as a team. In the far more exacting conditions of offensive operations, where only the master craftsmen could hope for consistent success, they climbed the individual score-board in a meteoric fashion, and established a record night bag for any one crew of twenty enemy aircraft destroyed.

In the hands of people such as Branse Burbridge and Bill Skelton, the AI equipped night fighter reached its highest level of efficiency, with the radar navigator exercising the greatest craftsmanship and skill. In the early days we used to speak of the German raiders who came over as customers who were coming to do business in our shops. The show that Branse and Bill put up on the night of the 4th of November 1944, I liked to think, was something that really spoke for all the men who reversed the order of things, who broke into the customer's premises and cheerfully assaulted his assistants, who ruined his trade, and who finally wrecked his shop.

That night Branse and Bill set out from Swannington as part of a mighty bomber effort. The main force of over 700 aircraft was to raid Bochrum, in the Ruhr, and there were be other smaller raids on the Dortmund-Ems Canal and on Hanover. Nearly four years had passed since that first successful AI combat of John Cunningham's; and what a difference those years had made. Those early night fighters of ours had fought back like stubborn full-backs defending a packed goalmouth. Now their successors were going out like an eager forward line thrusting aggressively into the enemy's penalty area.

At 20,000ft above the cold waters of the North Sea, Branse and Bill set course eastward for the Rhine. In the darkness with them the Pathfinders were dog-legging their way to the targets inside Germany, and then came the heavies, shaking the windows of the East Coast towns with the deep thunder of their engines as they streamed out in their hundreds. The night fighters were in their appointed places along the flanks, forming a cordon through which the German night fighters would have to pierce before they could get at the bombers. And in carefully-planned positions there were all the other aircraft of 100 Group, special aircraft loaded to the gills with all sorts of fanciful radio and radar equipment, all designed to mislead and jam the German radar screens and radio communications.

For a while, until they reached a pre-arranged position, and in order not to betray by their transmissions their presence to the enemy's monitor stations, 5 degrees east Bill reached forward to the control panel of his AI set and switched on, his fingers ranging over the mass of controls and buttons, finding them automatically in the darkness. The Mosquito was no longer blind and groping, a helpless target; it had become a questing and deadly hunter.

They were over the enemy coast, and keeping a sharp lookout for anything that might come their way. The German fighters were probably all off the ground by now, but their radio and radar must have been hopelessly bedevilled by interference. Bill was getting plenty of German interference on his own Gee set, making it difficult to fix his position; but the AI was quite free of it as the Germans had not yet caught on to a means of jamming our later types of radar such as Mark X.

Suddenly Bill stiffened, and his right hand slid along the control panel. Something had come into the radar vision of the Mosquito, and he warned Branse that he thought he had a contact.

Branse instinctively switched on the gun-sight, carefully and deliberately adjusting its brilliance. Bill was watching the little blob of light of the blip on the cathode ray tube as it smeared its glowing, snail track across the face. He was shrewdly weighing things up, waiting for the right moment to act. Then he gave a few instructions, and the Mosquito went curving down after its target. They began to close in with suspicious ease, which caused Branse to comment that it might be a new boy they were after.

When they were 1,500ft behind their target they started to slow down; and when they were in to 1,200ft Branse caught sight of it, identifying it as hostile.

As with all good crews, Branse and Bill always made a point of each of them identifying separately the aircraft they were intercepting and then making up their minds about it. With this one Bill needed only a quick glance through his night binoculars to decide that it was a Ju 88G.

Neither of them said a word as they pulled up behind the still unsuspecting German and Branse opened fire. Flames leapt from the engine cowlings as the Junkers was hit, and it began to wilt. But it still flew on, wallowing and undecided, and the flames dwindled. Branse hit the Junkers again in the same place, the port engine, and the fire broke out afresh. The enemy aircraft sagged and went into an ever-steepening dive, and then it exploded into the ground.

Only the glowing wreckage of their victim, scattered across the fields, disturbed the darkness below them. Branse banked the Mosquito around, and started to climb back towards their patrol line. They reached their beat and settled down to wait, keeping station in that wide arc of unseen fighters ringing the target. Inside, the Pathfinders were lining themselves up, making sure of their aiming points, and then the target indicators went down.

The German fighters would now come heading in from miles around and, after a while, their flares began to stab the darkness. Branse and Bill went off to search around one or two that were fairly close. But they did not pick up any contacts, so they went on waiting and watching, curbing their impatience and resisting the temptation to rush off in the direction of the fireworks. They knew that they must not leave a dangerous gap in the ring of night fighters which was standing guard out there in the darkness.

Nearly three-quarters of an hour passed after their first combat, and the bombers were already heading for home before Bill got another contact. They turned off in pursuit, and as soon as they straightened out behind their target Bill realized that this one was not going to be so easy. The blip showed from its position that the other aircraft was 4miles away, and it was swinging about the tube in a way that suggested that regular, routine evasive action was being taken. But there was nothing half-hearted about the evasion, and even at long range Bill had to start taking quite severe counter-action in order to follow it. The closer they got the harder they had to work. This one was an old hand, taking no chances. Branse had scarcely got the Mosquito twisting into one manoeuvre than Bill was pouring out instructions for another.

And all through Bill's commentary, woven into the constant stream of instructions, there were clear-cut word pictures which told Branse where to look for the target, and how it was behaving.

The occasional acknowledgements Branse made were scarcely noticed by Bill. The tubes told him far better than any words how short the time lag was between his calling an order and its execution by Branse, and slowly they closed in. Bill was getting dry in the mouth, but at 1,200ft Branse raised his voice to stem the torrent of words and said that he could see their target.

Bill was longing to have a look, but there was a note of warning in Branse's voice, and he kept his head down on the set. The blip had locked itself in that fixed position that it always did when the pilot could see and follow the target; but even then the Mosquito was being thrown about in the heat of the chase, and Bill was being lifted out of his seat at one moment and having his face jammed down on the visor the next.

Branse was having difficulty seeing the other aircraft against the ground when it went below the horizon, but he was closing in, and just as Bill reported that they were only 600ft behind Branse called on him to identify it. They agreed that it was another Ju 88. It was twisting, climbing and diving in a regular, corkscrew motion. Branse timed his final approach carefully, diving a little as the German levelled off at the top of the next swoop so as to bring the target above his horizon. Quickly he brought the sight on to his favourite aiming point – the port engine – and pressed the button. But instead of a roar from the cannon all he got was the mocking buzz of the camera-gun. By mistake he had pressed the camera-gun button. He adjusted his grip on the stick and pressed the second one. The cannon crashed into life, and the deadly burst struck home. But the target showed no signs of blowing up or even of hesitating in its course. Instead it instantly dived out of sight below the horizon. But it could not escape from the vision of the AI set. Although the German pilot had reacted quickly, Bill was even quicker in getting back on to the set. They twisted and dived with the frantic urgency of the hunted and the hunter. But Bill held on, and five minutes later, when they had lost a lot of height and were down to 3,000ft, Branse again had the other aircraft in sight.

Opening fire, Branse scored more hits; but again the Junkers dived away out of sight. This time Bill could not hold it: they were getting close enough to the ground to be handicapped by the ground returns. His voice was becoming hoarse, and despondently he remarked that they could claim that one as nothing more than damaged. But even as he spoke the darkness was broken by the familiar splash of red along the ground as something went in a mile or so ahead of them.

Bill made another brief entry about it in his log. The bombers must have been on their way home by that time, and they should have been thinking about it too. But Branse had other views. There was an established plan used by all night fighters in this situation. They would turn on to the homeward route followed by our bombers and fly back in towards the target area with the object of trying to intercept any head-on contacts, hoping that these would turn out to be German night fighters looking for stragglers from the bomber force.

They continued on the new heading for about two minutes, and then Branse saw, far to the eastward, the twinkling lights of an airfield. Then a cluster of red and white stars dropped from the sky. The German fighters, finding that our bombers were all well on the way back, were themselves returning home to roost.

Branse pushed the stick forward, and the Mosquito went howling down towards the distant lights, quickly losing all the height they had only just gained. Bill identified it as the aerodrome at Bonn-Hangelar. And then they saw an aircraft touching down.

Freelancing at a height of less than 1,000ft, even with the best radar set made, was a bit of a gamble, although all our crews were well practised at that game. It was hardly surprising, therefore, that they lost the snap contact and very fleeting visual which caught them on the wrong foot a few minutes later. But again they had a plan to meet the situation, a plan that had been worked out and practised with the other crews of the squadron. Branse turned and began to orbit the airfield in a right-hand circuit, flying into the stream of returning traffic. They kept below 1,000ft, scanning upwards to try and pick out a head-on contact from the swamping ground echoes.

Their chance came a few minutes later. Bill seized on the contact, and Branse hauled the Mosquito around into the left-hand circuit, turning as hard as he dared so close to the ground. Glancing shrewdly at the airfield ahead, he saw that there was certainly no time to lose, and he hesitated about slowing down as they closed in. But a rising note in Bill's voice carried its own warning, and Branse started pulling back the throttles. Immediately afterwards there was an almost panic urgency in Bill's voice, and Branse quickly dropped the wheels and put on a few degrees of flap; and the Mosquito came slithering in with the engine speed warning horn blaring away and the exhaust stubs crackling.

Bill kept his head down on the set, watching the blip as it slid down the trace. He went on reporting its position until finally, at minimum range, it disappeared from view. Then, instinctively, he looked up. Just above the windscreen, and still creeping back towards them, there was the ominous black shape of a Me 110, the most efficient of the German night fighters, known to the Luftwaffe as the Destroyer. Even without his night binoculars he could see all too clearly the black crosses and the bristling array of radar aerials; and the wheels and the flaps of the 110 were already down in preparation for landing.

The German crew were far too absorbed in their approach towards the runway to notice the menace beneath their tail, and hanging precariously on its flaps, the Mosquito slowly dropped away behind it. Branse began to breathe more easily. He pulled up behind his target. There was no time to spare for any fancy shooting, and his shells riddled the Messerschmitt. Blazing from end to end, it plunged into the river just short of the aerodrome.

Although time was running short, Branse decided that there was too much trade about to leave unattended, so they flew away from the aerodrome for a while to let the consternation on the ground die down. Then they turned back, and the radar scanner swept once more across the countryside of the approaches to the airfield, picking up and flooding the tube with an assortment of echoes from the ground. Then, as it swept the sky above, yet another contact appeared. On Bill's instructions, Branse opened up and they followed it around the circuit, cutting the corners as they got the measure of things. They closed in quickly, and as they came around on the final leg Branse throttled back and lowered his flaps a little so as to make sure that he would not overshoot. But when he did finally see the other aircraft there was no sign of its wheels being down ready for a landing. Patiently he stalked it while Bill checked its identity. Even at this late hour they could take no chances; there was always the possibility of another Mosquito joining in the same game. The seconds that were ticking by were precious enough; but they had to be sure of what they were attacking. Then Bill confirmed that it was another Ju 88.

The Junkers was nearing the airfield when Branse got his sight on and fired straight into the fuselage. The whole cockpit cover broke away. Branse set his teeth, and pulled up through the scattering debris. Almost on the perimeter, he banked the Mosquito steeply away from their fourth victim as it smacked down in a mass of blazing wreckage just outside the wire and in full sight of the waiting ground crews.

After that they realized that time was running short so they turned away and set course for England. Bill settled down to some navigation, juggling with fuel consumption and cruising speeds and times, and Branse followed the course he gave him.

Many years later Bob Wright described to me the way Branse came into the crew-room after they landed, quietly, almost unobserved. Bob saw him at the door and went across to him and asked him what luck they had had. Branse smiled and gently polished his nails on the lapel of his jacket, and then he held up three fingers.

"Three," he said; "possibly four!"

And from the evidence of what other crews had seen that night it was confirmed that they had indeed destroyed four in that one patrol. Moreover, in doing it Branse had fired only 200 rounds out of the total of 700 rounds of ammunition carried by the Mosquito night fighter.

Branse and Bill finished their second tours of flying early in the new year of 1945. They were both awarded Bars to their Distinguished Service

Orders – they had already received Bars to their DFCs – and in the citation for Branse it was recorded that of the twenty victories he had achieved at night in just over ten months, all but four of them had been over enemy territory. During the time he was with 85 Squadron in 100 Group he completed thirty offensive patrols, and on four occasions he destroyed two or more aircraft during one patrol. On one out of every six patrols he had to make a single-engine return, and on every occasion he landed safely back at Swannington. In the citation for Bill's award it was pointed out that under his able leadership the standard of AI operating reached such a high pitch that 85 Squadron destroyed sixty enemy aircraft at night during the ten months that he was Navigator Leader.

Immediately after the war and their release from the RAF, Branse and Bill went on with their studies. Branse became a lay preacher with a particular interest in the formation of religious groups in schools and the organizing during the holiday periods of camps and house-parties for schoolboys. Bill was ordained as a clergyman in the Church of England, and became the chaplain of Clare College, Cambridge.

CHAPTER THIRTY

No Joy

WITH the surge forward of the Allied armies from the east as well as from the west, and the crumbling of the Reich that Hitler had built to last a thousand years, the Luftwaffe found themselves within a shrinking perimeter. Driven from one aerodrome after another, starved of fuel, and with communications and the supply services breaking down, they were hard put to it to offer any sort of opposition at all to the fleets of our bombers pounding day and night at the few targets that remained. Our own night fighters even began to jostle one another as they went elbowing in; and just as the bombers were beginning to run short of targets, so were these fighters running out of what we had known for so long as "joy".

In April of that last year of the war, John and I went on another visit to the Continent. While we were at 85 Group Headquarters we heard the scarcely believable news that 604 Squadron was to be disbanded. We rushed up to Lille-Vendeville, where the squadron was stationed, and we found that they were stunned by the news. The whole thing had been very badly handled, the squadron merely being told without any explanation that their days were numbered. The explanation was, in fact, simple enough: the scaling down process had started, and the first to be affected were the Auxiliary squadrons. It was intended that they should be reformed on the old basis as soon as the peace broke out.

But simple explanations did not help much, and it was a bitter blow, both to the serving members and to those who had seen the squadron built up before the war and then win its first battle honours. Jack Baker, still with the squadron at the end, was almost in tears.

"This is a sad day, Doughy," I said to him.

"It's terrible!" he replied. He looked really shocked. "I can't understand it. Why the first day we got back over here we got four. It doesn't make sense."

I tried to explain to him that there was no reproach implied in what was going to happen, and that the squadron would be re-formed as soon after the war as possible. He brightened a little at that.

"Ah, well…that puts a different complexion on it," he said. "I suppose you'll be rejoining? And you must come to the reunion. We're just trying to fix something up."

There was a farewell dinner in the Mess at Lille that night during which strenuous efforts were made to polish off the champagne left behind by the Luftwaffe. I vaguely remember incurring the displeasure of the management by trying to perpetuate the motto of the squadron in candle smoke on a newly-decorated ceiling, balancing with some difficulty upon a swaying edifice of tables and chairs.

The next morning, as John and I bucketed back to England in the Oxford across a gusty Channel, I paid heavily for my evening's pleasure. But even then my outraged pride insisted on blaming it all on the shellfish and not on the champagne.

And so, with a rapidly gathering momentum, the end came in sight. So much seemed to happen in such a very short time; and in those last days of the war it was difficult to keep track of events.

The news of Hitler's death came to us one evening in the Mess at 11 Group. One of the Norwegians called for Pimm's all around, and very quickly a party blew up. Some of the stronger and heartier types rushed out and gathered up one of the heavy stone balls that decorated the gate of the outer wall. They trundled it back to the Mess and into the anteroom, finally hoisting it on to the large mantelshelf. It seemed to fly up to its resting place without any apparent effort on the part of the lifters, but one of John's fingers was never the same afterwards. And then across it there was scrawled in chalk: "Hitler dropped a clanger – May 1st, 1945". The mood with all of us was understandably one of jubilation. But I knew that at the back of the minds of many there lurked troubled thoughts about the future. In my own case I had a job waiting for me, although I should much rather have stayed in the Air Force.

It was only natural, of course, that John's services should have been very much in demand. He was offered a permanent commission in the RAF, and for a while he seriously considered it. He also received an offer from de Havilland's to go back there. It did not take him long to make up his mind that he preferred the idea of the greater freedom of civilian flying, and he was released from the Service and he returned to his pre-war job of testing. Eventually he became Chief Test Pilot of de Havilland's, and, based on the earlier work done by Geoffrey de Havilland, he did all the testing and development work on the Comet.

On the eve of VE Day, John and I went on leave. John, in his wisdom, rightly went to Swannington to be with 85 Squadron for their final celebration; but somehow I felt that I could not face it. I should have liked very much to have joined in the fun, but it was really more than just pricks of conscience that stopped me from going. The thought that I had not earned the right to be there was due mainly to a dissatisfaction with my own showing and the feeling that I had not measured up to the standards I had set myself. But on top of that I was also feeling rather overwhelmed by the overall picture of what the peace had brought. We were in a mess, and the world was far from being the happy place we had hoped and worked and fought for. It was not a matter of disillusionment: I was too old and too experienced for that. But we had set out to accomplish something, and in the course of trying to do that there had been many and great sacrifices and terrible losses. So many of my closest friends were either maimed or dead, and in my own mind I was tormented by the thought that it had all been in vain. The state to which Europe had been reduced, and the prospect of what there was ahead, left me feeling sick and ashamed.

With the vague idea of getting away from it all, I headed for the mountains. I met Micki in London and we had dinner at a restaurant in Soho before we caught the night train for the north. The crowds celebrating the peace were already gathering in Piccadilly Circus. An American soldier had got off to an early and too rapid start, and was spewing into the gutter, his attendant British harpy clinging to him like a bloated fly.

It seemed such a long, long time since I had stood on the same spot with Tommy, Sandi, Stan Hawke and Jack Love one day in the first week of our call-up in August 1939. We had tried then to explain to a rather bewildered American gentlemen and his wife what it was all about, and how close London was to the threat from the Luftwaffe.

So Micki and I went north, and in the quiet valley of Borrowdale, with the gaunt, grey hump of Gable, splendidly aloof, looking down on us, we heard the announcement made by Winston Churchill that the war in Europe was over. The other war in the Far East nagged for attention, but for that day at least peace of a sort had settled over the wreckage of Europe.

At dinner that night in the Scafell Hotel, we produced our carefully hoarded bottle of champagne. The pop of the cork sounded almost unseemly in the hush of the dining-room. I made an effort to arouse a little party spirit by offering some of the wine to a Corporal of the Royal Air Force and his friends sitting at the next table. But, rather churlishly, he refused it. He obviously did not approve of civilian types who drank champagne.

Perhaps it had been a mistake to try to get away. There began to creep over me a feeling that it was intolerable not to be with those with whom I had experienced so much. It was with them that I belonged. And yet, I wondered, where did one belong? Where, if not on an airfield? Or should we, any of us, really belong anywhere again?

After dark we joined in the general movement up the hillside towards the flickering red of the beacon fire, built on a crag looking down the valley to distant "Skidda". Here at least was something I could understand. Just one more bonfire, and let it be a good one, a blazer, a bonfire worthy of Sid. Let it be a fire for all the Sids and the Bills and the Stans and the Peters and all the rest of them.

More fuel…more fuel! Every man a log! We toiled up the hill with our loads, and we fell down the steep slopes in the darkness, and we staggered up with more fuel. We flung the sweet-scented wood into the leaping flames, and we capered and yelled in the pungent smoke. But through all our hilarity I was conscious of the memory of all those other bonfires.

And what of that splendid Sonnwendfeuer that had burned so brightly above the Rhine gorge on a midsummer night so long ago? How many of those starry-eyed children who had marched so fanatically up the hillside then would be dancing tonight?

More fuel...more fuel! The flames leapt higher and we danced and shouted. Nearby a supercilious onlooker sneered: "What fools some people become on a few beers."

And later, when the night was still and the fire had died down to nothing but embers, I thought of something from Rudyard Kipling that I had once quoted to John. It was from "The Changelings", and it spoke of the temporary sailors of the First World War; and John had agreed with me that it was very apt.

> Now there is nothing, not even our rank,
> To witness what we have been;
> And I am returned to my Walworth Bank,
> And you to your margarine.